Averroës
and the
Enlightenment

Averroës and the Enlightenment

Edited by
Mourad Wahba & Mona Abousenna
Foreword by UN Secretary General Boutros Boutros-Ghali

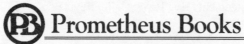

Prometheus Books

59 John Glenn Drive
Amherst, New York 14228-2197

Published 1996 by Prometheus Books

00 99 98 97 96   5 4 3 2 1

Library of Congress Cataloging-in-Publication Data

Averroës and the Enlightenment / edited by Mourad Wahba and Mona
    Abousenna.
        p.   cm.
"The First Special International Philosophy Conference on Ibn Rushd (Averroës) and the Enlightenment which is, at the same time, the fifth Afro-Asian Philosophy Conference organized by the Afro-Asian Philosophy Association." Also includes papers delivered at a follow-up conference on "Averroës and His Influence: Remembering George Hourani" held at the Center for Inquiry and the State University of New York at Buffalo.
    Includes bibliographical references.
    ISBN 1–57392–084–3 (alk. paper)
    1. Averroës, 1126–1198—Influence—Congresses. 2. Enlightenment—Congresses. 3. Developing countries—Civilization—Congresses. 4. Islam and humanism—Congresses. 5. Philosophy—Developing countries—Congresses. I. Wahba, Mourad. II. Abousenna, Mona. III. Afro-Asian Philosophy Association. IV. Special International Philosophy Conference on Ibn Rushd and Enlightenment (1st : 1996 : Cairo, Egypt)
B749.Z7A73   1996
181'.9—dc20   96–8856
                                                                        CIP

Printed in the United States of America on acid-free paper

Contents

---

*Averroës is the Latinized version of the Arabic name Ibn Rushd. Throughout this volume both names are used interchangeably, depending on each author's preference.

5

Foreword

Boutros Boutros-Ghali
Secretary General of the United Nations

This introduction serves as a substitute for my presence at the international conference organized by Dr. Mourad Wahba under the auspices of the Afro-Asian Philosophy Association, on the topic "Ibn Rushd (Averroës) and the Enlightenment." Although I am more a philosopher by inclination than by training, I have always been an admirer of the Arab philosophers who served as bridges between the heritage of Greece and the needs of the political philosophy of their times. In particular, I have long meditated on the importance of al-Farabi's *Ahl al-madina al-fadila,* not only as a commentary on the *Republic,* but also as an exploration of the role of the philosopher, of the thinker, in political life.

Dr. Mourad Wahba's request led me to reread the work of Ibn Rushd, and I turned, naturally for me, not to his dispute with al-Ghazali, *Tahafut al-tahafut (The Incoherence of Incoherence),* but to his own commentary on the *Republic.* It is there, in my opinion, that one finds the most important pages of Ibn Rushd, in the necessity of organizing the state according to the principles of philosophy, or reason, but also according to the moral law, to what would be later defined as categorical imperatives. Indeed, there are pages of Ibn Rushd which speak to us all today, on the importance of the masses in politics, on the need to address their problems and their happiness. Ibn Rushd also makes a strong case for the advancement of women, and their full participation in political and economic life.

9

Although I might be accused of professional deformation, I cannot but note the similarity of these ideas with the work being carried out at the United Nations. In particular, the Social Summit held at Copenhagen in 1995, and the Fourth World Conference on Women held at Beijing, highlight the dangers of exclusion and marginalization, and call for the advancement of women in all aspects of life, be they economic, political, social, cultural, and others. As for the moral aspect of politics, I have long held that the role of the Secretary General is to serve as a conscience, as a moral voice that will not be silenced, calling the world's attention to the fate of the victims of war or its sequels, struggling to end discrimination, working toward the realization of general and complete disarmament, and calling to the attention of the world the forgotten or orphan conflicts of this century.

These are moral imperatives as well as political necessities. Ibn Rushd, I know, would have understood.

Preface

In 1993, during the Nineteenth World Congress of Philosophy in Moscow, the executive committee of the Afro-Asian Philosophy Association (AAPA) held a meeting in which it was decided to organize its fifth international conference in 1994 in Cairo under the theme: "Ibn Rushd and the Enlightenment" (December 5–8, 1994). It was proposed that this fifth conference could be declared as the "First Special International Afro-Asian Philosophy Conference," and for three reasons:

First, it deals with a historic Islamic figure and not with a general theme.

Second, to use Ibn Rushd's (Averroës's) philosophy as an international platform for establishing a dialogue between the West and Islamic culture.

Third, this conference could be a prelude to the World Congress that will be held in Cairo in 1998 to commemorate the eight hundredth anniversary of Ibn Rushd's death.

In organizing the conference, we sent the following announcement of our goals:

The present stage of development in the world—East and West, North and South—is characterized by the predominance of factors of disintegration. The only means of overcoming disintegration and achieving in-

11

tegration, from a philosophical perspective, is by the cultivation of critical reason.

The history of human civilization provides strong evidence to support this thesis. The origin of philosophy has been the outcome of critical reason, which was fully crystallized in the eighteenth century, the epoch known as the Age of Enlightenment. If Immanuel Kant represents the summit of the Enlightenment, it is because he profoundly analyzed critical reason in his three books: *Critique of Pure Reason, Critique of Practical Reason,* and *Critique of Judgment.*

It is also noteworthy that the Islamic philosopher of the Middle Ages, Ibn Rushd (Averroës), had contributed to the emergence of the European Enlightenment—largely because of his commentaries on Aristotle. His philosophy had been the focus of intensive debate among theologians in religious universities in Europe. He did not perform the same role in the Arab societies, however, for he was persecuted and his books were burned.

Today, as we approach the twenty-first century, we may ask whether the Enlightenment can become a factor by overcoming cultural stagnation and disintegration in the Arab-Islamic world. Can the philosophy of Ibn Rushd help to develop an appreciation for the Enlightenment in the Arab-Islamic world—and could this be a basis for establishing a bridge between Afro-Asian and European culture?

To answer these questions, it is necessary to identify the importance of the Enlightenment, not only for Arab-Islamic and Afro-Asian culture, but also for the world at large. The overall purpose of our conferences is to discover the efficiency of the Enlightenment in revitalizing the cultural development of the Arab-Islamic world. In this way, perhaps Arabic-Islamic culture can be better integrated into world civilization by influencing it and being influenced by it. Hence, it is hoped that the golden ages of Islamic intellectual civilization can be revived within the context of the twentieth century and through the philosophy of Ibn Rushd.

It is therefore essential that we analyze the writings of both Ibn Rushd and the European philosophers of the Enlightenment, particularly Kant.

The European participants would therefore present their analysis within the context of European philosophers of the Enlightenment and their critics (especially Kant and his critics). Another kind of analysis could be presented within the context of the twentieth-century supporters of the Enlightenment and its critics, e.g., the Frankfurt School, postmodernism and, more recently, Christian and Jewish fundamentalism.

The Arab participants would equally present their analyses of Enlightenment and its critics within the context of Ibn Rushd, al-Ghazali, and Ibn Taimeya, and within the context of the twentieth-century supporters and critics of the Enlightenment, particularly the representatives of Islamic fundamentalism.

Both analyses will emphasize the influence of the philosophy of Ibn Rushd on the European Enlightenment. In a similar way, opposition to the Enlightenment can be highlighted in both cultures.

Within this context, we invited scholars from all over the world representing divergent viewpoints in order to present the pros and cons. In this sense, we could claim that the conference succeeded. Reference to some representative views expressed in the pages below illustrates this point. For example, Paul Kurtz states that Ibn Rushd was one of the key figures in the development of the Enlightenment and a precursor of the modern scientific outlook. Oliver Leaman thinks that there is little difficulty in seeing Ibn Rushd as a thinker who was in harmony with the main principles of the Enlightenment. Stefan Wild criticizes the term, coined by Mourad Wahba, "the paradox of Averroës"; that is, the "Latin" Averroës played an acknowledged role in the development of the philosophy of the European Enlightenment, whereas the Arab Ibn Rushd was neglected and disavowed by Islamic culture, the very culture that had produced him. Wild argues that the history of the reception of Ibn Rushd in nineteenth and twentieth-century Europe shows that the question what Ibn Rushd "really stood for" is unanswerable. One more controversy. Mona Abousenna declares that Ibn Rushd is the founder of hermeneutics, whereas Alfred Ivry objects to the reinterpretation of historical figures for contemporary purposes.

We are publishing the proceedings of the conference to pursue the dialogue. The proceedings are divided into two parts. The first part includes the papers presented at the Cairo conference in 1994 and the second part includes the papers presented at the Amherst, N.Y., conference as a follow-up to the first one under the title "Averroës and His Influence: Remembering George Hourani." The Amherst conference, held at the Center for Inquiry and the State University of New York at Buffalo (Amherst campus) on April 12 and 13, 1996, did honor to Ibn Rushd on the one hand and on the other hand, George Hourani, who devoted most of his time to working on Ibn Rushd and Islamic rationalism. Hourani was a former professor in the Department of Philosophy at the State University at Buffalo and a dedicated scholar of Islamic philosophy.

In conclusion, we would like to thank and gratefully acknowledge first, our partner, Paul Kurtz, representative of the Center for Inquiry and the State University of New York at Buffalo, and the Egyptian ministries of Foreign Affairs and of Culture, the Supreme Council of Culture, the League of Arab States, Goethe Institute, UNESCO, and the Cultural Development Fund for the generous financial assistance, which helped to make the conference the success that it was. The Amherst, N.Y., conference was made possible by grants from the Hourani Fund of the Department of Philosophy at the State University of New York at Buffalo, the International Humanist and Ethical Union, and the Center for Inquiry.

The Editors
1996

PART ONE

THE FIRST SPECIAL INTERNATIONAL PHILOSOPHY CONFERENCE ON IBN RUSHD (AVERROËS) AND THE ENLIGHTENMENT

1

Opening Addresses

Amir Moussa
Egyptian Minister of Foreign Affairs

When I was invited to take part in this conference, the theme of which revolves around the Enlightenment, I deemed it befitting to share with you some thoughts which, I hope, may present a new perception to the paradigm of the Enlightenment. I naturally anticipate that some of you would legitimately wonder as to the interrelationship, if there is any at all, between foreign policy and the Enlightenment. I hasten to say in response that there is indeed a solid common thread connecting foreign policy with the subject you will be discussing during the next few days. To elucidate, allow me to make the following observations.

Until recently, the relationship between foreign policy and development was looked at with apprehension and incredulity. Today, as we are all aware, it is virtually impractical to deal with foreign policy in the absence of coming to grips with the economic situation, be it local, regional, or international.

The Enlightenment, in my judgment, should represent a third dimension to complement the triangle confined hitherto to foreign policy and world economy. The Enlightenment represents the intellectual dimension, which is organically connected with that of development, in the sense that both of them dread war and international anarchy as irrational disturbances

17

of the calculable mechanisms of world economy. It was none other than Immanuel Kant—whose name and philosophy will no doubt be frequently invoked throughout your conference, being the towering pioneer of the Enlightenment—who stated that the spirit of economy and the welfare of man cannot coexist with war.

The Enlightenment attaches significant importance to concepts of peace and international harmony. It equally preaches values of human rights and interdependence among units of the human family. In practicing diplomacy, we are doing just the same: consecrating peace, promoting human rights, and recognizing the validity of interdependence among nations. From this angle, I could not possibly have missed making my contribution to your conference today.

I must equally pay tribute to your insightful selection of the Third World as a cardinal model in examining and exploring its relationship with the Enlightenment. Egypt not only belongs to the Third World, but happens to play an instrumental role in formulating all facets related to its diplomatic, economic, institutional, and environmental affairs. Your conference introduces yet one more dimension to Egypt's role among Third World countries; the role of enlightening the minds so as to help turn this part of the world to a more promising future.

Your conference could not have been convened in a more propitious time. Nor could it have chosen a more relevant venue. As you are fully aware, our region is currently embroiled in a host of unsettling currents and approaches which, in essence, run contrary to the spirit of the Enlightenment. Fundamentalism is conspicuously permeating many circles in our region. Symptoms of bigotry and intolerance are decomposing the otherwise compassionate and benevolent tenets of all monotheistic religions embraced by millions in the Middle East. Terrorism is resorted to in lieu of persuasion and dialogue. Enlightened thinkers and writers have increasingly become a prime target of extremists who emanate from convoluted value judgments and arbitrary interpretations of our luminous heritage. The Enlightenment can serve as an efficient antidote to all such aggravations, since extremism basically describes the impulse which is inimical to a pluralism of social harmony and the coalition among all religions and dogmas.

I highly commend if only from this sole attitudinal prism the pertinence of your pivotal and timely theme. Within the course of your deliberations you are bound to touch upon such notions—inextricably connected to foreign policy—as peace, disarmament, and human rights.

Present-day problems are so complex that we must come up with unconventional and sophisticated solutions for them. I can think of no more prestigious forum than yours that is sufficiently competent to devise the level of solutions desired. By employing your collective wisdom and insightful approaches to issues related to the Enlightenment, you are in fact rendering a helpful contribution towards saving our region from the menaces of regression and atavism. You are, moreover—though unwittingly—beckoning further light onto areas tangentially addressed by our foreign policy.

From that premise, I wish you success in your endeavor.

Essmat Abdel-Maguid
Secretary General, League of Arab States

It gives me great pleasure to participate in the inauguration of this important international conference on "Ibn Rushd (Averroës) and the Enlightenment."

On behalf of Dr. Essmat Abdel-Maguid, I am pleased to convey to you his Excellency's wish to attend the conference in person which he could not realize due to earlier commitments.

Please accept my deepest respect for and appreciation of the Afro-Asian Philosophy Association for organizing the First Special International Conference on "Ibn Rushd (Averroës) and the Enlightenment," and an equal sense of appreciation and gratitude to the eminent professors who traveled from different parts of the world for the sake of reviving the thought of this great Muslim philosopher whose influence surpassed the boundaries of the Islamic world and reached as far as Europe. The European mind, through the impact of Averroës, was capable of reading developed forms of philosophical and scientific debate. This is because Averroës, being a great man of knowledge, could develop and promote the legacy of reason and wisdom. He could also actively contribute to the emergence of the Enlightenment and to the building of bridges between the Arabic Islamic culture and other world cultures. Therefore, Averroës's influence has survived until our present age. This is testified to by the abundance of books, articles, and researches currently being published worldwide in different languages.

The main objective of your conference is to analyze the philosophical works of Averroës as well as those of the philosophers of the Enlightenment in Europe with the purpose of rediscovering the merits of Averroës's philosophy and the Arab roots of modern European culture. The study of this important period, that is, the twelfth and thirteenth centuries, is indeed of vital necessity in order to discover the common factors that unite the Islamic and the Western cultures.

Undoubtedly, this conference, comes as a prelude to the world celebration of Averroës's eight hundredth anniversary due to take place in 1998.

The League of Arab States, due to its keen interest in all that has been written about Averroës as the leading Muslim philosopher who has greatly contributed to the building of bridges of knowledge between various cultures, published in 1978 a book entitled *The Works of Averroës* (*Moalafat Ibn Rushd*), which is a bibliography that includes all published works as well as the unpublished manuscripts with reference to all the old and recent studies on Averroës.

The League of Arab States hopes that your conference will set up an international committee which will undertake the publication of Averroës's works in Arabic and English and to make them available to the researchers who are interested in developing Averroës's thought. We hope that such research would provide some guidelines for young researchers on the threshold of the twenty-first century.

To conclude, I wish you all a very successful conference and hope that you will reach the results for which you are convening today.

Farouk Hosni
Egyptian Minister of Culture

Ladies and Gentlemen, I feel extremely happy to attend this special International Conference organized by the Afro-Asian Philosophy Association in cooperation with the Supreme Council of Culture on the theme "Ibn Rushd (Averroës) and the Enlightenment." The reason for my happiness is due to the fact that the theme of this conference is in accordance with the Ministry of Culture's strategy and objectives. We are greatly concerned with publishing the legacy of Ibn Rushd, and we have so far published through the Supreme Council of Culture, Ibn Rushd's masterpiece on Aristotle's logic, the "Colliget," and "Epitome Meteorologica De Anima." Last year the supreme council published a voluminous memorial book on Ibn Rushd containing articles by eminent Egyptian professors of philosophy. A seminar was held to discuss the memorial book. It reasserted the Enlightenment values embodied by Ibn Rushd's philosophy throughout the Arab Islamic tradition. The Ministry's commitment to the Enlightenment was the motive behind publishing, through the General Book Organization (one of the Ministry's institutions), a series of low-priced books revolving around the tradition of the Enlightenment in Egypt, the Arab World, the Islamic World, and Europe. The slogan that we adopted for this series was "Confrontation" (*Al-Mowagaha*) by which we meant the confrontation of terrorism, extremism, and dogmatism: We confront these negative phenomena with the values of the Enlightenment such as rationalism to counterbalance the dangers of backwardness which were behind what happened to our eminent international novelist Naguib Mahfouz, when he faced an aborted attempt on his life because of enlightened views, which he expressed in his creative writings. Perhaps I should emphasize, on this occasion, that the major concern of the Ministry of Culture is to seek continuously the reconfirmation of the values of Enlightenment, freedom, and progress, which are also the values of creativity.

Ladies and Gentlemen, this is our concern and our commitment, which is not isolated from the concerns and interests of others working in the field of culture. There are plenty of books on Ibn Rushd published in foreign languages. Many seminars and conferences are held on the theme of Enlightenment. We Egyptians have recently celebrated the first centenary of the Egyptian Enlightenment, while Europe celebrated the second centenary of its own Enlightenment.

Within the context of this intellectual environment, we hold this conference to be distinct from any other conference because it relates Ibn Rushd to the Enlightenment and proceeds from the fact that this great Islamic philosopher has made an active contribution to the emergence of the Enlightenment in Europe. His philosophy constitutes an authentic foundation of the European Enlightenment. Ibn Rushd shortened the march of civilization which began in the twelfth century, the century in which Ibn Rushd confronted dogmatism and fanaticism by writing his books. When his books were translated into Latin and Hebrew in Europe in the thirteenth century, they had a great impact in transforming Europe from the Dark Ages to the Age of Enlightenment.

Ladies and Gentlemen, it gives me great pleasure to announce to you that the Ministry of Culture has decided to hold a world congress in Cairo on December 10, 1998, to commemorate the eight hundredth anniversary of Ibn Rushd. We expect to receive your recommendations and suggestions, which will be of great benefit to us in the organization of this world congress.

Finally, I congratulate you for your concern with Ibn Rushd and I would like to express my deep appreciation to the Afro-Asian Philosophy Association for organizing this conference. I also deeply thank all the participants who have contributed papers to the conference and welcome you all to Cairo and wish you a pleasant stay and a successful conference.

Ioanna Kuçuradi
Secretary General of the
International Federation of Philosophical Societies

It is an honor and a pleasure for me to welcome, on behalf of the International Federation of Philosophical Societies, all of you to this international conference on "Ibn Rushd (Averroës) and the Enlightenment," organized by the Afro-Asian Philosophy Association.

This is a conference in a chain of conferences which Prof. Mourad Wahba, founder and now honorary president of the Afro-Asian Association, and Prof. Mona Abousenna, Regional Secretary for Africa, started organizing toward the end of the 1970s and which show a continuity in the march toward the same objective, that is, highlighting the need for Enlightenment in Afro-Asian societies—a need which in the meanwhile has become a global one.

To better understand what is going on in this respect in our day, at the end of the twentieth century, a study of the question of how the medieval world (medieval philosophy and culture) emerged from the classical world could be helpful; since if we take a look at what is going on just at this moment on the global level, keeping in mind the history of ideas, we see, to our astonishment, striking *factual* similarities between the intellectual climate of the period of transition from classical to medieval thinking and the intellectual climate of our day.

In this short address I shall not dwell on this question, nor shall I repeat the analyses I made on other occasions concerning the intellectual developments throughout our century, lying in the background of the problems we face now.* I shall confine myself to pointing at only one fact, a

---

*One of these analyses can be found in my "Modernity as a Concept and as a Project, or 'Modernity,' Modernization and Beyond," published in *Cultures in Conflict or in Dialogue? Proceedings of the Third Afro-Asian Philosophy Conference,* held in Cairo in October 1990.

discrepancy or a paradox we have witnessed in the past two or three decades—which is, to my mind, directly connected with the problem of our conference, but which we are not sufficiently aware of.

This fact is our *simultaneous* promotion of human rights and of the so-called fundamental freedoms, as universal principles—that is, as principles deduced from the assumption of the *unity* of human beings—on the one hand, and on the other hand our well-minded but *not sufficiently scrutinized* promotion of cultural-ethnical identities based on the cultural differences of groups, which are a fact, *not* an ideal—our promotion of the so-called "respect for all cultures," and on top of all our promoting the development of cultural identities as a human right.

This discrepancy appears to be one of the main causes—if not the main intellectual factor—behind the increasing spread of religious fundamentalism(s), nationalisms, racisms, and ethnic prejudices, whose "embers of hatred" were "rekindled by the winds of freedom," as Federico Mayor, the general director of UNESCO, observes in one of his articles connected with the proclamation of 1995 as the "Year of Tolerance."

Thus in our attempts to fight them, without taking this discrepancy into consideration, we find ourselves helpless, and these calamities gain ground more and more.

Put very briefly, what happened seems to be the following. The failure of the development policies to fulfill the expectations for which they were introduced on global level was ascribed to understanding development only as economic development; thus the idea to bring "a cultural dimension" to this development or the idea of "cultural development" gained ground.

"Cultural development" was nevertheless understood differently in different categories of countries. In Western countries it was understood as "broadening for the masses of the possibility to have access to and participation in culture," that is, in activities considered to afford individuals the possibility to develop their potentialities as human beings—to artistic, scientific, philosophical activities. In the decolonized developing countries, mainly African countries, it was understood as being allowed to develop—to identify and reconstruct—their own culture, that is, the world view, the conception of man, and the norms prevailing in them before the colonization era. Also this understanding was globally supported and the demand for "equal respect for all cultures" came to the fore. It escaped, and still escapes, attention that respect for all human beings as human beings, whatever their cultures might be, and respect for cultures *themselves*, that is, to all world views and norms, whatever they be, demand respect for two quite different things.

Meanwhile, the peoples of countries "on the way to modernization" which earlier had opted for "modernization" or "westernization"—in fact certain groups in such countries—conceived "cultural development" as resurrection or revival of the culture, that is, of the world view and norms prevailing among them before they came into touch with the West.

Thus in this latter category of countries we observe the tendency to divorce modernization from what was called earlier "westernization," and as a result there was a confrontation and conflict of different cultures *within* the same country, within the same society, which leads people even to unscrupulous murder—to the kind of terrorism we observe in many such countries.

These systematic or programmatic attempts to resurrect an old world view and old norms in the latter category of countries, coupled with the "winds of freedom," that is, the demands which the so-called fundamental freedoms express, makes it possible for those who try to achieve this resurrection to use these "freedoms" for spreading world views and norms damaging to basic human rights. Governments attempting to limit such actions are accused of violation of human rights. This is an accusation that democratic governments, or governments claiming or wishing to be democratic, in such countries are, at this moment, mostly unable to face and which puts them in front of a dilemma.

In all these, it escapes attention that the idea of human rights, as universal principles, is used for defending empirical—nonuniversal—norms, which, in the conditions prevailing when they were deduced many centuries ago, might have been useful, but are now damaging to human rights. In other words, it escapes attention that the ideas of the Enlightenment are used for spreading norms preventing enlightenment, as it escapes attention that what makes this use possible is—so far as I can see—the prevailing understanding of freedoms as basic *rights* of the *individual*.

This same understanding of freedoms makes democratic governments in European countries unable to face increasing racism and nationalism, which leads even to killing people from other cultures—immigrant workers for example. It makes just now those governments unable to forbid racist propaganda, which contributed to the increase of ethnic and racial discrimination and which has "rekindled the embers of racial and ethnic prejudices" we observe now in Europe.

Something else also escapes attention in the global promotion of democracy, which *presupposes* enlightenment in the Kantian sense, that is, "man's leaving his self-caused immaturity" and using his own "intelligence without the guidance of another": it escapes attention that democracy is based on the concept of *citizenship*, the idea of the equal *political* rights of *enlightened individual citizens*, for the better fulfillment of the implications of basic human rights; while the demand for respect to *different* cultures and ethnicities in a country amounts to a demand for respect of different norms, which are not only discrepant among themselves, but sometimes in contradiction with human rights, and tends to lead to a new communalism, based on acknowledging equal rights to communities which are differentiated by the difference of their norms.

In order to tackle this and many other similar problems not mentioned here, we need a new enlightenment.

In our age, in which democracy has become a motto, we need enlightenment so that democracy can function. We have recently witnessed where democracy without enlightenment can lead. And for enlightenment, we need philosophical education, that is, an education which by training young people to use their own intelligence and to become able to relate every action they are about to perform to philosophical-ethical knowledge, aims at helping them become conscious of their *human identity* before any other identity they might have—a consciousness which is a *sine qua non* for the enlightened protection of human rights at national and global levels.

Mourad Wahba
Founder and Honorary President of the
Afro-Asian Philosophy Association

I have the honor and the privilege of opening the First Special International Philosophy Conference on Ibn Rushd (Averroës) and the Enlightenment, which is, at the same time, the Fifth Afro-Asian Philosophy Conference organized by the Afro-Asian Philosophy Association (AAPA).

As the founder and honorary president of the AAPA, I would like to say a few words about the birth of the association. Its birth was due to a paper presented by me at the Seventeenth Pakistan Philosophical Congress held in Lahore in October 1975, entitled "Authenticity and Modernization in the Third World." The pivotal idea in this paper could be presented in a nutshell as follows: the civilizational gap between the developed and the developing countries passes through two phases that have been already undergone by the developed countries: that is, the sovereignty of reason, and commitment to reason to change reality for the benefit of the mass man. Consequently, the crucial question that has to be raised is the following:

How can the two phases come into existence?

In my opinion this is impossible without the Reformation and the Enlightenment. The Reformation is based on free inquiry into the sacred books. The Enlightenment, which surpassed the Reformation, liberated reason not only from the religious authorities but also from any authority except that of reason itself. This is the real challenge that confronts the developing countries.

In 1977 in San Francisco I presented a paper in an Islamic philosophy conference entitled "Averroës and the Enlightenment." The pivotal idea in this paper is that Averroës's philosophy helped in breeding the Enlightenment in the West, whereas it failed to do the same thing in the East. Consequently, two questions have been raised:

1. Are the developing countries in need of enlightenment?

2. How far can the philosophical spirit of Ibn Rushd be a factor in generating the Enlightenment in the developing countries?

The Afro-Asian Philosophy Association has found that these questions are relevant to what is going on today, where religious fundamentalists are spreading all over the world. My colleagues in the AAPA shared with me the view regarding the importance of these questions as well as other, related ones which we decided to put under international discussion. Within this context, this first special international conference is held on the theme "Ibn Rushd (Averroës) and the Enlightenment."

To conclude, let me offer my deep, heartfelt thanks and my gratitude to His Excellency Amre Moussa, minister of foreign affairs; His Excellency Dr. Essmat Abdel-Maguid, secretary general of the League of Arab States; His Excellency Farouk Hosni, minister of culture and head of the Supreme Council of Culture. My thanks also to Professor Ioanna Kuçuradi, secretary general of the International Federation of Philosophical Societies; Dr. Hubert Hohl, director of the Goethe Institute; Mr. Thomson, representative of the British Council; and Mr. John Macullough, manager of educational services at the British Council. I am greatly indebted to all of them for their invaluable help and great support, without which this conference could not have been held. Special thanks are due to Professor Paul Kurtz, representing the State University of New York at Buffalo, our academic partner in the organization of the conference.

I would also like to welcome our colleagues who are participating in the conference for their enthusiasm and for their valuable contributions to the conference theme. I thank you all and wish you a pleasant stay in Cairo, and a fruitful and interesting conference.

2

Intellectual Freedom, Rationality, and Enlightenment: The Contributions of Averroës

Paul Kurtz
Professor Emeritus of Philosophy,
State University of New York at Buffalo

The Philosophy of Averroës

We do honor to a great thinker and philosopher, one who has had considerable influence on world civilization; and we come from various corners of the world to do so. As we approach the eight-hundredth anniversary of his death, it is time that his important contributions be better appreciated. Indeed, one can make the case that Ibn Rushd (1126–1198), or Averroës, his Latinized name, was one of the key figures in the development of the Enlightenment of the seventeenth and eighteenth centuries; at the very least he was a precursor of the modern scientific outlook.

Unfortunately, he was a prophet without honor in his own times, and it is only now that we can fully evaluate his contributions. It is well known that classical Islamic philosophers (from the ninth to twelfth centuries) added immeasurably to our common philosophical heritage. Their most important role was to preserve and transmit an appreciation for ancient Greek philosophy, especially Aristotle, to the world at a time when it was in danger of being lost. Al-Farabi (873–950) and Ibn Sina (Avicenna) (980–1037) pondered and commented on the works of Aristotle, but they provided a Neoplatonic interpretation. It was Ibn Rushd who constructed the most elegant, systematic interpretation of Aristotle, "The Philosopher," as he would later be called. Ibn Rushd's meticulous commentaries on Aristotle were a rich source of astute insights that later generations, particularly in Europe, found to be valuable.

Ibn Rushd presented Aristotle as a natural philosopher, interested in explaining the universe. *Falsafa*, or Greek philosophy, was conceived of as a demonstrative science, not a merely speculative activity per se, yielding objective knowledge of reality; for its conclusions were based on empirical observations and logical inferences. Aristotelian natural philosophy was thus advanced by Ibn Rushd as a rationally organized scientific study of the universe. Aristotle's cosmic outlook and his theory of human nature were in contrast on several key points with the world view that dominated Islamic, Christian, and Jewish theology in the medieval period. The Aristotelian universe was eternal, not created; there was little room for personal immortality, as the passive intellect was absorbed by the active intellect; and man could obtain ethical perfection in this life. For an age overwhelmed by faith, these views were innovative, even radical, so much so, indeed, that Ibn Rushd's works were condemned at one point by his compatriots.

Ibn Rushd was born and lived in Cordoba in the midst of intense philosophical and cultural creativity. Spain was then a pluralistic society in which three great religions subsisted side by side. Coming from a family of distinguished jurists, Ibn Rushd was commissioned by Caliph Abu Yaqub Yusuf to comment on and interpret Aristotle's works. This he began doing when he was forty-two, providing a constant stream of short, intermediate, and long commentaries. Nearing the end of his life, however, the attitude toward Ibn Rushd's work changed, a prohibition against his studies was issued, his books were burned, and he was insulted by a mob.[1] This ban was of short duration and he was restored to favor just before his death at the age of seventy-two.

The censorship of Ibn Rushd was not unique in the annals of philosophy; nor was it particularly harsh by comparison. Socrates, for example, was condemned to death by his fellow Athenians and he became a martyr to the life of reason. Spinoza was excommunicated from the synagogue and ostracized by the Jews of Amsterdam during his entire adult life because of his liberal views; Giordano Bruno was burned at the stake for advocating an unorthodox scientific cosmology; and Galileo was placed under house arrest by the papacy and forced to abjure the Copernican theory.

What a pity that Ibn Rushd's influence in the Muslim world waned after his death. Ibn Rushd/Averroës had a profound influence among Jewish and especially Latin scholars between 1200 and 1650. As such, he helped to contribute to the modern philosophical and scientific revolution that was then brewing in Europe. This occurred in part because a great number of translations from Arabic and Hebrew into Latin of Aristotle's writings, and especially the commentaries of Averroës, were made available to scholars. These were found to have a kind of autonomous logical coherence and they could be interpreted only by the rigorous exercise of rational analysis. The intellectual crisis provoked by the rediscovery of Aristotle challenged Christian theology on many fundamental issues. As a consequence, the works of Averroës were banned at the University of Paris in 1210 and 1215 and permitted only if corrected in 1231. Aristotle and Averroës stimulated theologians such as Albertus Magnus and Thomas Aquinas to try to reconcile the demands of scriptural faith with the standards of reason. The influence of Averroism on the Italian universities, particularly those at Padua and Bologna, had a direct impact on the emergence of modern science. Padua was host to a medical faculty that took Aristotle seriously; out of this context Galileo emerged. Granted, Newtonian-Galilean physics overthrew the Aristotelian heliocentric universe; nevertheless the methods of science were already implicit in Aristotle's natural philosophy.

One of the great intellectual tragedies of philosophy is the fact that Averroës's philosophy did not have any significant impact on the world of Muslim scholarship. Had it done so it might have led to a new Muslim Renaissance and Enlightenment, and perhaps to an outburst of scientific discoveries similar to that experienced by Western Europe and America.[2]

No doubt Averroës was thought to be dangerous to religious faith. Averroës himself wrestled with this problem. In his treatise *Incoherence of the Incoherence*[3] he attempted to respond to the attacks made by Al-Ghazali (1058–1111), a Muslim theologian who criticized Greek philosophical rationalism and defended spirituality as the primary source of truth. In his treatise *On the Harmony of Religion and Philosophy*, Averroës attempted to respond to Al-Ghazali and to reconcile the two domains. He argued that there is a unity of truth, though there are several modes of access to it: (1) rhetoric, which was available to ordinary people by means of teachers; (2) dialectics, which involves arguments in defense of revelation and Scripture; and (3) demonstration, which involved the rational inference of conclusions from indubitable premises. Philosophy in this third sense provides us with scientific truths about the world. Ibn Rushd did not advocate the thesis of a "double truth," as many later Averroists held; he thought that both philosophy and faith had a consistent role to play. What shall we do if we encounter a contradiction between philosophical demonstration and scriptural revelation? Ibn Rushd argued that in this case Scripture should be given an allegorical interpretation and is not to be taken in a strict literal sense. In *On the Harmony of Religion and Philosophy*, he insisted that he believed in the Qur'an and he indeed attempted to find additional scriptural sources for his defense of rational science.

Ibn Rushd was no revolutionary, and he did not criticize the Qur'an. All that he wished to defend was the importance of rational philosophical and scientific inquiry.[4] This inquiry he wished to restrict to a qualified group of philosophers and not the masses. There was no demand for democratic freedoms in society at large. The calls for democracy were only to come later, in the seventeenth and eighteenth centuries as a product of the Enlightenment. What is significant in reading Averroës is his conviction that man is a rational animal and that freedom for rational investigation needs to be defended. It is this defense of rational objectivity and free inquiry that is of crucial significance, for it puts forth key values as the basis for any scientific and philosophical search for the truth; it is this principle that is later taken up and defended during the Enlightenment.

What Is the Enlightenment?

One may ask, "What is the meaning of *enlightenment*?"

The term has been used by cultural historians to refer to certain intellectual trends that emerged in the seventeenth and eighteenth centuries in Western European culture. Its origin has been traced back to René Descartes, who is often considered to be the father of modern philosophy. But its roots appeared earlier in the views of the Latin Averroists. Many philosophers have been identified with the development of the Enlightenment, including Bacon, Hobbes, Locke, and Hume in Britain; the *philosophes* Voltaire, Diderot, Condorcet, d'Holbach, and the Encyclopedists in France; Kant and Goethe in Germany; and among the founders of the American Republic, Jefferson, Madison, Franklin, and others.

Immanuel Kant (1724–1804) was one of the leading proponents of the Enlightenment and perhaps Germany's greatest philosopher. In his critical philosophy he attempted to defend intellectual scientific objectivity. In an essay entitled "What Is Enlightenment?" Kant defines "enlightenment" as follows:

Enlightenment is man's release from his self-incurred tutelage. Tutelage is man's inability to make use of his understanding without direction from another . . . . *Sapere aude!* "Have courage to use your own reason!"—that is the motto of enlightenment. . . . For the enlightenment, however, nothing is required but freedom. . . . It is a freedom to make public use of one's reason at every point.[5]

Kant was heralded in his lifetime throughout the world. He was encouraged by Frederick the Great, king of Prussia and patron of the Enlightenment. Upon his death Frederick was succeeded to the throne by his nephew, Friedrich Wilhelm II, who issued a censorship edict in 1788, which forbade Kant to write anything about the Christian religion.[6] Kant agreed to be silent about such matters, at least until 1797, when Friedrich Wilhelm II died. By that time the Western Enlightenment commanded such a great hold on the Western intellectual community that liberty of thought and conscience could no longer be easily suppressed.

Today the Enlightenment has had an enormous impact on world civilization. It is usually identified with modernity itself, for it is said to express the essence of the modern philosophical and scientific outlook. What does this entail? First and foremost, an explicit quest for an *objective method of inquiry*. Descartes is significant here, for he details in his autobiography how he proposed to use a method of unlimited doubt, to question all of his beliefs, and re-establish them on firm rational foundations.[7] This, he thought, was best exemplified in mathematics, for it based its theorems on indubitable, clear, and distinct ideas and deductive inferences from them. Bacon, Locke, and Hume embarked on a similar program, although as empiricists they emphasized observations and the evidence of the senses. Philosophers of the modern period debated whether reason or experience was the foundation of human knowledge. By the time of Immanuel Kant it was recognized that *both* reason and experience are necessary criteria for validating knowledge claims. Added later was the pragmatic criterion of experimental verification.

These philosophers of the Enlightenment were reflecting on the new science, which had burst on the intellectual horizons and reached its culmination with the works of Galileo, Kepler, and Newton in astronomy and physics. The success of the natural sciences was attributed to the use of the hypothetical-deductive method in evaluating theories. The new science differed from Aristotle's conception of nature on important points: (1) it sought to use mathematics to interpret nature, (2) it used experiment, not simply observation, to test hypotheses, and (3) it rejected all final teleological causes. The new science used mechanical, materialistic, and efficient causes to unravel nature, and, unlike Aristotle's form and matter, it postulated material atomic structures. Unfortunately, many medieval scholars by that time took Aristotle as the ultimate authority in scientific knowledge; thus the heliocentric theory and the laws of motion were first opposed by them on the grounds that Aristotle held contrary views. But this appeal to authority violated the very spirit of Aristotle, which sought to base knowledge on empirical observation and rational inference.

A key point of modern philosophy and the Enlightenment is the view that there are objective methods of inquiry, and that these could be extended beyond the physical sciences to biology, psychology, and the social sciences. The expansion of scientific inquiry to these fields occurred in the nineteenth century, especially with the Darwinian theory of evolution, and in the nineteenth and twentieth centuries with the emergence of the social and behavioral sciences. Thus science was applied not only to the understanding of nature, but to human behavior. It was also believed by defenders of the Enlightenment that reason could be used to deal with our ethical values, and that we could resolve social problems by applying the methods of science and reason.

It was widely held that the advancement of science would have positive benefits for human life. Since that time the rapid development of industry and technology has transformed the globe, and is improving the standard of life of humankind, at least in affluent societies. The Enlightenment also led to the democratic revolutions of our time; parliamentary democracy and democratic governments are replacing autocratic dictatorships throughout the world.

A fundamental principle of modern democracy is the ideal of *intellectual freedom*. This means that no group has the right to prohibit free inquiry or suppress the right to knowledge and the free use thereof.[8] The case for intellectual freedom—and concomitantly civil liberties, including liberty of speech, the press, and of voluntary association—has been made by the philosophers of democracy such as John Stuart Mill, John Dewey, and Sir Karl Popper.[9]

Some important epistemological considerations are especially relevant. First is the recognition that truth is a product of a process of inquiry and that it depends on continuing research and investigation in a community of inquirers. This is vital in the sciences, whether physics or biology, medical science or geology, history or economics. For the validity of scientific theories is a function of the evidence and logic brought to support them.

One must have an open mind and be prepared to revise one's theories in the light of criticism. Scientific principles should be treated as hypotheses: they are not absolute or final laws of nature, but tentative principles tested by their experimental consequences. Hypotheses therefore need to be constantly reformulated in the light of empirical discoveries and new theories introduced to account for them. Any effort to enunciate absolute truths or ultimate first principles beyond question is hazardous. Skepticism is an essential ingredient in scientific inquiry. The principle of fallibilism, according to Charles Peirce, America's leading philosopher, plays a central role: Do not block reason, or inquiry, he argued, by saying that this, that, or anything else has reached a final formulation or is beyond further questioning or revision.[10] The whole history of modern scientific thought—from Newton to Einstein and beyond—demonstrates the need for a questioning attitude in every field of research. Science is predicated on free, untrammeled inquiry; it could not go on without it. No society can participate in the modern world and benefit from the progress of science and technology if it continually denies intellectual freedom. Those societies that seek to block creative inquiry will stagnate.

Attacks on the Enlightenment in the West

I have been asked to outline some of the attacks on the Enlightenment in the West in the contemporary world. They are, of course, legion:

We have been witness in the twentieth century to awesome totalitarian ideologies that have denied the ideals of the Enlightenment and repressed human freedom. Fascism violated basic human rights, including intellectual freedom, and it substituted violence for reason. Communism attempted the same. Paradoxically, Marx claimed to be heir to the Enlightenment; yet the Marxist-Leninist state imposed by terror its vision of the ideal utopia, based on the dialectic, and it thus betrayed freedom of thought and conscience. Fortunately, both of these movements have been discredited, and the virtues of the open, democratic society vindicated worldwide. There exist still other powerful forces, many of them very ancient, that have been unleashed in the world. These include nationalism, ethnic rivalries, tribal animosities, and religious fundamentalisms. In exciting the passions of chauvinism and hatred, reason disappears. These social phenomena are of course well known and I only mention them without elaboration.

I wish to focus instead on some philosophical trends in recent decades that I find particularly troubling: that is, the attacks on science and reason from within the intellectual world. These objections are not without precedent. We are aware of the fact that the Age of Reason was followed by the Romantic protest, and that philosophers, artists, and poets argued that man is not really a rational animal, but in need of expressing his poetic feelings and passions. I surely am sensitive to this indictment. We must appreciate the whole person and the wide range of human experience, including aesthetic and moral dimensions. Reason is but one of many components of human nature. It has a valuable role to play, but this does not mean that it should extinguish other genuine human needs and aspirations.

It is paradoxical that today, when the sciences are advancing by leaps and bounds and when the earth is being transformed by scientific discoveries and technological applications, a strong antiscience counterculture has emerged in the Western world. This contrasts markedly with attitudes toward science that existed during the Enlightenment. There have always been two cultures existing side by side, as C. P. Snow has shown.[11] Historically there has been a debate between those who wish to advance scientific culture and those who claim that there are "two truths." According to the latter, there exists along with cognitive scientific knowledge a mystical realm and/or aesthetic and subjective aspect of experience. The two cultures do not always live in peaceful coexistence; in recent decades there have been overt, radical attacks on science that threaten its position in society.

From within philosophy dissent has come from three influential areas. First, many philosophers of science, from Kuhn to Feyerabend, have argued that there is no such thing as scientific method, that scientific knowledge is relative to sociocultural institutions, that paradigm shifts occur for extrarational causes, and that therefore the earlier confidence that there are objective methods for testing scientific claims is mistaken.

This critique is, in my view, greatly exaggerated. It is true that science functions in relation to the social and cultural conditions from which it emerges, and I have conceded that we cannot make absolute statements in science. Nonetheless, there are reliable standards for testing claims and some criteria of objectivity, and these transcend specific social and cultural contexts. How does one explain the vast body of scientific knowledge we possess? A specific claim in science cannot be said to be the same as a poetic metaphor or a religious tenet, for it is tested by its experimental consequences in the real world.

The second philosophical attack comes from the disciples of Heidegger, especially the French postmodernists, such as Derrida, Foucault, Lacan, and Lyotard. They argue that science is only one mythic system or narrative among many others. They maintain that by deconstructing scientific language, we discover that there are no real standards of objectivity. Heidegger complained that science and technology were dehumanizing. Foucault pointed out that science is often dominated by power structures, bureaucracy, and the state, and that the political and economic uses of science have undermined the pretensions of scientific neutrality. Some of these criticisms are no doubt valid, but they are overstated. If the alternative to objectivity is subjectivity, and if there are no warranted claims to truth, then the views of the postmodernists cannot be said to be true either. Surely we can maintain that the principles of mechanics are reliable, that Mars is a planet that orbits the sun, that cardiovascular diseases can be explained causally and preventive measures taken to lower the risk of them, that the structure of DNA is not simply a social artifact nor insulin a cultural creation.

The postmodern critics of modernity are objecting to the rationalist or foundationalist interpretations of science that emerged in the sixteenth and seventeenth centuries, and perhaps rightly so. For the continuous growth and revision of scientific theories demonstrates that any quest for certainty within science is mistaken. Nonetheless, they go too far in abandoning the entire modern scientific enterprise.

A third area of antiscience is the growth of multicultural and feminist critiques of knowledge. The multiculturalist view is that science is not universal or transcultural, but relative to the culture from which it emerges. There are, we are told, primitive and other cultures that are as true and valid as the scientific culture of the world that has emerged. This movement supports the complete relativization of scientific knowledge. The radical feminist indictment of "masculine bias" in science maintains that science has been the expression of "dead, white males"—from Newton to Heisenberg, Descartes to Bertrand Russell. They defend instead what they call "feminine epistemology." What we must do, the extremists of these movements advise, is liberate humanity from cultural, racist, and sexist expressions of knowledge, and this means from scientific objectivity as well. The positive contribution of these movements, of course, is that they seek to open science to more women and minorities and I would strongly defend minority and women's rights. The negative dimension is that multiculturalist and feminist demands tend to weaken an understanding of the rigorous intellectual standards essential for effective scientific inquiry. Clearly we need to appreciate the scientific contribution of many cultures and the role of women in science throughout history; on the other hand, some multicultural critics undermine the very possibility of objective science. I submit that science provides us with universal knowledge that transcends the limits of culture or gender.

Science presupposes that there *are* objective methods by which reliable knowledge can be tested. This means that hypotheses and theories can be formulated and that they can be warranted (1) by reference to the evidence, (2) by criteria of rational coherence, and (3) by their predicted experimental consequences. Modern scientists find that mathematical quantification is a powerful tool in establishing theories. They hold that there are causal regularities and relationships in our interactions with nature that can be discovered. Although knowledge may not be universal, it is general in the sense that it goes beyond mere subjective or cultural relativity and is rooted in an intersubjective and intercultural community of inquirers. As the progressive and fallible character of science is understood, it is seen that it is difficult to reach absolute or final statements, that science is tentative and probabilistic, and that scientific inquiry needs to be open to alternative explanations. Previous theories are therefore amenable to challenge and revision, and selective and constructive skepticism is an essential element in the scientific outlook. Last is the appreciation of the fact that knowledge of the probable causes of phenomena as discovered by scientific research can be applied, that powerful technological inventions can be discovered, and that these can be of enormous benefit to human beings.

We are of course well aware of the classical schools of skepticism that flourished in the ancient Greek and Roman world, which reemerged at the beginning of the modern period, and which influenced philosophers as diverse as Descartes and Hume. There are various forms of skepticism, from extreme nihilism to selective skepticism within the contexts of inquiry. I have argued that some form of skepticism is essential to scientific inquiry. This is positive and constructive; it emphasizes *inquiry* rather than doubt.

The recent critics of scientific objectivity and rationality, however, seem to me too nihilistic in their skepticism, for they would undermine the very integrity of science and rational philosophical discourse. If all knowledge is utterly subjective and relative to culture or gender, then would not this pertain to their own indictments, which are equally subjective and no more worthy of validity than any other? Their arguments pale to insignificance in comparison with the continued progressive growth of scientific knowledge.

In my view, Ibn Rushd's epistemology in modified form provides a more adequate framework for approaching the questions of epistemology. He is in a very real sense one of the heroic figures in the pantheon of world culture, for he played an important role in defending the integrity of rational inquiry. We can still read him with profit today and appreciate all the more his great contributions to objective knowledge, freedom, and human enlightenment.

Notes

1. Ibn Rushd's biographer Ansari records Ibn Rushd's plight at that time. See: George Hourani, ed., *On the Harmony of Religion and Philosophy* (London: Luzac and Co., 1967), p. 39.

2. Perhaps an explanation of this was the fact that the Spanish Inquisition was embarked upon to root out all "non-Christian" influences. Thus the Moors and the Jews were expelled from Spain and their works banned by Roman Catholic monarchs.

3. *Tahafut al-tahafut* (1180). See Averroës, *Destructio Destructionum Philosophiae Algazeelis in the Latin Version of Calo Calonymus*, Beatrice H. Zedler, ed. (Milwaukee, Wisc.: Marquette University Press, 1961).

4. Ernest Renan in *Averroës et Averroisme: essay historique*, 3d ed. (Paris, 1866) interpreted Ibn Rushd as a freethinker, though this interpretation has been criticized by others.

5. Immanuel Kant, "What Is Enlightenment?" in *On History*, Lewis White Beck, Robert E. Anchor, and Emil L. Fackenheim, trans., a volume in the "Library of Liberal Arts" series (Indianapolis, Ind.: Bobbs-Merrill, 1957), pp. 3–10.

6. Johann Christian Wöllner, minister of state and justice to the king, sent a letter to Kant dated October 1, 1794. It read: "For some considerable time Our Most Exalted Person has observed with great displeasure how you have misused your philosophy to the misrepresentation and depreciation of many of the principle and fundamental teachings of Holy Writ and of the Christian Religion, to whit in your book, *Religion Within the Limits of Reason Alone*, as well as in other short treatises. We expected better of you, since you yourself must be conscious of your lack of responsibility both toward your duty as a teacher of youth and our

sovereign intentions, of which you are fully aware. We immediately demand of you the conscientious acceptance of your responsibilities and we expect you, on pain of our highest displeasure, not to allow yourself to be guilty of any future acts of this nature, but rather, in accordance with your duty, to devote your authority and your talents to the ever-increasing achievement of our sovereign purposes; if, on the contrary, you persist in your rebellion, you will suffer disagreeable consequences." Quoted in Willibald Klinke, *Kant for Everyman* (New York: Collier Books, 1962), p. 70.

7. *Meditations* and *On Method*.

8. It is a right recognized by the United Nations' Universal Declaration of Human Rights.

9. See especially John Stuart Mill, *On Liberty*; John Dewey, *Freedom and Culture*; and Karl Popper, *The Open Society and Its Enemies*.

10. See Charles Peirce, "Notes on Scientific Philosophy," in C. Hartshorne and Paul Weiss, eds., *Collected Papers of Charles Sanders Peirce*, vol. 1 (Cambridge, Mass.: Harvard University Press, 1931).

11. C. P. Snow, *The Two Cultures and the Scientific Revolution* (New York: Cambridge University Press, 1959).

3

Medieval Scholasticism and Averroism: The Implication of the Writings of Ibn Rushd to Western Science

Vern L. Bullough
Distinguished Professor Emeritus,
State University of New York (USA)

Western Christianity up to the twelfth century was essentially Augustinian and Neoplatonic. Aristotle, with the exception of his treatises on logic, known collectively as the *Organon,* was unknown. There was, however, a tradition of rational thought, best exemplified by the writing of John Scotus Eriugena in the ninth century C.E. While he recognized the authority of the Scriptures and the Fathers, he put reason first. This is because though authority is earlier in time than reason, reason is by nature older than authority and superior to it. In fact authority, Eriugena said, comes from reason, and reason does not come from authority. Reason needs no support from authority but authority must have the support of reason.[1] To follow reason, however, does not mean to break with authority. Eriugena's often quoted statement on this is that, "True authority does not oppose right reason, nor right reason true authority. For it is not to be doubted that both come from one source, namely the divine wisdom."[2]

This assumption led some Western theologians to try to prove the existence of God, and to a major battle over universals, simply put, the recognition that the human mind has the capacity to take a group of somewhat different individuals or things and represent them under one thought or at

41

least under one name. The issue on which the medieval theologians (and philosophers) disagreed was whether universals existed apart from their ideas in finite minds or whether they had no existence in themselves but were categories of convenience developed by humans. Notable in this respect was the eleventh-century archbishop of Canterbury, Anselm, a dialectician, who attempted to demonstrate the existence of God on the basis of reason alone without appealing to religious authority. The result was his ontological proof for the existence of God, essentially that because we can conceive of a supreme being, such a being must exist.[3]

Anselm was a realist (idealist) in the Platonic sense and much of his work was written in response to the ideas of his contemporary Roscellinus, who was an advocate of nominalism, holding that individuals alone are real and universals nothing but words. This led Roscellinus to hold that the three persons of the Trinity were real but that the common divine nature that they were supposed to share had no actual existence.[4] Neither Anselm nor Roscellinus were very good logicians although there is a great show of logic in their discussions. Both, however, operated on a lot of unfounded assumptions.

The issue is further complicated by the efforts of Abelard at the end of the eleventh century. He was a pupil for a time of Roscellinus, later of the realist William of Champeaux (who picked up on Anselm). Abelard criticized both of his teachers, although his ultimate position was closer to Roscellinus than to William. He held that the individual alone is real in the strict sense, and that there was no general substance but only particular substances. Still, genus or species has reality in a secondary sense, in that the individuals that constitute such categories are bound together by the possession of identical qualities that actually reside in the things themselves, which are not merely the product of imagination. Abelard was not a strict rationalist, however, for he believed in a divine revelation and recognized the authority of the Scriptures.[5]

Abelard's views are more important for their criticism of his contemporaries than for solutions. The problem was how to deal with the debate and it is with this background that the writings of Aristotle begin to permeate into Western Europe, primarily at first through Islamic commentators. They were seized upon to give answers through what might be called moderate realism, which, put simply, argues that there are no real and actual universals in themselves but there are actual universal ideas in the intellects of humans and these concepts had an objective basis in the real similarities of individuals and of real classes of things.

Ibn Rushd

The key Islamic transmitter was Ibn Rushd, known in the West as Averroës, and his commentaries on Aristotle remained more or less standard until the late seventeenth century. This in spite of the fact that many of his writings were condemned by various Church authorities. Sometimes it is not so important what a person actually says as what he is believed to have said, and this is particularly true of Western ideas about Ibn Rushd. In the Islamic tradition, Ibn Rushd might be characterized as representing the culmination of the efforts of the philosopher scientists. He regarded Aristotelianism as the truth, at least in so far as the truth is accessible to the human mind, and his commentaries on Aristotle are the most comprehensive that were made. Aristotle's texts often posed difficulties and usually it was Ibn Rushd's version that prevailed. The key to the difficulties Ibn Rushd had in the West was his view of Aristotle's metaphysics. He felt that metaphysics in general was almost impossible to understand, and that it was difficult to grasp either metaphysical truth as a whole or even one of its important parts. The one exception to this was Aristotle, who in Ibn Rushd's mind seemed to have grasped the truth, or at least most of the truth about this area, and that what his predecessors grasped was very little in comparison, whether it be the whole or the most important part. For this reason, the best thing to do in Ibn Rushd's mind was to assume that Aristotle comprehended the entire truth, and by the entire truth he meant that quantity which human nature—insofar as it is human—is capable of grasping.[6]

It was the logical demonstrations in Aristotle's philosophical and scientific writings that led Ibn Rushd to this conclusion. Ibn Rushd, however, made an important qualification in his evaluation of Aristotle, cautioning that while the Greek philosopher possessed the totality of the truth available to man, he did not possess the Truth itself. In short, he allowed for faith in revealed truths.

Ibn Rushd apparently had not read Aristotle in the original Greek but had depended upon Arabic translations, some of them quite garbled. He tried to make sense of these confused areas, and it is his interpretation which was generally followed in the West. Ibn Rushd emphasized the opposition between Aristotle and Plato and criticized and corrected the erroneous positions he felt Ibn Sina had taken. He felt the key to Aristotle was his physics, and it was that which gave the foundation to metaphysics.

In his *Tahafut al-tahafut* (*The Destruction of Destruction*)[7] Ibn Rushd criticizes al-Ghazali's religious criticism of Ibn Sina's version of Aristotle on the ground that the criticism is not demonstrative. Though he thinks al-Ghazali's refutation of Ibn Sina is worthless, Ibn Rushd nevertheless concludes that Ibn Sina's ideas should be combatted and he marshals a number of demonstrative proofs against the major themes of Avicennian thought. In the process, Averroës presents virtually an entirely philosophical treatise in which he seeks to replace Arab Neoplatonism with what he thought were Aristotle's real views while at the same time taking into account the demands of religious faith. In spite of this Ibn Rushd's philosophical works fell out of favor in Islam and many of them were banned or burned. The writings of al-Ghazali against the principles of Greek philosophy were probably a factor in changing even the medical curriculum, where Greek concepts were gradually supplanted by Islamic theology.

But as Ibn Rushd's influence declined in the Islamic world, it rose in the Western Christian world, where he became recognized as the great authority on Aristotle's philosophy. Ibn Rushd's reputation was so great that he became known simply as "the Commentator." A school rose around Ibn Rushd's commentaries on Aristotle that came to be known as Averroism and this became a vital force in European philosophy. Interestingly, however, Ibn Rushd's ideas, abstracted from his own Islamic framework and belief, were interpreted as that of a skeptic oriented towards nominalism. or empiricism, rather than that of the realist (or idealist) that he was. In Europe, Ibn Rushd was associated with the so called "two truths," that there is one truth for philosophers and another for the masses, that is, religion. Averroës, however, always held that the higher truth lay in revelation and the lower in the formulations of theology, and so he was not the "free thinker" he was accused of being.

When Aristotle reached the West in the last part of the twelfth and first part of the thirteenth centuries via translations from Spain and interpreted through the words of Islamic commentators, Western thinkers were in a quandary. These Islamic commentators, particularly Averroës, were alleged to have interpreted Aristotle in such a way as to deny free will to man and even to God himself. According to Western versions of Averroës (and other Islamic commentators) the world had been created not directly by God but by a hierarchy of necessary causes starting with God and descending through various Intelligences which moved the celestial spheres until the Intelligence moving the moon's sphere caused the existence of a separate Active Intellect that was common to all men and the sole cause of their knowledge. The form of the human soul already existed in this Active Intellect before the creation of man and after death each human soul merged again into it. At the center of the universe within the sphere of the moon, that is, in the sublunary region, was generated a common fundamental matter, *materia prima,* and then the four elements. From the four elements were produced, under the influence of the celestial spheres, plants, animals, and man himself.[8]

Many of these assumptions were unacceptable to the philosophers of Western Christendom in the thirteenth century. They held that Ibn Rushd denied the immortality of the individual human soul as well as human free will, and such views allegedly gave scope for the interpretation of all human behavior in terms of astrology. They claimed that Ibn Rushd was rigidly deterministic, denying that God could have acted in any way except that indicated by Aristotle. Averroës was quoted as saying that, "Aristotle's doctrine is the sum of truth because his was the summit of all human intelligence. It is therefore well said that he was created and given us by Divine Providence, so that we should know what it is possible to know."[9]

Since the commentaries of Ibn Rushd and the writings of Aristotle reached the West at about the same time, they were treated as one and the same. In 1210 they were both forbidden by a provincial council at Paris; in 1215 the prohibition was confirmed with special reference to the *Metaphysics*; in 1231 a papal injunction interdicted the reading of their works until their complete expurgation. Condemnation, however, did not make the writings either of Ibn Rushd or of Aristotle disappear, and in fact a whole series of ideas came to be associated with what was called Averroism. In 1217 the bishop of Paris specifically condemned 219 errors in these troublemakers.

It was in part to deal with the problems raised by the translations of Aristotle and the appearance of the commentaries of Averroës that there was an attempt to separate Averroës from Aristotle. Though initially there had been a categorical condemnation of Aristotle, before the end of the century Aristotle had been accepted as the most important of philosophers. We can trace the growing influence of Aristotle largely through the use of translations of Averroës. For example, translations reached the West in the middle of the career of Robert Grosseteste and we tend to date his writings by whether or not they mention Averroës.[10]

Essentially there were at least five different responses. One school, centered around a group of Franciscans at Oxford in the thirteenth century, tended to remain loyal to the main features of Augustinianism regarding the theory of knowledge and of universals, but accepted Aristotelian additions in order to explain such natural phenomena as the movements of the heavenly bodies. They were hostile to Aristotle as a whole. A second group, also of Oxford, was symbolized by Roger Bacon, who was keenly alive to the mathematical, physical, astronomical, and medical learning of Aristotle and his Arabic commentators, but was less concerned with Aristotle's metaphysics, the heart of the problem. A third school, mainly of Dominicans, centered at the university of Paris and represented by Albertus Magnus and Thomas Aquinas, accepted the main principles of Aristotle's physics and philosophy of nature, but rejected his absolute determinism and tried to separate him from Ibn Rushd. A fourth school of thought represented by Siger of Brabant, a thoroughgoing Averroist, accepted an entirely determinist interpretation of the universe. Yet a fifth group was in the Italian universities of Padua and Bologna, where theological matters counted for less, and where Aristotle, Averroës, and other Islamic writers were studied principally for their medical learning.[11] In all of these responses, the writings and interpretation of Ibn Rushd played an important role.

Those mainly responsible for making Aristotle acceptable to the Christian West were Albertus Magnus (1193–1206) and Thomas Aquinas (1225–1274). The main problem confronting them was the relation between faith and reason. To resolve this Albertus accepted two certainties: the realities of revealed religion and the facts which had come within his own personal experience. Building on this was Aquinas and neither Albertus nor Aquinas regarded Aristotle as an absolute authority as Averroës was believed to have done, but simply as a guide to reason. Where Aristotle, either explicitly or as interpreted by Latin translations of Islamic commentators, conflicted with the facts either of revelation or observation, he must be wrong. The world could not be internal, the individual soul must be immortal, and both God and man must enjoy the exercise of free will. Aquinas also argued that theology and natural science often spoke of the same thing from a different point of view, that something could be both the work of Divine Providence and the result of a natural cause. In this way they established a distinction between theology and philosophy that assigned to each its appropriate methods and guaranteed to each its own sphere of action. There could be no real contradiction between truth as revealed by religion and truth as revealed by reason. Albertus believed that the apostolic and Church Fathers should be followed in terms of faith and morals and that

Aristotle and other scientists should be followed in medical and scientific questions, for they knew more about nature. What we had was the Christianizing of Aristotle and the Aristotelianization of Christianity, something that came to be known as scholasticism. I think Averroës, in spite of Aquinas's objections to him, was a major influence in the development of scholasticism and the elevation of reason to an official standing within Christianity. This then was one of his major contributions to the West.

The Aquinas version obviously was not quite the Aristotle of Averroës, but Averroës was not necessarily thrown aside because of Aquinas's writings. His influence is demonstrated by another condemnation of his ideas in 1277 by the bishop of Paris for promulgating the Aristotelian idea that the gods were no more than "unmoved movers" of the celestial spheres. This doctrine, it was claimed, led to the conclusion that since matter was eternal, there could not have been a creation *ex nihil,* nor could the universe ever run down. Stephen Tempire, the bishop of Paris, specifically condemned as execrable errors beliefs that, "God cannot impress translational motion on the heavens for the simple reason that such motion would produce vacuums," and "The primary cause cannot create a multitude of worlds."[12]

Such a condemnation was contrary to the widespread belief that celestial spheres underwent some translational motion, and the condemnation of something that was so widely accepted is indicative of the fear that Averroism caused. Interestingly, in spite of its broad scale, Pierre Duhem claimed that the 1277 condemnation made modern science possible. He argued that it was a condemnation of Greek "necessitarianism" and thus permitted scientific or philosophical views that were traditionally judged incompatible with the essence of nature to be thought of as possible. By allowing new mental experiences, the theological notion of an omnipotent God liberated the intellect from the finite field into which Greek thought had imprisoned the universe.[13] In short, the condemnation meant that Aristotle was not the final word. In fact, Duhem claimed that the condemnation not only allowed but encouraged all the theoretical work about impetus physics to be carried out in the fourteenth and fifteenth centuries. I am not so sure I agree with Duhem, who in many ways was a Christian apologist, but this view emphasizes that, even in the opinion of his most severe critics, Averroës had at least a negative force in the development of modern science. He forced the critics to come up with new answers.

Did Averroës have a more positive force? I think he did. Though the condemnation of Averroism by the Paris diocese was followed by a condemnation by the archbishop of Canterbury in 1278, this did not prevent the teaching of what came to be called Averroism. Unfortunately several things are sometimes called Averroism. In the thirteenth century it was, as indicated above, responded to by Aquinas. Sometimes the appellation Averroist was given to any philosopher or scientist who consulted the works of Ibn Rushd, which remained the dominant source for Aristotle. For others Averroism was the doctrine of the double truth. Probably the most accurate use of the term is the description of those who adopted almost in its entirety the whole system of Ibn Rushd. This group came to be centered in Italy, where, interestingly, the condemnations made at Paris and in England did not apply.

The most complete Averroism can be found in the writings of John of Jandun (died 1328), Taddeo of Parma (flourished circa 1320), and Angelo d'Arezzo, all of whom might be called rationalists, and one critic has gone so far as to claim that they had "no Christian belief behind their learning."[14] The fact that John of Jandun was at Paris meant that even in Paris, despite the condemnation, Averroës remained influential. With the death of Jandun, however, Averroism found its strongest supporters in Italy, particularly at Padua. Among the major teachers were Paul of Venice (1368–1428?), Cajetanus de Thienis (1387–1465), Alessandro Achillini (1463–1512), Marantonio Zimara (1460–1523), Augustino Nifo (1469–1538), and, into the seventeenth century, Cesare Cremoni (1550– 1661). Nifo marks somewhat of a change, however, since he emphasized the importance of reading Aristotle in the Greek instead of depending entirely on Averroës.

The most important doctrine of these "Latin" Averroists was the supremacy of reason over faith. This led them to argue among other things: (1) the eternal and necessary creation, both for the world of spirit and for the world of matter, (2) the human intellect as a separate substance, one throughout the human species, yet at the same time the substantial form of the individual to whom it is united (sometimes called the unicity of the human intellect), which implied a negation of belief in individual immortality, and in the transcendent destiny of man, and (3) psychological determinism.

It was not so much the so-called Averroists themselves who were important in the history of science, but those influenced by their teaching. At Padua, a number of medical professors applied the logic advocated by their physician predecessors Ibn Sina and Ibn Rushd to medicine. This led to the development of the method of "resolution and composition," something which I think was essential to the development of modern science since it emphasized the importance of experiment, a far more sophisticated concept than the simple observation with which Aristotle and some of the earlier scholastics had been content. Starting from observation, complex fact was "resolved" into its component parts: "the fever into its causes, since any fever comes either from the heating of the humour or of the spirits or of the members; and again the heating of the humour is either of the blood or of the phlegm, etc.; until you arrive at the specific and distinct cause and knowledge of the fever."[15] Nifo and others amplified on this. Some of the theories of Averroës were put to the test.[16] For example, Averroës had developed a theory of color which held that colors were attributed to the presence in varying degrees of two pairs of opposite qualities: brightness and obscurity, bounded and unboundedness. This led a number of individuals, including Isaac Newton, to examine and test his theories and to counter with their own.

Averroës had also investigated the problem of magnetic attraction and this had been explained as a form of multiplication of species. That is, the lodestone modified the parts of the medium touching it (that is, air or water), and these then modified the parts next to the iron, in which a motive virtue was produced, causing it to approach the loadstone. This is somewhat similar to John Faraday and J. C. Maxwell's tubes of force of a much later date, although I have not attempted to trace a direct connection. Averroës was also interested in embryology, at least tangentially, and one of the first treatises on the subject in the West, by Giles of Rome, took up one of Averroës's concerns—when the soul appeared in the body. Ibn Rushd had held that the soul was generated together with the body but manifested itself only with the first movement of the fetus. This idea was ultimately accepted by Western Christianity in the nineteenth century.

Averroës's ideas also exercised great influence on Galileo as well as on Giordano Bruno, both of whom studied with Averroists. In short, the influence of the Averroists gave rise to the kind of questions which in the seventeenth century led to the downfall of Aristotle. It is one of the contradictions of modern science that disciples of Averroës, the very person most responsible for interpreting Aristotle to the Latin West, were among those most responsible for undermining the assumptions of the Aristotelian universe.[17] I guess this only emphasizes that once a person accepts the importance of reason, it is not always possible to predict what the findings will be. In sum, Averroës, whether as a positive or negative force, was extremely influential in the development of the forces which went into the Enlightenment.

Notes

1. John Scotes Eriugena, *De divisione naturae,* book 1, ch. 69, in Jacques-Paul Migne, *Patrologia Latina,* vol. 122.

2. This is the translation of Eriugena, *De divisione naturae,* book 1, ch. 66, by Arthur Cushman McGiffert, *A History of Christian Thought* (New York: Charles Scribner's Sons, 1954), p. 169.

3. His arguments appear in his *Monologium* and in his *Proslogium.* These can be found in Migne, *Patrologia Latina.* There is an English translation of both of them by S. N. Deane (1903).

4. The writings of Roscellinus are no longer extant and his ideas are known from others, primarily his critics.

5. There is a tremendous literature on Abelard. Many of his writings were condemned, first at Soissons in 1121 and later at Sens in 1141. His collected writings are in Migne, *Patrologia Latina,* but many other writings have been discovered and published since then. For example his *De unitate et trinitate divine* was discovered by R. Stolzle and published in 1891.

6. Tafsir ma ba'd at-Tabi'at, as quoted in P. M. Bouyges, "Inventaire des textes arabes d'Averroës," *Melanges de l'Université Saint-Joseph* 8 (1) (1922): 3–54; 9 (2) (1924): 43–48; quote is from (1), p. 7.

7. A Latin translation of this with commentary by Augustinus Niffus (Nifo) appeared in Venice in 1497. The Medieval Academy of America is currently publishing medieval Latin and Hebrew translations of his works.

8. This is essentially the argument of A. C. Crombie, *Augustine to Galileo: The History of Science A.D. 400–1650* (Cambridge, Mass.: Harvard University Press, 1953), pp. 39–40.

9. Quoted by A. C. Crombie, *Augustine to Galileo,* p. 40.

10. See, for example, A. C. Crombie, *Robert Grosseteste and the Origins of Experimental Science* (Oxford: Clarendon Press, 1953), p. 49.

11. Crombie, *Augustine to Galileo,* p. 41.

12. This translation is based upon René Taton, *History of Science* (New York: Basic Books, 1957), p. 590.

13. Ibid., p. 43. This statement is in P. Duhem, *Le Systeme du Monde* (Paris: Hermann, 1958). The quote is from Taton, *History of Science,* vol. 1, 501.

14. Fernand van Steenberghen, a professor of philosophy at the Catholic University in Louvain, in his short article on Averroism in the *Encyclopedia Britannica,* vol. 1, 892–93.

15. Jacopo d'Forli, *Super Tegni Galeni,* comm. text 1.

16. This led to some of the experiments outlined in my book, *The Scientific Revolution,* Vern L. Bullough, ed. (New York: Holt, 1970). Summaries of some of these can be found in Ernest A. Moody, "Galileo and His Precursors," in *Galileo Reappraised,* Carlo L. Golino, ed. (Berkeley: University of California Press, 1966), pp. 23–41; Alexander Koyré, "The Origins of Modern Science," *Diogenes* 16 (Winter 1956): 1–22; and *Critical Problems in the History of Science,* Marshall Clagett, ed. (Madison: University of Wisconsin Press, 1959). There are many others.

17. This concept was not original with me, but advocated earlier by Charles Singer, *A Short History of Scientific Ideas to 1900* (London: Oxford University Press, 1959), pp. 156 and 218–68.

4

Averroës and the West

Oliver Leaman
Reader in Philosophy,
Liverpool John Moores University (UK)

It is a commonplace in the history of Islamic philosophy that the career of Ibn Rushd in the West took a totally different form from that in the Islamic world. In the latter, even students of Ibn Rushd such as Ibn Tumlus did not mention the name of the great philosopher in works which were clearly influenced by him.[1] Ibn al-Arabi famously recorded a presumably apocryphal conversation with him which resulted in Ibn Rushd's total humiliation at the hands of the younger thinker.[2] There are very few references to Ibn Rushd at all by any writers in the Islamic world until he was rediscovered in the relatively recent past, and even then there is a good deal of evidence that he was rediscovered through the translation into Arabic of a book on Averroës written by a Frenchman.[3] He has played much more of a role in the Islamic world in this century, largely through his assumed participation in the *Nahda* movement, as a symbol of the possibility of reconciling modernity with Islam. It has to be said also that some of the more contemporary interest in Ibn Rushd is in admiration of his role as an intellectual who was prepared to present his views in unreasonable circumstances. Despite the dangers, he was not dissuaded from going ahead and carrying on the philosophical work to which he was committed, and in these days where

53

intellectuals are so often constrained by the political apparatus of which they are a part, this has come in for much praise by many in the Islamic world who operate in conditions which are not that dissimilar.[4]

In the West, Ibn Rushd came to have a rather different career. His works were rapidly translated into Hebrew and Latin, and there were a number of different editions of these translations, bearing witness to a continuing interest which persisted right up to, and to a certain extent beyond, the Renaissance.[5] Much of this interest was due to his status as the chief commentator on Aristotle. Once Aristotle became important for the development of Western philosophy, the main thinker who had devoted himself to understanding him in the Islamic world became important himself. In some ways, the fluctuations of Ibn Rushd in the West represented the fluctuations in the regard in which Aristotle was held. Although some of his views survived to form a remote part of the development of modern Western philosophy, it was not until his rediscovery in the last century by Renan and Munk that he came to play much part in the continuing philosophical debate. Munk was impressed by the importance of Ibn Rushd in lying at the basis of medieval Jewish and Christian philosophy, while Renan valued his role in defending a role for reason as against faith, thus identifying him with the contemporary struggles in France of the secularists against the influence of the church.[6]

Were Ibn Rushd to be known as no more than a commentator on Aristotle, he would be consigned to a minor, although doubtless worthy, role in the history of philosophy. What makes him such a major figure is his participation, or apparent participation, in some of the most heated and controversial debates in philosophy and religion. These debates led to the creation of the so-called Averroist movement, and this movement called for a radical approach to the relationship between faith and reason. For one thing, it argued for an understanding of some of the key religious concepts in ways which do not leave them making much religious sense. Secondly, it suggests that the sort of approach to issues followed by religion is entirely different from that followed by philosophy, and the implication is that the former is of far less significance than the latter. After all, the Averroists make clear that the whole purpose of religion is to represent philosophical truths in ways which accord with the limited intelligences and aspirations of the ordinary members of the community. Religion is there to preserve social harmony, very different from the rigorous and demanding versions of truth which are attainable through the pursuit of philosophy.

Who were the Averroists? It is difficult to be specific here, since there are thinkers who mention Averroës with great respect and discuss his views in depth, but who are certainly not Averroists (Aquinas, for example), while their work reveals the deep impact which he made on virtually every facet of their thought.[7] There are thinkers who refer to Averroës approvingly, but one suspects that it was to Averroës the commentator that they were referring, since there is no reason to think that they adhered to the more daring of the ideas of Averroism.[8] There are other thinkers, and this is especially frequent in Jewish Averroism, who combine Averroës with a whole variety of thinkers, such as Maimonides and Abraham ibn Ezra, who put forward incompatible views. We need to bear in mind all the time when considering the impact of Ibn Rushd on the West that he entered the West in two forms, as the Aristotelian and as the polemicist.

It might be argued that this is a mistaken approach, since it is not possible to distinguish between these different aspects of his thought. Much of what is taken to be controversial in his views is more Aristotelian than it is Averroist. We have to remember here how difficult it was for the medieval thinkers to reconcile some of the leading principles of Aristotelianism with their religions. After all, Aristotle seemed to argue that the world is eternal, that there is no soul independent of the body, and that the idea of a corporeal afterlife is vacuous. Even the notion of an individual afterlife is disparaged, and Aristotle's God is an uninterested and uninvolved being as far as the world of generation and corruption is concerned.

Now, it is certainly true that the form of Aristotelianism which arrived in the Islamic world was far from pure and unadulterated. As is well-known, it was replete with Neoplatonic influence, and many works were ascribed to Aristotle which would have horrified him. Yet if any philosopher was capable of distinguishing between the Aristotelian gold and the Neoplatonic dross, it was Ibn Rushd, and he is forever complaining about the way in which Ibn Sina takes as Aristotelian material which clearly is not. This is not to suggest that Ibn Rushd's Aristotle is the same as the Stagyrite himself, since he certainly was not. Ibn Rushd was working at a time when the very notion of a philosophical curriculum was Neoplatonic, and he had to employ the conceptual tools of that philosophy to try to cleanse himself of it and return to the genuine thought of the First Master himself, and often he is unsuccessful.[9]

This does not answer the point, though, as to whether Ibn Rushd was regarded as such a radical thinker because he really was a radical thinker, or because he was an Aristotelian. What might be regarded as radical about his thought is precisely its Aristotelianism. It is difficult today to think about Aristotle as a radical thinker, yet when one considers the context within which Ibn Rushd was working, the effort is worth making. The point which should be made about Aristotle is that he is a profoundly areligious thinker. By contrast with Plato, who gave a transcendental role to the spiritual and the religious, Aristotle is a down-to-earth thinker, someone who thinks that the world is a subject which we can quite easily understand. He has no time for the idea that the meaning of the world is outside the world, and although he does have his more spiritual moments, these are few and far between, and do not represent in any way the general thrust of his metaphysics. Of course, in the fervor of Neoplatonism which dominated the ancient world for so long, any hint which could be made more mysterious and transcendental was pounced upon and developed. One has only to examine the long career of the "active intellect," a Neoplatonic construction from a vague reference in an Aristotelian aside.[10] Even the Neoplatonized Aristotle with which Ibn Rushd worked, and was obliged to work, reveals his areligious teeth. The basic problem, as al-Ghazali so acutely pointed out in his *Tahafut al-falasifa*, is that there is very little if any role for God in the world of the *falasifa*, and it has to be borne in mind here that al-Ghazali's main target is Ibn Sina, very far from an orthodox Aristotelian, but rather a Neoplatonist who incorporated a good deal of religious and mystical thought into his metaphysics. Yet even he was sufficiently representative of the Greek tradition of *falsafa* to find it difficult to give God much to do in his account of the world.

It looks as though we are going to conclude that what is radical in the thought of Ibn Rushd, given the context within which he was working, was its Aristotelian basis. Ibn Rushd, as the thinker within the Islamic world who was most committed to the real Aristotle, as he thought, thus turned out to be the most radical philosopher. It would be pleasing to be able to accept this view, since then one could bring the varied works of Ibn Rushd under just one description, Aristotelian, and then look for the common strands which link them all together in that way. We should be careful here, though, since this is very far from the truth. Ibn Rushd's works are so varied in their form and content that they do not neatly fall under such a description. This is even true of the commentaries, which are not all the same in their approach or content. The short commentaries are very different from the long ones, and the middle ones are distinct from both the short and the long. The differences are not just of size either, but in the views which Ibn Rushd presented. As a rule of thumb, it can be said that the shorter the commentary, the freer Ibn Rushd felt to express what he thought the implications of the original text were. He is most free, perhaps, when he is writing his short theological works, which certainly bear the influence of Aristotle, but which could hardly be called Aristotelian. When we look at the writings of Ibn Rushd we are in contact with a remarkable and original thinker, someone who is far from being a slavish follower of even Aristotle.

It is important to bear in mind these points about Ibn Rushd before we examine his impact on the West, since we want to be able to differentiate between the impact which he had as an Aristotelian and the impact which he had as Ibn Rushd. As I have suggested, some of the ideas which came to be seen as threatening in the West are primarily Aristotelian ideas, and once established religion is confronted with a *Weltanschauung* which is so different, it reacts with surprise and shock. This certainly was the case in the thirteenth century in Paris, where the introduction of Averroës into the university curriculum led to great excitement and hostile reaction on the part of the authorities, but the nature of the propositions to which they were responding were essentially Aristotelian rather than anything else. It was Aristotle through the medium of Averroës, and not the other way around, which led to the form of philosophy in Western Europe known as "Averroism," a type of thinking which led to a strong and conclusive response in the Christian world. The theological and legal texts of Ibn Rushd, which really represent a very radical approach to the relationship between faith and reason, were not much translated into Latin, and did not achieve currency in Christian Europe, so the influence which Averroës was able to have during the medieval period was largely based upon his skill as a commentator.

The position in the Jewish world was different. Here there was a great deal of interest in Ibn Rushd's theological works, and there were many translations of them. Jewish thinkers were also interested in his commentaries, of course, but the number of translations of the shorter theological and more polemical pieces indicates a strong current of discussion within the Jewish community about the precise relationship between faith and reason. It is interesting that although the Christian and Jewish worlds had only the commentaries in common, they both produced numbers of philosophers who came to be called Averroists, and who did have rather similar views. Are these views essentially Aristotelian, so that the theological writings turn out to be rather unimportant in the elucidation of the thought

of Ibn Rushd as a whole? I think the best formulation of the relationship
here between Aristotle and Averroës is to say that the latter used the language and philosophical structure of the former in order to present his
views and arguments. The relationship between a major thinker and his followers is always difficult to pin down precisely; one has to steer a course
between the Scylla of seeing the follower as just derivative throughout his
work and the Charybdis of regarding him as breaking entirely new ground.
This is certainly the case with Ibn Rushd. He clearly did set out to establish a form of thought which was more than merely Aristotle's, and yet it
is clearly an Aristotelian form of thought.

What was the impact of this thought on the West? As we have seen, it
is not easy to distinguish between the influence of Ibn Rushd the commentator and Ibn Rushd the philosopher. Despite this, some have argued
that the way in which his thought was received in the West bears little relationship with the thinker himself. Some of the radical directions in which
his thought was pushed does indeed seem to have little in common with Ibn
Rushd himself. Radical Averroism is taken to hold that the truths of religion and philosophy can both be accepted even though they are incompatible, that religion is a formulation of philosophical truths for the masses,
and that the most basic concepts of religion need to be reinterpreted if they
are to be in any way acceptable. What lies behind radical Averroism is the
idea that religion and philosophy are two very different enterprises, and the
latter is far superior to the former. One aspect of Ibn Rushd's work which
is clearly transmitted to the Averroists is the idea that the world is basically
a comprehensible place. There is no mystery about the world, and accordingly, no necessity to seek transcendental explanations. As was argued
earlier, there is clearly no set of specific ideas which anyone who is de-
scribable as an Averroist has to share, since they are a very varied group,
but the three propositions which appear here do seem to be something of
a common theme running through the writings of Siger of Brabant, Al-
balag, Caspi, Narboni, and Nifo. The interesting question is whether these
propositions represent the views of Ibn Rushd himself.

Most of the literature tends to argue that the Averroists go some distance from Ibn Rushd. This is hardly implausible, since they did not have
the complete corpus of works by Ibn Rushd in any case, and often their access to his writings was quite limited and partial. They often had to make
up in enthusiasm for what they missed in depth. Since the study of the Arabic works of Ibn Rushd has only become possible fairly recently in any-

thing like their original state, we now know how distinct many of the ideas of the Averroists are from those of Ibn Rushd himself. Yet this does not show that they were not following in a relatively faithful fashion his philosophical principles, and it will be argued here that there is little if anything to distinguish the Averroists from Averroës himself.

The main target of those who criticize the link between the Averroists and Averroës lies in the doctrine of the relationship between religion and philosophy. If we examine one of Ibn Rushd's key works on this topic, the *Fasl al-maqal*, we can see that he presents a subtle account of this relationship. He does not argue that philosophy is superior to religion, nor that philosophers are superior to theologians. He argues here, and in many other places, that both faith and reason present routes to the truth, and that they both end up in the same place, albeit that they get there by different routes. The point of religion is to present the truth in such a way that everyone in the community can understand it, as is surely only fair given the creation of a world with people of very different abilities and interests. The point of reason is to give those who are capable of employing it a very real understanding of why things are as they are, since the universe is essentially rational and was constructed along rational lines. Through seeking to understand it rationally we participate, albeit in a limited way, in the divine processes which themselves went into the creation and construction of the world. But the majority of the population, who are not capable or interested in exploring the processes of demonstrative argument, do not suffer as a result. They have ways of finding out how they should live and what they should believe, and these ways are capable of giving them all the information they need. If they received too much information they would not be able to cope with it, and would come either to lose confidence in their religion or in the acceptability of philosophy. Neither alternative is desirable, and philosophers should be careful about who they contact with their arguments.

Now, this doctrine does not sound very radical. It is in fact something of a theme in Islamic philosophy that you pay careful attention to the nature of the audience before you decide what you are going to say and how you are going to say it. Actually, Ibn Rushd goes a bit further than this, because he makes it quite clear that it is the philosophers rather than the theologians who are capable of deciding how to sort out difficult issues of interpretation. This is hardly to put philosophy and theology in a position of equality, and it does imply that religion is just a pale reflection of the truth which the philosophers can see quite clearly. Actually, this is not really the case, because what Ibn Rushd is arguing here is that the dialectical ways of thinking of the theologians are far weaker logically in resolving arguments than are the demonstrative arguments of the philosophers. This does not directly affect the status of religion, since the latter may be secure as a route to truth while the activities of the theologians may be regarded as unduly confusing. That is, the theologians are seen to cloud the issues even further by their attempts at explaining difficulties, while the philosophers can resolve these problems finally through the application of demonstrative reasoning. The best thing of all is for ordinary believers just to go along with the beliefs and practices of their faith and not raise issues which are inappropriate for them.

This has often been criticized as a patronizing and dubious doctrine, and I know that when I teach this topic to my students, they invariably react in rather hostile ways. The students who are particularly annoyed by this approach are those who are religious, since they feel that Ibn Rushd is downgrading the truth and significance of their faith. Is he? Those who argue that the Averroists are not representative of Ibn Rushd himself do think that they downgrade the significance of faith, in contrast with Ibn Rushd himself, who, as we have seen, merely suggests that faith and reason are two very different approaches, and that their diversity must be respected in any attempt at grasping their relationship. The Averroists are taken to argue, and they often do argue, that religion is in fact false, while philosophy is true, but that this is not a state of affairs which should be widely broadcast.

Now, this is certainly far from the doctrine of Ibn Rushd. He nowhere goes as far as this, but reiterates constantly throughout his work that religion and philosophy are compatible, and that the philosopher is obliged to play a part in the everyday religious and social activities of the community of which he is a part. This hardly seems to pack much of a punch, and certainly not the sort of punch which the Averroists, with their radical separation of religion and philosophy, accomplish. What is important here is to distinguish between the doctrine that religion and philosophy are different routes to the same truth, and the doctrine that only one of them is capable of reaching that truth. The Averroists often upheld the latter, while Ibn Rushd clearly supported the former. It appears, then, that it is wrong to identify the philosophy of Ibn Rushd with the Averroists.

Is this really true, though? Perhaps the Averroists are saying explicitly something which Ibn Rushd is only thinking implicitly, but which is undeniably there in his work. There is a lot to be said for this argument. We have to appreciate the radical nature of the distinction which Ibn Rushd establishes between philosophy and religion. They may both be routes to the same truth, but the nature of the routes themselves is very dissimilar, and it is clearly the case that philosophy is in a privileged position. Only the philosopher really understands the situation which is in front of him, only the philosopher really has the ability to key into the basic thought processes of the deity, only the philosopher grasps the real nature of the truth. The philosophical route represents by far the quicker and the straighter journey. Those on the ordinary route do not get where they are going at all directly, and even when they get there and confine themselves to the practice of their faith and the adherence to basic religious ideas, they do not have much insight into what is going on. They are obliged to remain content with the version of the truth which is all they can understand, and one remains with the feeling that the level of understanding they receive is rather poor.

Perhaps we could illustrate this by thinking of a particular example. It is clear that in Ibn Rushd's view there is very little if any scope for thinking about the individual immortality of the soul, or any other part of us, in the afterlife. On the contrary, the only role which immortality plays within his system is a sort of global immortality in which the individual merges his individuality to participate in an immortality of the species. This was clearly one of the most controversial ideas of Ibn Rushd in the West, and much effort was made to try to refute him on this point. Although he sometimes equivocates on this point, there can be little doubt that he does not adhere to a view of the afterlife which fits in at all well with religious conceptions. Al-Ghazali is quite justified in arguing that the views of the *falasifa* on this point are incompatible with Islam. They are certainly incompatible with Christianity also. Now, what is one to make of this difficulty? The Averroists would argue that the belief in individual immortality is perfectly acceptable for the masses, since it will help them fulfill their religious duties and have a respectful attitude to the deity. Strictly speaking, however, as the philosophers realize, it is false, and the ordinary religious understanding of the afterlife has to be discounted in favor of a more sophisticated version which takes account of the more complicated nature of personal identity. Ordinary believers are just wrong in what they take the afterlife to be. They are not entirely wrong, because there are aspects of their beliefs which are acceptable, and the value of their beliefs lies in their pragmatic thrust. They are capable of moving people to act in ways which are in accordance with their duty, ways which in the absence of such beliefs those people would find very difficult to understand.

Is the belief in individual immortality held by the Averroists to be literally false? It is, and it is not. It is false in the sense that it sets out as possible and indeed actual a state of affairs which could not take place, because it goes against the nature of the concepts involved. Not even God can go against the laws of logic, and if the religious account of the afterlife involves changing the notion of personal identity, then even God cannot accomplish this. There is an essence of humanity which makes a particular view of personal identity right, and other views wrong, and even God is constrained by the existence of this species to respect its characteristics when he decides on the nature of life after death. Of course, most people would not really understand this, and if they were told that the nature of the afterlife was totally different from the nature of this life, they would not be able to follow the point that was being made, and this theoretical lacuna would lead to practical difficulties also. Yet the ordinary belief in individual immortality seems to be literally false. How could one justify asking people to accept something as true which is literally false? One can see good instrumental reasons for such a policy, but nothing more, and the suspicion is that Ibn Rushd and his followers really seek to disparage faith by contrast with philosophy.

The position is not quite so clear-cut, though. It is possible that Ibn Rushd would argue that there are two ways of assessing the acceptability of a proposition, a theoretical and a practical way. All propositions have some sort of theoretical content. It is worth remembering here that even poetic and sophistic propositions have some propositional value on the approach to the Aristotelian organon followed by most of the *falasifa*. It is just that their value declines progressively the further they distance themselves from the level of demonstrative reasoning represented at the apex of the logical system. For propositions with a weaker logical content, what has to be done is to work out what they mean. Since one is dealing here with material whose theoretical content is low, it is reasonable to conclude that the main element of meaning in such propositions is primarily intended to be practical. For example, the sort of rhetorical language used by a superb politician, the Prophet Muhammad, was designed to move and inspire the greatest number of people who came into contact with it. It was not the purpose of such language to present theoretical truths to that audience, who certainly would not have known what to do with them.

But surely, it will be said, what is at issue here is whether the language which is used is true. How could one suggest that the language which the Prophet Muhammad used was not true, but just used to bring about a certain effect in its hearers? This is not what Ibn Rushd is suggesting. He is arguing that the practical implications of the propositions at issue (what Austin called its elocutionary force) is part of the meaning of the whole proposition. It is of the nature of that sort of language that the meaning should be structured in such a way as to give priority to its practical impact, as compared, say, with the propositions of natural science. So when the Prophet tells us something about the afterlife which goes against the philosophical understanding of that notion, he must be doing something which has as its focal meaning changing people's behavior. That is what the proposition means. One cannot say that he is producing a false proposition to get over a practical message, since this is not the case. There is nothing false about the proposition, since the content of the proposition is quite true, that people should act in particular ways. The philosopher, and only the philosopher, is able to understand how the very minimal theoretical content of the proposition is translatable into practical language, and this is why Ibn Rushd stresses in the *Fasl* that only the philosophers should have the responsibility for interpreting difficult passages. Such passages, he suspects, are really dealing with ideas which seem to be theoretical but in fact are practical, and only the philosopher is aware of the rules to convert the theoretical into the practical. This is because only the philosopher grasps the precise distinctions between the different logical forms of judgment, and so only he can work out what the precise logical structure of a particular proposition is.

This brings us to what is perhaps most interesting about what has been called the "double truth" theory. The theory has often been taken to be that religious and philosophical statements may contradict each other yet both be true. It is difficult to see how this could work, since if two propositions are contradictory, they cannot both be true. The Averroists were often taken to argue that although one can say that religious statements are true, really they are not, since they go against the conclusions of philosophy. They were left accepting that people could say religious statements are true if they want to, but this does not prevent the philosopher from realizing what is wrong with them. The Averroist philosopher would have sufficient grace not to attack the faith of the believer, but he would acknowledge to himself the falsity of the other's beliefs. As we have seen, this is hardly Ibn

Rushd's position. He would argue that we do have two routes to the truth, and both are routes to the truth, neither being a misguided and erratic path to error. What we have are two different notions of truth, one which is theoretical and one which is practical. The philosopher has access to the former, while the ordinary believer can make contact with the latter. While the truths may appear to contradict each other, in fact this is not the case, since there are two ways of interpreting what is true.

This may seem far-fetched, and an evasion, but when we think of the principles of Aristotelianism, it becomes quite plausible. Two Aristotelian principles become crucial here. Firstly, Aristotle argues that the level of exactness which applies to particular forms of discourse are relative to the nature of those forms. There is no one standard of exactness which applies to all ways of speaking.[11] So the criteria which apply to a theoretical issue, for example, need not be replicated by the criteria which apply to a related practical issue. Secondly, Aristotle stressed the importance of the "mixed" way of life, the sort of life which is replete with duties, obligations, and political activity.[12] Although he sometimes suggests that this is a secondary activity on the road to perfection through contemplation, both he and his followers in the Islamic world constantly emphasize that a sine qua non of intellectual perfection is the satisfactory expression of our social needs and obligations. What is easier to understand, then, is that there are (at least) two ways of understanding our most important beliefs, a practical way and a theoretical way. The latter certainly has the advantage that it is capable of comprehending the structure of the former, yet the former has the advantage of representing the theoretical principle in a way which it is unable to do itself, that is, practically.

Where does Ibn Rushd stand in relation to the Enlightenment? We have seen that the Averroists provide a generally accurate account of the thrust of Ibn Rushd's philosophy, and they emphasize the significance of philosophy as compared with faith. Faith has an important, but essentially subsidiary role as a popular and practical interpretation of philosophy. This clearly fits in nicely with what has become known as the Enlightenment project, and the sorts of reaction which were made to the project in the West were effective in entirely submerging Ibn Rushd's contribution to the Islamic world.[13] As Hegel put it in the preface of the *Philosophy of Right,* "The owl of Minerva spreads its wings only with the falling of the dusk." It obviously was dusk in the West a bit earlier than nightfall came in the Islamic world! It is important to realize that the sort of thinking which emerged in the Enlightenment did not come from nowhere, but arose as a result of extended and extensive discussions taking place over many centuries in the West, and there can be little doubt that Averroism played a large part in establishing a tradition in which it became possible to question the status of religion by comparison with reason. The Enlightenment has often been criticized as failing to establish on a secure footing the validity of the application of reason itself, since if the justification of such application is given in terms of reason itself, the process seems to be entirely circular.

I am not sure that this criticism of the Enlightenment project as a whole is as decisive as its supporters, ranging from Pascal to the postmodernists, believe. But it is not at all clear that it applies to Ibn Rushd anyway. After all, he does not just claim that reason is to be employed to comprehend the nature of religious statements. He argues that only philosophy is capable of understanding those statements, and we are forced to this conclusion by the failure of any other methodology to deal satisfactorily with the problem. So, according to the Averroists, there is evidence which can be used to vindicate reason, and the trust which is held in reason is based on that evidence. This is far from being an uncritical acceptance of the importance of reason. Of course, it may be said that this process itself is rational, and we might demand some prior justification of the value of rationality itself, but there is nothing which can be done that would satisfy this demand, since any justification could only succeed if it is rational in form. This is where the significance of Averroism in the development of Western philosophy lies, in its balanced yet determined support for the integrity and independence of reason itself, a position which was to resonate through the creation of modern Western philosophy.

Where the thought of Averroës really struck home was on the notion of the world as a place which is far from a mystery. He had no time for the idea that one should look for transcendental explanations for what is around us. This is not because there are no such transcendental explanations, because there most certainly are, and they are represented in the language of religion. From a theoretical point of view, these explanations are really superfluous. They have a place, certainly, but their place is practical, and we should bear this in mind whenever we confront the potential conflict which exists between religion and faith. We should remember here that in Ibn Rushd's theory of meaning, language consists of terms which are equivocal in a limited sense. The ways in which we use language are restricted by the limitations in our point of view, since we are finite and limited creatures. As a result, our language is not always capable of being precise and perspicuous.[14] Yet it does not follow that we should abandon language, or seek to replace it with some other form of expression, or that we should look in some other direction for guidance as to how to understand what is around us. Ibn Rushd had the same attitude to the mystics of his time as Kant did to those of his, whom he thought guilty of *Schwärmerei*. The mystics represent something which is capable of explanation in principle as though it were not and end up by devising strange and exotic techniques to try to get into contact with the meaning of the world. All that they had to do was to examine it rationally.

The argument here, then, is that there is little difficulty in seeing Ibn Rushd as a thinker who was in harmony with the main principles of the Enlightenment. It is difficult to know how significant the works of the Averroists were in forging the path to the Enlightenment, since it is always very difficult to understand how particular periods of intellectual history bring about particular results. What we can say is that the Averroists were in line with the views of Ibn Rushd himself on the main issues, and we have seen how subversive the basic thrust of the Averroistic argument is. It does not explicitly disparage religion, it does not even implicitly disparage religion, but it provides religion with a role which is essentially secondary and demeaning. Averroism proclaims the overwhelming importance of reason, and in this way sets the scene for the identification of modernity with secularism. It is not surprising that in the Islamic world of Ibn Rushd's time there were few takers for this thesis. Ibn Rushd set us an intellectual and practical problem which modern culture is still struggling to address.

Notes

1. Ibn Tumlus, Abu al-Hajjaj Yusuf b. Muhammad, *Al-Madkhal li-Sina at al-Mantiq,* ed. and trans. M. Asin (Madrid: Matba at Ibiriqa, 1916).

2. See the section on Ibn Rushd by Dominique Urvoy in *The Routledge History of Islamic Philosophy*, S. H. Nasr and O. Leaman, eds. (London: Routledge, 1995).

3. E. Renan, *Averroës et l'Averroisme* in *Oeuvres complètes de Ernest Renan,* vol. 3 (Paris: Calmann-Levy, 1949).

4. A. von Kugelgen, *Averroës und die arabische Moderne* (Leiden: Brill, 1994).

5. For more detail here, see the chapter "Averroism" in my *Averroës and His Philosophy* (Oxford: Clarendon Press, 1988), pp.163–78; the section "Jewish Averroism" in Nasr and Leaman, *Islamic Philosophy*; and my "Is Averroës an Averroist?" in *Averroismus im Mittelalter und in der Renaissance*, F. Niewohner and L. Sturlese, eds. (Zurich: Spur Verlag, 1994), pp. 9–24.

6. S. Munk, *Melanges de philosophie juive et arabe* (Paris: Franck, 1859); and Renan *Averroës et l'Averroisme*.

7. Thomas Aquinas, *Tractatus de unitate intellectus contra averroistas*, L. Keeler, ed. (Rome: Pontificia Universitas Gregoriana, 1957).

8. Gersonides is a good example here. See G. Freudenthal, ed., *Studies on Gersonides* (Leiden: Brill, 1992).

9. See my *An Introduction to Medieval Islamic Philosophy* (Cambridge: Cambridge University Press, 1985), pp. 39–40.

10. Alexander of Aphrodisias really created the concept of the active intellect. All that Aristotle talked about was the "passive intellect" (*De anima,* 430a 14ff).

11. See here Aristotle's *Nicomachean Ethics,* 1094b, 12–28.

12. *Nicomachean Ethics,* 1178 passim.

13. For critics of the Enlightenment project, see A. MacIntyre, *After Virtue* (London: Duckworth, 1981) and O. O'Neill, "Vindicating Reason," in P. Guyer, ed., *The Cambridge Companion to Kant* (Cambridge: Cambridge University Press, 1992), pp. 280–308.

14. For more detail on Ibn Rushd's theory of meaning, see my *Averroës* and "Continuity in Islamic Political Philosophy: The Role of Myth," *Bulletin of the British Society of Middle Eastern Studies* 14, no. 2 (1988): 147–55.

5

Averroës and Inquiry:
The Need for an Enlightened Community

Timothy J. Madigan
Executive Editor, Free Inquiry *Magazine*

Critics of Enlightenment

While the conference we are participating in is focusing on Averroës and the Enlightenment, it would also be helpful to briefly examine some of the main *criticisms* of the Enlightenment project, and see how Averroës's philosophy might address these. Critics of the Enlightenment such as the Frankfurt School scholars Theodor Adorno and Max Horkheimer have charged that its near-deification of human reason has totalitarian and repressive tendencies that are inimical to human freedom. There is an assumption—especially evident in Descartes's methodology—that all people reason alike and should arrive at the same conclusions. In their 1947 book *Dialectic of Enlightenment*, they write that, "The difficulties in the concept of reason caused by the fact that its subjects, the possessors of that very reason, contradict one another, are concealed by the apparent clarity of the judgments of the Western Enlightenment."[1] That is to say, the Enlightenment thinkers had a difficult, if not impossible, task of dealing with the fact that individuals seem to understand the world in different ways, by using different methods.

One of the most vigorous critics of the Enlightenment's adherence to rationalism was Arthur Schopenhauer (1788-1860). One area he dealt with particularly was the prevalence of religious belief. He scoffed at the Enlightenment notion that superstitions and false beliefs could be eradicated. We are metaphysical creatures by our very nature, doomed to ask unanswerable questions about the meaning of our existence. While a scant few may be able to overcome superstitions, the vast majority of humans take solace in their illusions—and it would be cruel to disabuse them of these, or encourage them to give them up. Rationalism is not a mode for the masses, who are unable to follow the dictates of truth tables or logical methodologies.

This critique is best expressed in Schopenhauer's dialogue "On Religion." In it, two atheistic characters, Demopheles and Philalethes, debate the merits of ridiculing religious teachings. It is clear that Schopenhauer favors the views of Demopheles, who states that,

> Religion is the metaphysics of the masses; by all means let them keep it . . . for mankind absolutely needs *an interpretation of life*; and this, again, must be suited to popular comprehension. Consequently, this interpretation is always an allegorical investiture of the truth. . . . Don't take offense at its unkempt, grotesque and apparently absurd form; for with your education and learning, you have no idea of the round about ways by which people in their crude state have to receive their knowledge of deep truths.[2]

One sees here a sharp condemnation of the Cartesian dream of individuals following the exact same path to knowledge and arriving at a common belief system. Such a method could well lead to contempt for those who are unable or unwilling to use it.

At first glance, the above passage seems to be similar to Averroës's views on the harmony of religion and philosophy. As Arthur Hyman and James J. Walsh point out in their *Philosophy in the Middle Ages*,

> Invoking Aristotelian logical principles, he divided the citizens into the rulers who can follow demonstrations, the masses who are persuaded by rhetorical arguments, and, between them, the dialectical theologians who can understand dialectical discussions. . . . Averroës insisted that each of the three classes must be taught on its own level. General philosophical enlightenment, according to him, is proscribed.[3]

Is Averroës, then, a critic of the Enlightenment project's critique of super-stitions and false beliefs? Certainly, like Schopenhauer, he valued the im-portance of symbolic and metaphoric language, and had a keen under-standing of the ways in which people in general are motivated. But his presentation of this is far more nuanced than that of Schopenhauer.

The irony of Schopenhauer's position is that it is he, and not the En-lightenment thinkers whom he castigates, who actually shows contempt for the masses. One cannot help but detect in the above-mentioned dialogue a sneering tone regarding the fools who cannot comprehend the world on ra-tional principles. For all of his avowal of compassion, Schopenhauer seems to have little real regard for the majority of his fellow suffering creatures—at least of the human species. Horkheimer and Adorno are likewise guilty of the very sort of condescending attitude they criticize Enlightenment thinkers for having. For instance, in their discussion of what they call the "culture industry"—films, radio, television, magazines and other media that essentially sell the general public a false identity in order to keep them passive—they write that,

> As naturally as the ruled always took the morality imposed upon them
> more seriously than did the rulers themselves, the deceived masses are
> today captivated by the myth of success even more than the successful
> are. Immovably, they insist on the very ideology which enslaves them.
> The misplaced love of the common people for the wrong which is done
> them is a greater force than the cunning of the authorities. . . . It calls for
> Mickey Rooney in preference to the tragic Garbo, for Donald Duck in-
> stead of Betty Boop.[4]

While it is unclear what tragic element Horkheimer and Adorno see in Betty Boop which would make her superior to Donald Duck, one can sense an attitude of superiority. Unlike the masses they critique, Hork-heimer and Adorno are not fooled by the system. Like Schopenhauer, they affect an air of detachment, an "above the battle" position which separates them fundamentally from the common herd. Indeed, Schopenhauer is often quite blunt in his estimation of the majority of human beings—"What the pathetic commonplace heads with which the world is crammed really lack are two closely related faculties: that of forming judgments and that of pro-ducing ideas of their own . . . they are capable of only *subjective* interest. It is precisely this that makes card-playing the most appropriate amusement for them—card-playing for money. . . . To be sociable with them is to be degraded."[5] He also adds that to expect most people to appreciate intellectual merit is like expecting a castrate to beget children.

It can be seen then that critics of the Enlightenment are themselves often prone to belittle the aspirations and intellects of the vast majority of human beings. On the one hand, we have an Enlightenment ideal of all people being encouraged to use rules and logical methodologies to lead their lives; on the other hand, we have an anti-Enlightenment, cynical view of most people being duped by their societies and a few intellectuals able to see the charade but unable to essentially change it. Neither of these scenarios (both of which are, of course, drastic oversimplifications) seem to fit the approach which Averroës himself advocated, for they each lack a sense of human beings attempting to learn the truth about their world by relying both on their own intellectual powers and by sharing information and freely discussing their points of view with others—in short, what is missing in these scenarios is the sense of a *community* of inquirers. This is an aspect which is perhaps best advocated by the American philosopher Charles Peirce (1839–1914), and I would like to close this presentation by briefly presenting Peirce's views on the human practice of inquiry, and show how these resonate with Averroës's own discussion of the importance of philosophy.

Peirce

Like the Frankfurt School, Peirce was a strong critic of the Cartesian way of philosophizing. In his article "The Spirit of Cartesianism," Peirce compared it unfavorably to the scholasticism it had sought to replace. He listed four key differences between these approaches:

1. Cartesianism teaches that philosophy must begin with universal doubt; scholasticism never questiones fundamentals.

2. Cartesianism teaches that the ultimate test of certainty is to be found in individual consciousness; scholasticism rests on the testimony of sages and of the Catholic Church.

3. Cartesianism replaces the multiform argumentation of the Middle Ages with that of a thread of single inference.

4. While scholasticism has its mysteries of faith, it nonetheless undertakes to explain all created things, whereas Cartesianism ultimately relies upon facts that are themselves absolutely inexplicable.

While not advocating a return to scholasticism—which he recognized had relied far too heavily on the method of authority—Peirce nonetheless called into question the supposed liberating element of Descartes's method of doubt. Doubts are not something that can be artificially generated. Rather, doubts cause us to question our previous habits of actions, or beliefs—they stop us in our tracks. Inquiry, then, is the struggle to attain beliefs. In order for inquiry to begin, there must be real and living doubts, which irritate us and which we struggle to free ourselves from. "Let us not pretend to doubt in philosophy what we do not doubt in our hearts," he writes.[6] In addition, Peirce questioned whether individuals on their own could arrive at conclusions that would truly satisfy this quest. "We individually cannot reasonably hope to attain the ultimate philosophy which we pursue; we can only seek it, therefore, for the *community* of philosophers. . . . Philosophy ought to imitate the successful sciences in its methods, so far as to proceed only from tangible premises which can be subjected to careful scrutiny, and to trust rather to the multitude and variety of its arguments than to the conclusiveness of any one."[7]

Peirce was also sensitive to the different ways in which people arrive at their beliefs, and the methods they use to preserve them in the face of doubts. Like Averroës, he held that there are three universal classes of believers:

> If we endeavor to form our conceptions upon history and life, we remark three classes of men. The first consists of those for whom the chief thing is the qualities of feelings. These men create art. The second consists of the practical men, who carry on the business of the world. They respect nothing but power, and respect power only so far as it is exercised. The third class consists of men to whom nothing seems great but reason. . . . For men of the first class, nature is a picture; for men of the second class, it is an opportunity; for men of the third class, it is a cosmos, so admirable, that to penetrate to its ways seems to them the only thing that makes life worth living. These are the men whom we see possessed by a passion to learn.[8]

Descartes's error was to assume that *all* people were or could be capable of joining the third class, with a disinterested desire for truth for truth's sake, seeking explanations, laws, and fundamental principles. An empirical examination of society ably demonstrates that this is simply not the case. The aesthetically minded believer tends to rely on feelings, intuitions, and instincts, and generally holds on tenaciously to previously accepted postulates. This type of person is easily moved by poetry and rhetoric. The practical person focuses on concrete, short-term situations, and is only interested in examining fundamental principles if there is (in William James's famous phrase) some "cash value" to doing so. Such people seek order and opportunity, and often rely upon the method of authority to fix their beliefs. Unlike the third class of believers, the first two both fear and abhor uncertainty and chance. The aesthete and the businessperson distrust the thoroughgoing fallibilism of the scientific attitude, and are unlikely to be moved by appeals to reason.

Yet Peirce was by no means sympathetic to Schopenhauerian elitism and resignation. He remarked that the school of Schopenhauer contained philodoxers almost as narrow-minded as Italian monks and Thomists, and rather uncharitably described Schopenhauer himself as having a "diseased mind."[9] Schopenhauer's misanthropy itself impedes inquiry. For Peirce, a community of inquirers involves people of all three classifications of belief interacting with each other, attempting to understand their differing perspectives and endeavoring to forge mutually satisfying structures. Each type is likely to see aspects of the whole situation that the others might miss (scientists, for instance, in their quest for facts, often overlook a question that business-oriented people would immediately raise—"what will this cost?"). Peirce, like his colleague James, calls for intellectuals to come down from their ivory towers and mingle with nonintellectuals, seriously listening to their concerns and sharing observations with each other. As Philip Weiner points out,

> Most important of all for understanding the man and the deep humanistic undercurrent of even his abstruse speculations and technical researches is Peirce's view of higher education. A college or university should be a community of scholars devoted to study and to enlarging the sphere of knowledge so that teaching may spread the desire to learn how things really are, instead of aiming at increasing the prospects of financial or social success for its graduates.[10]

Peirce forswore Schopenhauer's intellectual self-satisfaction and would have had little patience for the Frankfurt School's highly specialized terminology and cliquish posture. In a sense, Peirce is far more sensitive to individualism, and sympathizes with Descartes's respect for the untapped intellectual powers of *all* members of society.

In a recent discussion of the book *Dialectic of Enlightenment*, Richard Rorty writes that, "Horkheimer and Adorno . . . suspect that you cannot have a moral community in a disenchanted world because toleration leads to pragmatism. . . . They think that pragmatism was the inevitable outcome of Enlightenment rationalism and that pragmatism is not a strong enough philosophy to make moral community possible."[11] Interestingly enough, Peirce himself grew disenchanted with the ways in which some of his contemporaries—especially James—used the term "pragmatism," making it seem as if it referred primarily to the second class of believers (the practically oriented). He disavowed the word, preferring to call his own philosophy "pragmaticism"—a word too ugly for anyone to kidnap. Philosophy, Peirce felt, needs to combine the aesthetic, practical, and scientific elements, not treat them as separate and distinct. A moral community is one in which all members respect each others' capabilities and try as best as possible to work together in a common search for satisfying and enriching beliefs.

Peirce's pragmaticism attempts to steer a course between the Scylla of romantic cynicism and the Charybdis of Enlightenment deification of reason. Yet, when all is said and done, his commitment to the quest for objective truth is deeply evident—a quest he urges all people to attempt, for their own good and for the good of society as a whole. For Peirce, the ultimate commandment is: Thou shalt not block the road of inquiry.

Averroës

Such a commandment is one which Averroës would equally espouse. Dominique Urvoy writes that,

> In contrast to the haughty isolation of the mystics and the advocates of illumination like Ibn Tufayl or Ibn Bajja's "solitaries," the process by which philosophy is carried out is, according to Ibn Rushd, the concern of humanity as a whole. . . . In short, the men of religion, like the philosophers before Ibn Rushd, failed to combine a personal perspective with a concern for the public good. Ibn Rushd's approach was more balanced.[12]

Urvoy points out that Averroës was not a marginal figure in his own time, but rather was fully involved in the affairs of his community as a physician and jurist. Even more importantly, he was both willing and able to communicate with and learn from the Christian and Jewish communities and appreciate the wisdom of the ancient pagans. He had a respect for all inquirers, and made it clear that even the educated elite must be receptive to the wishes of the masses. Reason should be used to harmonize society rather than enslave it. The Law has provided a way to truth suitable to every person's nature, and a good community is one where hatreds and misunderstandings are overridden by a shared love for the truth. "Indeed," he writes,

> God has already removed many of these ills, ignorant ideas and misleading practices, by means of this triumphant rule. By it He has opened a way to many benefits, especially to the class of persons who have trodden the path of study and sought to know the truth. This [he has done] by summoning the masses to a middle way of knowing God the Glorious, [a way] which is raised above the low level of the followers of authority but is below the turbulence of the theologians; and by drawing the attention of the elite to their obligation to make a thorough study of the principles of religion.[13]

In a time of increasing culture clashes and renewed tenacity in belief-fixation, Averroës's espousal of collegiality is all the more relevant. He presents a method which avoids both Cartesian isolationism and Schopenhauerian contempt for the masses. The Enlightenment project, if it is to remain relevant to the present day, needs to be aware of Averroës's sensitivity to the different avenues of knowledge and belief.

Notes

1. Max Horkheimer and Theodor W. Adorno, *Dialectic of Enlightenment* (New York: Continuum, 1991), p. 83.

2. Arthur Schopenhauer, *Essays and Aphorisms* (London: Penguin, 1970), p. 96.

3. Arthur Hyman and James J. Walsh, *Philosophy in the Middle Ages* (Indianapolis, Ind.: Hackett, 1973), p. 285.

4. Horkheimer and Adorno, *Dialectic of Enlightenment,* pp. 133–34.

5. Schopenhauer, *Essays and Aphorisms,* pp. 127–29.

6. Charles Peirce, "The Spirit of Cartesianism," *Collected Papers*, vols. 5 6, Charles Hartshorne and Paul Weiss, eds. (Cambridge, Mass.: Harvard University Press, 1931–35), p. 157.

7. Ibid.

8. Peirce, "The Scientific Attitude," *Collected Papers*, vols. 1 and 2, p. 19.

9. Peirce, *Collected Papers*, vols. 5 and 6, p. 330.

10. Philip P. Weiner, introduction to Charles S. Peirce, *Selected Writings* (New York: Dover, 1958), p. xvii.

11. Richard Rorty, "The Priority of Democracy to Philosophy," in *Objectivity, Relativism, and Truth* (Cambridge: Cambridge University Press, 1991), p. 177.

12. Dominique Urvoy, *Ibn Rushd* (London: Routledge, 1991), p. 110.

13. Averroës, "The Decisive Treatise Determining the Nature of the Connection Between Religion and Philosophy," G. F. Hourani, trans., in *Philosophy in the Middle Ages*.

6

Understanding Religion:
The Contribution of Ibn Rushd

Iman Sodibjo
Professor of Philosophy, Jakarta University

In 1993 Samuel Huntington published an article entitled "The Clash of Civilizations" in the magazine *Foreign Affairs*.[1] That article has caused a lot of reactions, for and against.

In short Huntington's thesis can be formulated as follows: political experts tend to regard ideology and economics as determining factors in global politics. Civilizations and cultural factors are not taken much into consideration. Present-day trends show that in the future those cultural factors will determine global politics. The most important of these cultural factors is religion. Future tensions and conflict will run along the "cultural fault lines" of Western Christianity, Orthodox Slavic Christianity, Islam, Confucianism, Hinduism, Buddhism, and the various religions in Africa and Latin America. But, according to Huntington, in the near future the most important conflict will be between the culture of Western Christianity and the culture of Islam-Confucianism.

Huntington's thesis arouses varied reactions because it is frightening. Donald Emerson of the University of Wisconsin calls Huntington's thesis a "phantastical phantasy."[2] However the *Economist* in August 1994 published a survey concerning Islam and the West that takes Huntington's thesis more seriously. Whatever the truth about their analysis of the current world situation it remains true that religion plays an important factor in determining war or peace. What for us is of importance is the suggestions of those authors who try to avoid the clash of religions and to secure world harmony.

Huntington: "In the future there will not be a universal culture. There will be only different cultures and each has to learn to live alongside the other."[3]

Emerson: "We, in our multicultural societies, have to safeguard openness and intercultural tolerance so that Huntington's phantasy remains a phantasy."[4]

The writer in the *Economist* suggests: Both sides have to see that this is a moment of change. The West should be more spiritual-religious, the Muslims should be more enlightened in their way of life, while remaining religious and spiritual: "Islam then reminded the West of the common underpinning of what they both stand for. . . . Islam and the West no longer regarded each other as, respectively, amoral and fanatic."[5]

Approaches to the Philosophy of Religion[6]

From the viewpoint of the philosophy of religion, the possibility of religion being the cause of disintegration or harmony consists in man's understanding of religion. Islamic circles distinguish natural religion and revealed religion. This distinction becomes of general use when talking about religion in countries where there is great Muslim community. As the Christian and Jewish religions are revealed religions (*samawi*) some Christians also use this distinction in understanding religion. This understanding of religion is the theistic inheritance from Judaism, Christianity, and Islam.

This understanding of religion is, in my opinion, the basic source of our present difficulty.

First: It divides mankind into those who do and do not have a natural religion, which is regarded as being inferior to religion revealed by God in Scriptures.

Second: It divides the believers themselves into the faithful and the heretic. This distinction is based on the different interpretion of Scriptures by the official, accepted authorities and by the scholars who follow their own reasoning and have different conclusions.

Third: It is the source of the present tension among the Jewish, Muslim, and Western Christian people.

However this theistic understanding of religion contains in itself the possibility of a way out of our difficulty.

The way out must be sought from the point of dissent concerning interpreting the Scriptures, which then becomes focused in the problem of the relation of reason and religion in revealed religions.

THE BASIC PROBLEM

This basic problem is common to all revealed religion (Judaism, Christianity, and Islam). The believers accept as an article of faith that their Scriptures are revealed by God. So those Scriptures (what they teach, what they command and forbid) have to be obeyed literally, and implicitly the meaning of the words is also to be taken literally, as God is the ultimate truth and his words must be literally true. As long as the founder of the religion is alive the believers have no difficulty. They just follow the founder in what he teaches and in what he does.

However, once the founder has died and the Scriptures have been put into a standard text, the believers encounter difficulty in understanding some of the words in the Scriptures, and encounter difficulty concerning the day-to-day reality of action for which they do not get any guidance from their Scriptures. In such cases official teachers and scholars arise who give the interpretation of the Scriptures based on the practice of the founder.

However, once interpretation starts there will arise different interpretations, some of which will seem more reasonable than others. Reason is then used to settle the questions of religion. The difference of interpretation comes about not only through different situations in cultural and local contexts, but also because the believers in their actual lives are living in a world with different ways of thinking. When they become believers they still carry the "old" way of thinking, and of course they try to find justification for their way of thinking in their new belief instead of "completely throwing away" their old way of thinking.

PHILOSOPHY AND RELIGION

Richard Schaeffler in his book *Religions-Philosophie* traces the relation between reason and religion and philosophy and religion.[7]

1. In Greek antiquity reason was used to get away from mythological

explanations of nature. Man started using the "scientific" method in explaining nature. However, the people of Greek antiquity did not throw away their religious outlook on life.

2. Later on questions of the *Arche* of Nature shifted into the question of Being. With Plato and Aristotle began the quest for the Supreme Being, the ground cause of all the beings in this world; and how the beings in this world were to be understood in relation to the Supreme Being; and how the beings in this world came about from the Supreme Being.

3. At the beginning of Christianity Aristotelian philosophy and Neoplatonism were well known among scholars while in the practical life Sufism and Gnosticism kept alive the practical wisdom and religious sentiment of the people.

When later Christianity and Islam started to become official religions, many of the believers had already adopted or learned about those philosophies and ways of life.

4. Both in Islam and in Christianity, the "philosophers" among the believers started to reevaluate the position of those "philosophies" and ways of life in relation to their newfound religion. They also started to try to explain the teaching of their religion and their Scriptures in terms of their philosophies.

5. When the teaching of Aristotle became more and more known many Christian and Muslim philosopher-theologians used the philosophy of Aristotle to explain the teaching of their religion. The pattern of approach is equating the God of their religion with the Supreme Being of contingent beings in nature. The relation of man to God is thought of as the relation of contingent beings to the eternal, necessary Supreme Being. This approach is called ontotheology.

6. Both in Christianity and in Islam the basic opinion was that the teaching of religion is superior to the wisdom and conclusion of pure reason. However, reason can aspire to the basic teaching of religion concerning God and the world. In my opinion this ontotheology is the root of all division in religions. Equating God with the Supreme Being has brought the philosopher-theologians into using rational ontology to explain God (God's existence, God's attributes, and so on). And their explanation and their method will be a rational method and a rational explanation. One rational explanation will lead to other rational explanations by those who disagree. So a lot of rational explanations came about. Since such explanations and conclusions might contradict the Scriptures taken in their literal meaning, the necessity arose to justify nonliteral interpretations of the Scriptures.

This process arouses the opposition of those official teachers and theologians who want to safeguard the purity of religious teaching by sticking to the official traditional teaching and adhering to the more literal interpretation of the Scriptures. Both Christian and Muslim philosopher-theologians underwent those oppositions, but in Christianity the impact has not been tremendous. In the Muslim world the impact has been considerable because of the belief that any "new opinion" (*bida'ah*) that deviates from official teaching should be banished, and its authors could be put to death. This was the fate of Ibn Rushd.

THE PRECARIOUS USE OF REASON IN ONTOTHEOLOGY—KANT[8]

Kant's teaching about religion can be found in his *Kritik der praktischen Vernunft* and in his *Die Religion innerhalb der Grenzen der blossen Vernunft*.[9]

The basic tenets of his philosophy of religion are that all ideas about God are only ideas, postulates of the mind. God is not an object of knowledge, because knowledge concerns itself with what is in space and time.[10]

For Kant the idea of God is a necessary idea for morality. However, morality for Kant is doing one's duty because it is one's duty, which man can attain from the use merely of his reason. Morality leads to the idea of God as being useful, but morality is not based on God but on the autonomy of the will and on human reason.

According to Kant man need not try to prove God's existence as the Supreme Being and then relate the other beings to this Supreme Being. Man has no need of ontotheology. For Kant religion is not dogma but morality. True religion is something in the inner man, a moral disposition. As such religion must be distinguished from church belief (*Kirchen Glauben*). It is those "institutional church beliefs" which cause clashes between religions. It is in this sense that man has to understand Kant's saying: "There is only one true religion but it is possible that there are many kinds of beliefs." In this theory Kant went so far as maintaining the opinion that Christ as Son of God is not a historical personality (*Historische Gestalt*). He is only the personified idea of principles of morality (*Personifizierte Idee des sittlichen Prinzips*). Of course, Kant was reprimanded by official church authority for this opinion.

The importance of Kant's teaching on religion is the teaching that reason does not concern itself with knowledge about God, connecting its result with obtaining the truth (which causes clashes between religions defending the truth). Reason postulates the idea of God as a motivation of reason in adhering to its own ethical principles with the strength of doing God's will, in the sense of acting on moral precepts with more conviction of duty.

So God is the inner motivation of reason to do good. All mankind will be regarded as having true religion if they use reason to promote good life among their fellowmen. So reason is still connected with religion but, released from ontotheology, will be able to build a bridge for harmony amongst religious beliefs.

We will now turn to Ibn Rushd.

Ibn Rushd on Reason and Religion

Ibn Rushd's treatment of this topic is found in his writing *Kitab fasl al-maqal wa taqrir ma bayn ash-sharia wal-hikma min al-ittisal*, meaning, "The book of the decision [or distinction] of the discourse, and a determination of the connection between religion and philosophy."

For this study I use the English translation by George Hourani published by the trustees of the E. J .W. Gibb memorial.[11] Ibn Rushd's teaching on this matter can be summarized into the following points.

1. If theological study of the world is philosophy, and if law commands such a study, then the law commands philosophy.

2. This study must be conducted in the best manner, by demonstrative reasoning.

3. To master this instrument the religious thinker must make a preliminary study of logic, just as lawyers must study reasoning. This is no more heretical in the one case than in the other. And logic must be learned from the ancient masters, regardless of the fact that they were not Muslims.

4. After logic we must proceed to philosophy proper. Here too we have to learn from our predecessors, just as in mathematics and law. Thus it is wrong to forbid the study of ancient philosophy. Harm from it is accidental, like harm from taking medicine, drinking water, or studying law.

5. For every Muslim the law has provided a way to truth suitable to his nature, through demonstrative, dialectical, or rhetorical methods.

6. Demonstrative truth and scriptural truth cannot conflict.

7. If the apparent meaning of Scripture conflicts with demonstrative conclusions then it must be interpreted allegorically, that is, metaphorically.

8. All Muslims accept the principle of allegorical interpretation; they only disagree about the extent of its application.

9. The double meaning has been given to suit people's diverse intelligence. The apparent contradictions are meant to stimulate the learned to deeper study.

10. In interpreting texts allegorically we must never violate Islamic consensus when it is certain. But to establish it with certainty with regard to theoretical texts is impossible, because there have always been scholars who would not divulge their interpretation of such texts.

11. Texts of Scripture fall into three kinds with respect to the excusability of error: (a) texts which must be taken in their apparent meaning by everyone. Since the meaning can be understood plainly by demonstrative, dialectical, and rhetorical methods alike, no one is excused for the error of interpreting these texts allegorically; (b) texts which must be taken in their apparent meaning by the lower classes and interpreted allegorically by the demonstrative class. It is inexcusable for the lower class to interpret them allegorically or for the demonstrative class to take them in their apparent meaning; (c) texts whose classification under the previous headings is uncertain. Error in this matter by the demonstrative class is excused. The unlearned classes must take such texts in their apparent meaning. It is unbelief for the learned to set down allegorical interpretations in popular writings.

12. Demonstrative books should be banned to the unqualified, but not to the learned.

13. The purpose of Scripture is to teach true theoretical and practical science and right practice and attitude.

14. Scripture teaches concepts both directly and by symbols, and uses demonstrative, dialectical, and rhetorical arguments. Dialectical and rhetorical arguments are prevalent because the main aim of Scripture is to teach the majority. In these arguments concepts are indicated directly or by symbols, in various combinations in premises and conclusion.

15. Where symbols are used, each class of men, demonstrative, dialectical, and rhetorical, must try to understand the inner meaning symbolized or rest content with the apparent meaning, according to their capacities.

16. To explain the inner meaning to people unable to understand it is to destroy their belief in the apparent meaning without putting anything in its place. The result is unbelief in learners and teachers. It is best for the learned to profess ignorance.

The most important points from Ibn Rushd's thoughts which I want to emphasize are those points which I would like to work out further into a philosophy of religion which will enable mankind to come out of conflict of religions:

1. His teaching that the law of religion commands the practice of philosophy.

2. His division of man's intellectual capacities into demonstrative, dialectical, and rhetorical classes.

3. Allegorical interpretation is allowed but limited to those people gifted with the capability of demonstrative reasoning.

4. The connection of Scripture to the different ways of interpreting it.

From the above-mentioned point springs to mind the closeness of Scripture and its rational interpretation. However, rational interpretation must be done only by people well trained in syllogistic logic and metaphysics learned from the ancient philosopher (Aristotle). As such it is not necessary that the master should be a Muslim. There is the openness of a rational mind in Ibn Rushd.

Using philosophy to explain Scripture should be done only by well-qualified philosopher-theologians. Allegorical interpretation liberates the interpreter from literal interpretation. This makes it possible to keep religion above sectarian dialectical and rhetorical interpretation. However, again, the possibility is open only to well-qualified people.

Final Reflection

CONTEMPORARY PHILOSOPHY OF RELIGION

Contemporary scholars of religion do not give a definition of religion based on theistic understanding. However, attempts to give a definition of religion which will cover all facts designated as belonging to religion, which will satisfy all people of all cultures, has not had any result yet. Nonetheless, contemporary scholars, tired of the existing quarrels among religions, tend to look for a designation of religion which could go above and beyond the official institutional religions.

In this connection I would like to explore the theory of John Hick in his book *An Interpretation of Religion* and the theory of Ken Wilbur in his book *A Sociable God*.[12] In the preface of his book Hick writes:

My hope is that this book will make it clear that a viable justification of religious belief, showing that it is rational to base our beliefs upon our experience, including religious experience, leads inevitably to the problems of religious pluralism; and that there are resources within the major world traditions themselves that can, when supported by important philosophical distinctions, point to a resolution of these problems. Insofar as such a resolution proves acceptable within the different traditions it provides a basis for the mutual respect that is necessary for fruitful inter-faith dialogue and for practical collaboration in face of the common threats.

Hick's solution to religious pluralism is rejecting ontotheology as giving actual proof to the truth of religion. The essence of religion is in the religious experience of men who strive forever to attain the Ultimate Real. Further, he maintains that the God of religions, whatever he is called, is a manifestation of the Ultimate Real not the Ultimate Real as it is in itself. (He uses Kant's distinction between *phenomenon* and *Das Ding an sich*).[13]

Ken Wilbur maintains that the peak experience of true religious people is being one with the Transcendence. So within each religion there are stages of religiosity among the believers. Implicitly he maintains that believers who are still at the lower stages will tend to act in a crude fashion, while people enjoying peak experience will act full of compassion to other people and other religions. At the higher level religions have no distinctions. Wilbur distinguishes six stages: the *physical* level, where religiosity is still closely bound with material things; the *emotional* level, where religiosity is connected with intimate relations amongst the believers, however, the relation is still exclusive; the *mental* level, where religiosity is connected with intellectual debate—there is some openness to other religions but it is still somewhat antagonistic; the *psychic* level, which brings meditation and insight into play—all religions tend to accept other experience of other religions; the *subtle* level, where the believer experiences the closeness of God and embraces all mankind in God; and the last stage, the level of *radical absorption in the Uncreate.*

It is interesting to note both authors use for the word God other very general terms, like the *Ultimate Real* and the *Uncreate*. This is part of the current tendency to go above and beyond traditional terms for God in the present official theistic religion.

Back to Ibn Rushd and Beyond Ibn Rushd

You may ask the question: What is the connection of all these theories of the philosophy of religion with Ibn Rushd? I would like to show how theoretically, using some points of thought of Ibn Rushd to arrive at Kant's philosophy, and from then on adapting the thoughts of Hick and Wilbur to arrive at an understanding of religion and reason that is conducive to establishing a cultural bridge.

Ibn Rushd was of course a child of his time. So his scholarly undertaking was still embedded in ontotheology. However, he managed to show that the use of reason was commanded by religion and to show that reason and religion were on the same level for the demonstrative class. Once this was established Ibn Rushd pointed out that allegorical interpretation was proper to demonstrative reason. Reason was then free to go beyond the limit of literal official interpretation.

Kant further established reason as beyond the knowledge of phenomena and put religion and reason on the level of morality. Again here Kant also took religion away from the sphere of official teachings, the church beliefs, and put it on the level of human conscience, on the same level as reason. Kant also put God beyond the God of official teaching. God became a transcendental idea.

For Ibn Rushd Muslims and non-Muslims are on the same level philosophically. Even Muslims must learn from non-Muslim masters of philosophy. For Kant all men of good morality and rational conscience are actually of the same true religion although belonging to different official beliefs.

Hick uses the same pattern of thought. He puts religion and reason on the same level, the level of religious experience, which makes possible the acceptance of pluralism in religion.

To avoid clashes of religion and reason Kant had to distinguish between *phenomenon* and *Das Ding an sich* and thus gave human reason the function of ordering the phenomena. Applying Kant to his understanding of religion Hick also takes away God from the realm of knowledge. He puts God beyond the grasp of knowledge, calls it the Ultimate Real, and regards the God of our official religions as manifestations (phenomena) of the Ultimate Real, so men of reason can serve God in their own particular religion without clashing with other religions because all actually serve the Ultimate Real. Wilbur shows only the psychological stages of becoming perfectly religious, however implicitly we can see that for the truly religious man all religions lead to the same Supreme Reality. The tendency to see differences and to clash because of differences in external factors and doctrines belongs only to those believers of the lower stages.

Actually Ibn Rushd was advocating the same pattern of thought, without calling his classes stages of religious development. To be able to accept philosophy and allegorical interpretation as in accordance with religion one has to overcome, go beyond, rhetorical and dialectical reasoning. One has to attain higher rational maturity above the level of the masses. We have to come to the level of demonstrative reasoning analogous to Wilbur's higher stages of religious life.

I am quite aware that Ibn Rushd, Kant, Hick, and Wilbur talked about different things. But using their pattern of thought we can hope to use reason and religious practices to go beyond the limits of our sectarian beliefs, to put God really at the highest place, above our human expressions, concentrate on doing good and exchanging religious experiences instead of quarreling about doctrines and formulations. We are the demonstrative class mentioned by Ibn Rushd, we are the people at the higher stages of religious life (not necessarily in accordance with Wilbur's stages). We can build the bridge between cultures, because cultures are only limited manifestations of the Ultimate Real.

Bibliography

Badawi, Abdurrahman. *Histoire de la philosophie en Islam.* Paris: Libr. Philos. J. Vrin, 1972.

Beversluis, Joel, ed. *A Source Book for the Community of Religions.* Chicago, 1993.

Eliade, Mircea, ed. *The Encyclopedia of Religion.* New York: Macmillan, 1987.

Gauthier, Leon, trad. *Ibn Rushd (Averroës): Traite decisif.* Algier, 1942.

Dasuki, H. A. Hafizh. ed. *Ensiklopedi Islam.* Jakarta: Van Hoeve, 1994.

Hick, John. *An Interpretation of Religion.* Hong Kong: Macmillan, 1991.

Hirschberger, Johannes. *Geschichte der Philosophy.* Freiburg: Herder, 1991.

Hourani, George F., trans. *Averroës: On Harmony of Religion and Philosophy.* London: Luzac & Co, 1961.

Kemp, John. *The Philosophy of Kant.* New York: Oxford University Press, 1968.

Peters, F. E. *Aristotle and the Arabs.* New York: New York University Press, 1989.

Schaeffler, Richard. *Religions-Philosophie.* Freiburg: Karl Aber Verlag, 1983.

Schmidt, Raymond. *Immanuel Kant: Die drei Kritiken.* Stuttgart: Kroner Verlag, 1969.

Sharif, M. M. *A History of Muslim Philosophy.* Weisbaden, 1963.

Wilbur, Ken. *A Sociable God.* London: New Science Library, 1984.

Notes

1. Huntington's article is also found in Indonesian translation in the magazine *Ulumul Qur'an* 4, no. 5 (1993): 11–25.

2. Emerson's article is translated into Indonesian in *Ulumul Qur'an* 4, no. 25 (1993): 44–55.

3. Huntington, p. 25.

4. Emerson, p. 50.

5. *The Economist*, August 6–12, 1994, Survey, p. 16.

6. See the article on "Agama," in *Ensiklopedi Islam*, pp. 63–65.

7. Richard Schaeffler, *Religions-Philosophie* (Freiburg: Karl Aber Verlag, 1983), pp. 47–63.

8. See Johannes Hirschberger, *Geschichte der Philosophie* (Freiburg: Herder, 1991), pp. 336–53; John Kemp, *The Philosophy of Kant* (New York: New York University Press, 1968), pp. 90–96; and Raymond Schmidt, *Immanuel Kant, Die drei Kritiken* (Stuttgart: Kroner Verlag, 1969), pp. 365–87.

9. R. Schmidt, *Immanuel Kant: Die drei Kritiken* (Stuttgart: Kroner Verlag, 1983), p. 381.

10. Hirschberger, *Geschichte der Philosophie*, p. 351

11. George F. Hourani, *Averroës. On the Harmony of Religion and Philosophy* (London: Luzac & Co., 1961), pp. 44–71.

12. John Hick, *An Interpretation of Religion* (Hong Kong: Macmillan, 1991), p. xv; and Ken Wilbur, *A Sociable God* (London: New Science Library, 1984), p. 44.

13. Hick, *An Interpretation of Religion,* pp. 236–49.

7

Ibn Rushd in the Islamic Context

Mokdad Arfa Mensia
Professor of Philosophy, Tunis University

Let us begin with a rapid comparison between the two situations of Averroës and Averroism in the two medieval Latin West and Islamic worlds. Certainly the same basic philosophy underlies the two situations, but the focus is different and even the Averroist corpus is not the same here and there. In his Western context the thought inspired by Averroës is considered a reaction against ecclesiastic authority and as a response to a need caused by emerging forces which led to the Renaissance. Starting from the Averroist treatises which were not translated in Latin (that is, those the author himself considered as nonapodectical works, especially *Fasl al-maqal* and *Manahij al-adillah*), I try to place Ibn Rushd in his Islamic context and to discuss his relation to pure Islamic sciences (especially *fiqh* and *kalam*) and to Islamic sects like the *Ash'arites* and especially the *Zahirites* (Literalists). I base my analysis on his own classification of literalism. Averroës made a distinction between theoretical literalism, based essentially on the negation of the *kayfiyya* (modality) and the *physis* in the dogmas, and practical literalism, based on the negation of the *'illa* (cause) and then the *qiyas* (analogy) as a source of *fiqh*. In his defense of philosophy, Ibn Rushd claims his proximity to the theoretical one.

91

In comparison with previous Islamic philosophers like al-Farabi, who tries, as does Plato, to organize the City on a philosophical basis, relative to people's convictions as well as to their practices, Ibn Rushd makes a very pessimistic diagnosis of the situation and the destiny of philosophy in Islamic countries. His principal concern is to save philosophy from extinction and to legitimate an area reserved for a restricted elite. Hence, he makes the defense with an admirable but rather artificial ability and sometimes uses the same methods as those whom he attacks. Indeed there is a serious rivalry between *al-falasifa* and *al-mutakallimun*, because they have opposite rationalist issues for the same topics, even though, always, the *falasifa* tend to accuse their opponents of logical inferiority.

To describe globally and formally Averroës's work we may say that he seeks to realize a double purpose in returning simultaneously to pure Aristotelianism beyond Hellenistic and Islamic commentators (like Avicenna) on the one hand, and to literalist Islamic dogmas beyond various historical interpretations (like that of the Ash'arites) on the other hand, thinking that, in this manner, a better *modus vivendi* between religion and philosophy will be realized.

I come to the conclusion that the role played by Ibn Rushd in developing rationalism and enlightenment is not greater than that of other Muslim philosophers like al-Farabi, Avicenna, or al-Ghazali. Of course, Ibn Rushd can really be a symbol for a kind of liberating thought, because philosophical truth pretends to be universal; but what is often considered as rationalism (here the Averroist Aristotelianism) can sometimes be an obstacle to the development of reason itself in science and thought.

8

The Averroistic Ethos
Beyond the Enlightenment

Joe Teffo
Professor of Philosophy,
University of the North (South Africa)

The onset of the twentieth and twenty-first centuries has led to the dis-integration of numerous systems that have survived for centuries. This development was both occasioned and necessitated by the dominant trends and movements that are characteristic of postmodernity. The Enlightenment, which began in the seventeenth century and flourished in the eighteenth, constitutes one of the great spiritual movements of modern Europe. In its ap-proach the Enlightenment was essentially revolutionary, directed against the authority of intellectual and religious traditions. The positive force at its core was a determined assertion of the freedom of the individual, freedom in af-fairs social and political, intellectual and religious. It gave prominence to the primacy of the individual and freedom to choose. To some extent it paved the way for phenomenology and existentialism.[1]

A brief excursion into some of the characteristics of the Enlightenment is in place here. During this era, reason dethroned faith. Faith in the old pre-suppositions and authorities for so long considered valid beyond question gave way to a spirit of criticism. Reason claimed to be autonomous and set itself up as the unique court of appeal. Though it is dangerous to rely too much on characteristics specifically for some given period, one could perhaps characterize this period as one of increasing emancipation of reason from faith, just as during modern times natural science gradually emancipated itself from philosophy.

At an early period, when philosophy amounted to little more than logic or dialectics, it was natural that theologians should tend to look on philosophy as the handmaid or instrument of theology (*ancilla theologiae*). For as long as logic had not been developed as a formal science in its own right, it was natural to look on it as providing tools for use elsewhere. And theology was then regarded as the highest science. But in the course of time the concept of philosophy was greatly widened, and its autonomy came to be recognized. In the thirteenth and fourteenth centuries the close union between philosophy and theology, between reason and faith, tended to fall apart. Metaphysical arguments were subjected to vehement criticism. The range of philosophical demonstration was greatly narrowed. Late medieval philosophers concentrated much more on logic and the philosophy of language. They were still religious believers, but they tended to relegate philosophy to the sphere of faith beliefs, which lay beyond the scope of philosophical proof.

The aforesaid trends and movements led to the abandonment of some ethical systems whose history is as old as humanity's. It should also be noted against the backdrop of this observation that some of the ethical systems traceable to the ancient Greek philosophical systems are being revisited for their relevance and validity in and for the contemporary human condition.

The Averroistic ethos, or the ethical doctrines propounded by Averroës, a distinguished neo-Aristotelian Muslim *falsifa* (philosopher), hinged on the Aristotelian doctrine of the golden mean, which today also dominates humanity's quest or search for an appropriate framework within which to locate ideal ethical systems. Having been immersed in the entire Aristotelian tradition of both theoretical and speculative thinking, it is also noticed that Averroës subscribed to the Aristotelian metaphysics, conceiving of God/Allah as the creator and the mover of substances. But the Aristotelian Averroistic metaphysical theorizing which dominated much of the later period of medieval scholasticism and the early times of the modern metaphysical speculation, as intimated in the introductory paragraph of this paper, has receded to the sidelines of philosophical discourse.[2] This is particularly so with the dominance of the detailed and penetrating forms of scientific inquiry. Well and good, the natural sciences are taking good care of that area of human inquiry into the nature of things.

Averroës, having interpreted and commented on the entire Aristotelian corpus, endeavored to relive the Aristotelian doctrines unaltered and thereby Islamize them.[3] This endeavor wasn't much of a problem for Averroës because there were attributes of similarity between the Islamic ethical systems and the Aristotelian ethics of moderation. Averroës himself, a physician and judge rather than a theologian, had applied a rigid legal method of interpreting Aristotle.[4] In Aristotle, Averroës found much cosmic mysticism and pantheism.[5] Islamic ethical doctrines, just like all other culturally decreed ethical systems, do bear imprints of absolutism in so far as the behavioral patterns of the subscribers to the system are concerned. From the ancient to the modern, cultures have produced deterministic ethical systems. The same development also obtains in the ethical doctrines that have evolved out of philosophical discourses. One of the contributory factors to the disintegration of most of these ethical systems is found to be the element of absolutism about them. It is the attributes of determinism, which often tend to be absolutist, that in actual fact led to the emergence of the rebellious existential movement in the history of humanity's speculative thinking processes.[6]

Today's everyday realities and trends in both the speculative philosophical movements and discourse are such that it is as though they are responding to the Marxian antithetical postulate that, throughout the history of philosophy, the philosophers have interpreted the world differently and that the time had come to change it. Yes, for centuries mankind has been subjected to the mighty intellectual storms of existentially inconsequential metaphysical accounts to such an extent that man ended up giving up hope for salvation, more especially of a philosophical nature. This observation was well captured by the equally disenchanted intellectuals who declared the discipline a poverty-stricken enterprise. This assertion is traceable to the fact that mankind today is already waiting for philosophy to come and assist man in finding citizenship in an ethos that is characterized by all the attributes of humanness.

In the face of the onslaught by the existential movement on the obsolete ethical doctrines, some of the said systems still survive, just like the Averroistic ethos of moderation. The observation can be made in the movements in the contemporary era, wherein numerous clarion calls are made for the abandonment of absolutistic political, social, and ethical systems as well. This basically suggests that there is a need for the invocation of moderation, which is one of the most pronounced attributes of the Averroistic ethos.

Today's movements, like democratization, with their existentialist declarations, postulate the avoidance of the pursuit of the good to the extremes, as the neo-Aristotelian Averroistic ethos maintains. The rejection of the absolutist ethical doctrines which have been reinforced by the positivism of the Enlightenment's ethical frameworks of inflexible rigidities is also in a measure an exhortation of humanity toward accomodationist outlooks like those of Averroës, which inevitably will not go down well with the absolutist perspectives, like those of the fundamentalists. It is also worth noting that, unlike other medieval philosophical traditions, Averroës took on the unspiritual characteristics of Aristotle's thought, as it is the case with Aristotle's ethical doctrines, and yet it is the very same Averroës who by virtue of his influence hastened the advent of integral Aristotelianism among Christian thinkers who felt much more comfortable in the confluence of reason and revelation.

If this is what emerged out of the influence of Averroës on the development of philosophy in both the Islamic and the Christian Western world, then humanity can as well settle for the Gadamerian hermeneutic postulates, in which philosophy Gadamer is beckoning all the diverse perspectives in the philosophical enterprise for the merging of these very diverse horizons of human conviction. After all, much of the philosophical enterprise today in numerous philosophical traditions is about the problems of human experience,[7] and it is in this very same enterprise that texts with an ethical import are simultaneously produced. Upon profound analysis it will still be established that the production of texts in different horizons of human experience is of and for the same purpose, a quest for solutions to the problems experienced by man, whether Muslim or Christian, Jewish or gentile. And quite often if not always the sociopolitical and ethical dispensations yearned for by all these traditions are life-giving. And if all these traditions are inspired by a willingness to give humanity life without being injurious to other traditions, then what on earth can forestall the formulation of a unifying ethos modeled on the neo-Aristotelian Averroism, with its attributes of universality, in a less exacting endeavor for the building of bridges?

It is the pluralism and accomodationism of both post-Enlightenment and postmodernity that make the revisitation, revival, and reconceptualization of Averroism, more especially on the ethical terraces, a worthy cause to pursue. The absolutism of the ancient and medieval doctrines that was reinforced by the sophisticated Enlightenment doctrines and postulates was geared to mobilizing humanity to revel in the anestheticizing logical categories of dehumanization, a pilgrimage in which few followers were drawn by these crusaders of positivism.

Postmodernism in general and deconstruction in particular demonstrate how discourse is not a neutral phenomenon but is very much involved in the construction, subjugation, and liberation of humankind. The panacea to this discourse is the ethics and politics of difference.

Morality implies respect for others. By emphasizing the process of differentiation, we can highlight not only the otherness of the other as a mere fact, but also the importance of the other as a precondition of the self's awareness and self-understanding. The respect for the other is partly based on the fact that the human relationship exposes contingency in the being of both parties.[8] Sartre further asserts that, "I am the proof of the Other. That is the original fact."[9]

Postmodern politics at least entails tolerance of difference. In actual practice there are, of course, limitations that should be set to all kinds of tolerance. Politics is an interplay of pressures within a society whose solidarity consists in the acceptance of a plurality of communities and in the resistance to the imposition of conformity onto society. It is referred to as "a communitarianism rooted in the liberal values of difference, that is to say, a political community whose solidarity is affirmed, and not denied, by the different ways in which the people within it choose to lead their lives."[10]

The Averroistic ethos can therefore come in handy as a very essential ingredient or component of the process of transformation with the production of a new world order out of the ashes that were deposited by the destructive and absolutistic systems of yesteryear. In conclusion, let all of humanity rise across the political, religious, and cultural divides, like the proverbial phoenix bird, from the ashes of sociopolitical and cultural totalism to the humanizing heights of the mutual recognition of each other's cultures and values, guided by the Averroistic determinism.

Notes

1. I. Kant, *Religion Within the Limits of Reason Alone,* Green et al., trans. (New York: Harper Torchbooks, 1960), p. 1x.

2. P. Edwards, ed., *The Encyclopedia of Philosophy* (New York: Macmillan, 1972), p. 226.

3. I. Husik, *History of Medieval Jewish Philosophy* (New York: Meridian Books, 1960), p. xx.

4. J. Randall, *The Career of Philosophy, Vol. 1: From the Middle Ages to the Enlightenment* (New York: Columbia University Press, 1970), p. 54.

5. Ibid.

6. D. Knowles, *The Long Evolution of Medieval Thought* (London: Longman, Green and Co., 1963), p. 202.

7. R. E. Palmer, *Studies in Phenomenology and Existential Philosophy: Hermeneutic* (Evanston, Ill.: Northwestern University Press, 1977), p. 203.

8. J. P. Sartre, *Being and Nothingness* (London: Methuen Press, 1958), pp. 361–64.

9. Ibid., p. 363.

10. G. Hawthorn, "Is Postmodernism Politics?" *History of the Human Sciences* 5, no. 3 (1992): 92–97.

9

The Politics of Logic

Mourad Wahba
Professor Emeritus of Philosopy,
University of Ain Shams (Egypt)

At the Third International Philosophy Conference held in Cairo in 1980 on the theme "Unity of Knowledge," I presented a paper entitled "Three P's Science," that is, three sciences in one, each beginning with "p": physics, politics, philosophy. This "Summa" does not mean the elimination of other sciences, but it means the reduction of natural sciences to physics in general and to nuclear physics in particular. The reduction of social and human sciences to politics is not meant in the sense of a theory of governance but of international relations. As for philosophy, it is looked at as a cosmic vision based on physics and politics.

In this context comes the title of my paper today: "The Politics of Logic," which could refer to a certain kind of reducing of logic to politics which is justified by Averroës. But this justification does not mean adopting Averroës as a model of this reduction. It means that his philosophy is considered the crowning of previous endeavors beginning with the Sophists. Logic, according to the Sophists, originated from "contradictory arguments," that is, approving an argument and its contradictory at the same time, which was in line with the contemporary climate, that is, the second half of the fifth century of the Christian era, where political dialogue had as its target conviction and rhetorical influence. A dictum was said to be attributed to Protagoras, namely, what the Sophists had to offer, teaching a man about matters of state so that he might become a real power in the affairs of the city both as a speaker and as a man of action. This kind of instruction was the reason why the Sophists were powerful in Athens.[1]

Then came Aristotle, who defined man as a political animal. But he divided men in *Politics* into free and unfree men. He then formulated this dichotomy into universal and necessary propositions: all Athenians are free by nature, and all foreigners are not free. Accordingly, logic has nothing to do except teach us how to formulate these propositions depending on the concept of "essence," which is the subject matter of science. And what the particular adds to the essence comes from the sensible matter and this is excluded from the field of science.

Averroës is in agreement with Aristotle on relating logic to politics, not within the context of the division between Athenians and foreigners, but within the division between the multitude and men of science. However, this dichotomy, though it is traditional in Islamic thought, is the pivotal idea in Averroës's logic. It could be stated that Averroës has two logics: the logic of multitude and the logic of men of science. The first is the logic of induction and the second is the logic of syllogism. He says: "Induction is more convincing than syllogism for it is based on the sensible, consequently it is beneficial to the multitude and easier in argumentation. On the contrary, syllogism is less beneficial and in particular to the multitude and is more difficult in argumentation. Therefore, its use is more beneficial to those who are experts in this art." By "those" he means men of science.

However, Averroës illustrates his favorable appreciation of syllogism and not induction due to its superiority. He means the demonstrative syllogism, or demonstration, which is based on true a priori premises. On the contrary, dialectical syllogism is based on premises that are considered to be accepted premises while in fact they are not, or are thought to be true but in fact are not.

Despite this dichotomy between induction and syllogism, Averroës does not consider it a dichotomy that is based on the discontinuity of both ends but rather on the continuity between both. He gives five proofs.

First: The universal premises that are the basis of syllogism cannot be known without induction; consequently, if there is no way to know these premises, there is no way to demonstrate them (certain syllogism).

Second: This is the result of Averroës's concept of accepted opinions.

He says men of science and philosophers believe in certain accepted opinions without being opposed by the multitude. He says there are reasons for doubt about the accepted opinions: one of these is due to the contradictory views among philosophers such as the undivided particulars; another is due to the contradictory views among the multitude. For example, some think that wealth is more favorable than poverty, while others think that poverty is more favorable than wealth.

Third: This proof concerns the contradictory views among the philosophers and the multitude, such as the view that virtue with poverty is preferable to the good life without virtue; the multitude thinks the opposite. From this it seems that if contradiction is possible among philosophers and among the multitude, it is possible among philosophers and the multitude. Therefore, contradiction is a human phenomenon and is not confined to certain classes of human beings.

Fourth: Philosophical concepts come from the multitude, such as substance. Philosophers think that the concept of substance comes from the multitude when they sell and exaggerate the price of certain stones. The similarity between the two terms is due to the fact that these stones are substances because of their superiority and because substance is the most dignified if it is named substance.

Fifth and last: The multitude appreciates the philosopher's thought, though they attack him for it. The philosophers start from accepted opinions.

Now the question is: If there is continuity between the multitude and the philosophers, why does Averroës speak about the discontinuity between them? The answer to this question is possible on the condition that we differentiate between the status quo and the pro quo, or the futuristic vision. To elaborate: historically, this discontinuity between philosophers and the multitude goes back to Euthyphro. Euthyphro says that after the condemnation of Socrates, his distinguished disciples dispersed. Among them was Plato, who left Athens, and when he returned after thirteen years, he established the Academy and on its entrance he inscribed, "Entrance is forbidden except for those who are competent in geometry." Thus Plato was separated from the multitude. As for Averroës, he claimed that the Prophet used to translate the sensible images into symbols so the multitude could understand the religious text. Concerning the philosophers, Averroës thought that they are competent to interpret. Thus, the question of the problematic of truth, according to Averroës, is as follows:

If contradiction is embedded in the problematic, the question is: where is the contradiction in the concept of truth? I think that the contradiction is in Averroës's definition of interpretation, which is "extension of the significance of an expression from real to metaphorical significance, without forsaking therein the standard metaphorical practices of Arabic, such as calling a thing by the name of something resembling it or a cause or consequence or accompaniment of it, or other things such as are enumerated in accounts of the kinds of metaphorical speech."

Thus we can understand Averroës's warning against the explicit declaration of the contradiction between what is real (sensible) and what is allegorical. The importance of this warning is due to the fact that philosophers, in his age, were ignored in comparison to jurists and politicians. Therefore, as a reaction, Averroës gives priority to the philosophers, although they are equal to theologians. This priority of philosophy over theology leads to the negation of the illusion of possession of absolute truth by the theologian (jurist), that is, by religious authority in its organic unity with political authority. And if the illusion of possessing absolute truth is negated, truth is turned into mere knowledge, which is liable to development. In this case, no one will have the right to charge the other of unbelief on the ground that he negates the absolute truth, and hence is deviating from *ijma'*, or consensus, and its concomitant certainty, *qati'a,* strictly, dogmatism.

If certainty is the essence of *ijma'* and if certainty negates demonstration, that is, refuses to be answered by demonstration, certainty then prevents demonstration. Consequently, *takfir,* the charge of unbelief, is a charge that will continue to be directed against any one who violates dogmatism. In this sense, Averroës is distinguished from Aristotle due to his introduction of the category of *takfir* into the field of logic and demonstrating that it contradicts interpretation. Therefore, I disagree with Gauthier and Gilson in their claim that Averroës did not contribute anything new in the field of logic. For logic, according to Aristotle, does not include the two categories of *takfir* and "interpretation" because it does not imply the dichotomy between *al-Rasikhoun fililm* ("well-grounded in science") and the multitude. This dichotomy, in turn, implies a problematic or, strictly, a contradiction between continuity and discontinuity.

The question now is: Is it possible to eliminate the problematic which is implied in the dichotomy, and hence, eliminate the category of *takfir*? Within the context of a pro quo, the elimination is possible. Averroës had envisaged such a possibility in his discussion of Plato's *Republic*. In the ideal city of Averroës the multitude practices the logic of syllogism.

The question is: How? Averroës answers by saying that if man's sole purpose is sensual pleasure, delight of the senses, in this case man is closer to the field of unexamined opinions, in contemporary terms, taboos. Due to this liberation, the multitude will be equal to the philosophers. The evidence is that Averroës, in his ideal city, evades the class divisions. Consequently, one could say that he wishes to involve the multitude in the field of philosophy, provided that the multitude is not involved in sensual pleasures, for such pleasures prevent men from controlling themselves. This means that this kind of control leads man to surpass what is sensual to what is reasonable, or to surpass what is rhetorical or poetic to what is demonstrative. This opens the door for the multitude to practice rational demonstration. And if the multitude enters that door it becomes possible for them to be governors in Averroës's ideal city, and, in this way, the discontinuity between the multitude and the governors is negated.

Therefore, Averroës attacks the Arab poets who call for sensual pleasures through their poetry. In this sense, the poets perform a role in bringing about the discontinuity between the multitude and the governors. He also attacks the theologians (*mutakallimun*), particularly the Asharites, describing them as having sick minds which influence the multitude; hence true harm comes from them and not from the philosophers.

Hence, according to Averroës, if we seek continuity between *sharia* (religion) and philosophy, it is imperative that we eliminate false problems which emanated from *kalam* (theology). It is also essential that the *fakih* (jurist) stop using *fikh* (jurisprudence) as a tool for either pleasure or authority. This means that if we succeed in eliminating theology, the opposition between religion and philosophy will consequently be eliminated. As a result, *takfir* will also be eliminated.

Now the question is: Was Averroës able to achieve this task? In other words: Was he able to convince the multitude?

My answer is that he failed, and the reason for this failure is his being unaware of the necessity of writing a sequel to *Fasl al-maqal fima bayn al-hikma wal sharria min al-ittisal,* to be entitled *Fasl al-maqal wa taqrir ma-bayn al-gomhour wal hukamaa min al-ittisal* (Decisive Treatise on the Continuity Between the Multitude and the Governors). The importance of such a book, in my opinion, is due to the fact that *takfir,* the charge of unbelief, will always be practiced by theologians against the multitude as long as the multitude continues to be under the control of the theologians. Therefore, writing such a book would have made the multitude conscious that this control is false and illusory. Accordingly, due to the absence of such a book, the charge of unbelief still prevails in the present age.

Note

1. G. B. Kerferd, *The Sophistic Movement* (Cambridge: Cambridge University Press.)

10

Ibn Rushd, Founder of Hermeneutics

Mona Abousenna
Professor of English,
University of Ain Shams (Egypt)

In November 1979, at the First International Islamic Philosophy Conference, organized by Mourad Wahba on the theme "Islam and Civilization," one of Egypt's most renowned philosophers, the late Zaki Naguib Mahmoud, presented a paper entitled "The Rational Aspect of Islam." Andre Mercier, then secretary general of the International Federation of Philosophical Societies, asked the Egyptian philosopher if there was hermeneutics in Arab Islamic culture. The late Egyptian philosopher answered by saying that Islam is a rational religion and therefore is not in need of interpretation. And he added that the parts in the Qur'an which defy rational demonstration should be taken on faith and not questioned. It is noteworthy that this late Egyptian philosopher is famous for being the founder of logical positivism in the Arab world.

In 1984, I was invited by the International Federation of Modern Languages and Literatures to deliver a plenary lecture at its sixteenth international congress, which was held in Budapest, on the theme "Change in Language and Literature." The topic I chose for my paper was "Language As Culture." The pivotal argument in the paper is the absence of hermeneutics in Arabic culture due to the predominance of a specific phenomenon, namely, permanence rather than change in language. This is due to an indigenous phenomenon, namely, absolutization of language due to its sacredness. These two organically related phenomena make it difficult for hermeneutics to rise and develop in Arabic Islamic culture because they are responsible for the growth of the phenomenon of *takfir,* or charge of blasphemy, with which anyone who attempts hermeneutics is accused and hence the attempt is aborted.

I had reached that conclusion through the analysis of two important texts, one by the Egyptian thinker Taha Hussein entitled "On Pre-Islamic Poetry," banned in Egypt in 1925, and the other by the Lebanese thinker and poet Adonis entitled "Permanence and Change," published in Beirut. The comparison between the two texts was conducted on the basis of one of the main principles of hermeneutics, namely, demythologization as propagated by Bultman, or the deobjectification of sacred texts through linguistic interpretation of allegories and metaphors within a rational historical perspective. In my paper, I called this attempt a reduction of language to culture, or reducing language of sacred texts to their secular, that is, cultural, roots. By so doing, the interpreter relativizes the texts, that is to say, humanizes them.

The previous two attempts were aborted; the first by banning and the second by being totally neglected. However, I chose to avoid, for certain reasons, another, more radical work by the Syrian philosopher Sadek Galal Al-Azm, which was another aborted attempt at establishing hermeneutics in Arabic culture in modern times.

At that time, I was totally unaware of Ibn Rushd as a possible source of hermeneutics in Arabic culture. All I knew about him was the common general knowledge that he was a uniquely rational Islamic philosopher, and that he explained and commented on Aristotle's philosophy.

When I started to become involved in the organization of this conference, I went back to my paper of 1984, which has had a deep impact on my academic career. On the international level, it had won me membership on the Executive Council of the International Association of Comparative Literature, to which I was elected three years after the Budapest congress as the first Arab scholar since the foundation of the association in the 1950s. However, on the local level, it was a completely different story. The same paper was the reason behind delaying my promotion to the post of full professor for a whole year because the committee of examiners, consisting of professors of English language and literature, dismissed it because it contained radical criticism of Arabic culture which, in their opinion, should never come from an Arab scholar against her indigenous cultural roots.

The circumstances surrounding my paper on "Language As Culture" established a kind of personal affinity between me and Ibn Rushd. They also reconfirmed my conviction regarding the absence of hermeneutics in Arabic culture, including academic circles. The elapse of eight hundred years could not erase a deeply rooted characteristic of the Arab mind, namely, a deep-seated hatred for secularization and an intrinsic antagonism toward any attempt to humanize the roots of its culture, namely, language.

Therefore, I would like, in my paper, to raise three essential issues:

1. Ibn Rushd as a forerunner and founder of hermeneutics through his theory of allegorical interpretation. Through this theory Ibn Rushd provided a synthesis between language and content in the interpretation of scriptural texts, within the overall context of his philosophy of demonstrative reasoning, which is also a heralding of the Enlightenment that took place in Europe six hundred years after Ibn Rushd's death. By so doing, Ibn Rushd went beyond the real meaning (that is, the sensory or literal meaning) of scriptural texts by giving priority to the understanding and interpretation of such texts on the ground of their allegorical or metaphorical significance.

2. The limitations imposed on Ibn Rushd by his contemporary cultural and political climate to a great extent prevented him from fully developing his theory of interpretation into the context of the theory of knowledge. This attempt was made four centuries later by Luther in the field of religious reformation, and later by the hermeneutical theorists Heinrich Bullinger and Matthias Flacius Illyricus in the sixteenth century and Dannhauer in the seventeenth. When hermeneutics became a broader discipline by the end of the seventeenth century, more jurists tried to establish rules of hermeneutics. These included Johannes von Felde, Christian Wolff, and Jean Alfonse Turenitus of Geneva. This trend culminated in the eighteenth century in three most significant theorists, Johann Chladinius, August Ernesti, and Semler of Halle. The three were paving the ground for Schleiermacher who in the nineteenth century set the foundations of modern hermeneutics by relating it to epistemology in the light of Kant's theory of knowledge.

3. The limitations imposed on Ibn Rushd by the climate of *takfir,* or charge of blasphemy, make him very much our contemporary in the twen-

tieth century, where the same phenomenon is still prevailing. Modern examples of Ibn Rushd range from Taha Hussein, who in 1925 adopted the Cartesian method to demythologize Arab Islamic culture and language, more recently Naguib Mahfouz, who presented his literary interpretation of the story of creation in a secular humanist way, and last but not least, in the field of art, when director Youssef Shahin presented his own creative interpretation of the story of Youssef in the film *The Immigrant.*

Based on the above three issues, I would like to raise the following questions:

Is it possible, today, to pick up where Ibn Rushd left off eight hundred years ago, by contributing to the field of hermeneutics starting from Ibn Rushd and linking him to the whole tradition of European philosophy?

I will attempt to answer this question by attempting to clarify the term "interpretation" by tracing its etymology in Arabic language and culture. By so doing, I intend to place Ibn Rushd in his Arabic-Islamic context before linking him to the European philosophical tradition.

The first meaning of "interpretation" is mentioned in the *Dictionary of Trimming Language (tahzib al-logha)* edited by al-Azhary, who died in 370 Hegira. It is cited under the item "interpret" (*awwal*), and is edited by Ibrahim al-Ibiary, who defines the meaning of "interpretation" or *ta'wil* as "referring to, going back to," hence, *a'al,* or "go back to," and *ya'oul you'awil,* "interpret," and *a'wlan.* All these meanings imply a sense of going back to the origins, going back to the traditions laid down by the ancestors. It thus stops interpretation at the level of the ancestors, leaving nothing for their followers, which negates the very essence of interpretation, namely, creativity and critical thinking.

The second meaning was then developed in the *Dictionary of the Arabs' Tongue (lisan al-arab)* published in 1092 Hegira and edited by Ibn Manzour. It shows the development of the word "interpret" to mean explain or explicate (*ta'awal*), and "interpretation" as explanation, cognate with the meaning of being discreet about something, or making a sound assessment of events. In this definition "interpretation" implies a value judgment based on common sense, which again contradicts "interpretation" in the sense of free inquiry and personal creativity.

The third meaning can be found in Ibn al-Athir's book *The End of Strange Discourse,* cited by Ibn Manzour in his dictionary. Here the meaning of "interpretation" is "to transform the word or expression from its surface or apparent meaning by providing the necessary evidence which is the reason for discarding the apparent meaning." The same meaning is transmitted by al-Zoubeidi in his book *The Bride's Crown* (*tag al-arous*). Quoting Ibn al-Kamal, Zoubeidi writes, "Interpretation means to refer the Quranic verse from its meaning to a probable meaning which accords with the Holy Book and the *sunna* [the Prophet's sayings and behavior]." This definition of interpretation means that the probable meaning should be equivalent to the meaning in the religious text. This equivalence negates plurality, which is an essential feature of interpretation.

The above three meanings of "interpretation" in Arabic represent the foundations of the prevailing traditional trend in Arabic culture and thought. This is confirmed by the famous lexicographer al-Gorgany, who defines "interpretation" in his book of *Definitions* as "originally the substance of interpretation is reduction," i.e., reducing to, going back to the ancestors. In religious texts "interpretation" means the transformation of a word or expression from its apparent meaning to a probable meaning if that probable meaning accords with the Book and the *sunna*. As an example al-Gorgany cites the following expression from the Qur'an, "He delivers the living from out of the dead," as an example of interpretation. He says that if the intended meaning is understood as "bringing the bird out of the egg then this would be explanation; whereas if the meaning is understood as bringing the ignorant out of the learned or the unbeliever out of the believer then this would be interpretation." This definition eliminates the probable meaning if it contradicts the Qur'an, and hence limits interpretation to the apparent meaning and does not surpass it to the hidden meaning.

Al-Mawardi similarly considers interpretation to be not simply "a going back to the origins or beginnings," but an "act of preference," or a preferring of one meaning over another. In other words, according to al-Mawardi, interpretation in this sense leads to difference of opinion and to controversy among those who prefer certain meanings over others which, in turn, "could lead to the division of nations." This view by al-Mawardi expresses in a nutshell the predominance of a purely Arab phenomenon, *ijma'*, or consensus, in the sense of unanimity, which totally rules out and incriminates difference of opinion and controversy, that is, pluralism.

This phenomenon prevailed up to the beginning of the twelfth century. In the thirteenth century came the Islamic fundamentalist and jurist Ibn Taimeya, who provided the ultimate justification for the elimination of interpretation as a religious necessity. He proposed two meanings of interpretation: the first one refers to external truth or the real or sensory effect of the significance of a word. Ibn Taimeya then claims that this is the meaning conveyed by the Qur'an. Hence interpretation for Ibn Taimeya is to explain the Qur'an within the context of the Qur'an itself. In case such an explanation is not possible, he maintains that it is possible to resort to the *sunna* to provide explanation of the Qur'an. Therefore, Ibn Taimeya rejects the view that interpretation means the transformation of the apparent meaning of a word because this sense of interpretation is tantamount to blasphemy because it casts doubt on the very role of the Prophet, which is to convey the message of Islam to the people, or *al-Balagh.* In other words, hermeneutics, which in Greek is the conveying of the message of the gods to the masses, according to Ibn Taimeya is heresy because it interferes with the Prophet's essential role. In other words, interpretation is blasphemous because it presupposes for individuals the role of the Prophet and, in this sense, is a kind of *shirk,* polytheism, and hence is *kufr,* or unbelief, and, therefore, calls for the death penalty.

Since then interpretation has been linked with the charge of unbelief or blasphemy, *takfir.*

Between the end of the eleventh and the thirteenth centuries Ibn Rushd came as an exceptional moment or a rare phenomenon in the history of Arab Islamic culture. Ibn Rushd's uniqueness appears from his own definition of interpretation, which should be understood within the context of his philosophical output. In *Fasl al-maqal,* chapter 2, entitled "Philosophy Contains Nothing Opposed to Islam," he writes:

If the apparent meaning of Scripture conflicts with demonstrative conclusions it must be interpreted allegorically, i.e., metaphorically. This being so, whenever demonstrative study leads to any manner of knowledge about any being, that being is inevitably either unmentioned or mentioned in Scripture. If it is unmentioned there is no contradiction, and it is in the same case as an act whose category is unmentioned, so that the lawyer has to infer it by reasoning from Scripture. If Scripture speaks about it, the apparent meaning of the words inevitably either accords or conflicts with the conclusions of demonstration about it. If this [apparent meaning] accords there is no argument. If it conflicts there is a call for allegorical interpretation of it.

Ibn Rushd then expounds his famous definition of allegorical interpretation: "Extension of the significance of an expression from real to metaphorical significance, without forsaking therein the standard metaphorical practices of Arabic, such as calling a thing by the name of something resembling it or a cause or consequence or accompaniment of it, or other things such as are enumerated in accounts of the kinds of metaphorical speech."

In the following pages Ibn Rushd tackles the problematic of what he terms *batin,* or hidden meaning, and *zahir,* the apparent meaning. He continues,

> So we affirm definitely that whenever the conclusion of a demonstration is in conflict with the apparent meaning of Scripture, that apparent meaning admits of allegorical interpretation according to the rules for such interpretation according to Arabic. . . . Indeed we may say that whenever a statement in Scripture conflicts in its apparent meaning with a conclusion of demonstration, if Scripture is considered carefully and the rest of its contents searched page by page, there will invariably be found among the expressions of Scripture something which in its apparent meaning bears witness to that allegorical interpretation or comes close to bearing witness.

After reiterating that all Muslims accept the principle of allegorical interpretation, and that they only disagree about the extent of its application, Ibn Rushd then tackles what he takes to be the reason for receiving a Scripture with two meanings, an apparent and a hidden one, which sometimes contradict each other. He says, "The reason why we have received in Scripture texts whose apparent meanings contradict each other is in order to draw attention of those who are well grounded in science to the interpretation which reconciles them."

However, in my opinion it was this problematic of the hidden and the apparent meaning of scriptural texts, or Qu'ranic texts, which created the crisis between Ibn Rushd and his adversaries, who antagonized Sultan Mansur against him. This problematic, which implies the contradiction between two meanings, one apparent and the other hidden, was attacked by the *mutakallimun* or Muslim theologians, the Ash'arites and the Mu'tazalites. However, the traditionalists, headed by al-Ghazali, regarded it as a formal contradiction and thus eliminated the hidden meaning and preserved the apparent meaning, or more commonly known as the "real" meaning, on the ground of safeguarding the dogma and consolidating the belief of the masses, which could be shaken if they were exposed to the contradiction between apparent and hidden meaning.

The creative contribution of Ibn Rushd regarding this problematic is that he treated the contradiction between *zahir* and *batin* in a dialectical way and not in a formal way, like the theologians who came before and after him. His dialectical method consists in the *Aufhebung* or supersession of the contradiction by a new synthesis. This new synthesis lies in Ibn Rushd's theory of allegorical interpretation, which preserves the Arabic language as a divine language while subjecting it at the same time to the rational scrutiny of the human mind through demonstration. However, here arises another contradiction, which Ibn Rushd himself has created through his theory of allegorical interpretation. The contradiction comes from the restrictions imposed by him on interpretation, which he calls the "standard metaphorical practices of Arabic."

The elimination of the contradiction between allegorical interpretation and the restrictions of language is possible only through the foundation of a theory of knowledge. For allegorical interpretation by its nature leads to plurality of visions and consequently leads to the negation of dogmatism, which is represented by *ijma'* or unanimity of understanding the religious text. In other words, allegorical interpretation can be said to be the cause of dedogmatization. However, the opposite is the truth, that is, dedogmatization permits allegorical interpretation; dedogmatization means admitting of the inability of the human mind to grasp the dogma. This necessitates the investigation of the ability of human reason, which is what Ibn Rushd did not do, but which Kant did seven hundred years later.

If I say that Ibn Rushd is the founder of hermeneutics, that is, interpretation as a discipline, we should mention that it is Kant who laid its foundation, by his theory of knowledge, which concludes that human reason tries to grasp the absolute but is nonetheless incapable of doing so. The reason behind writing *Critique of Pure Reason* is to justify the failure of the attempt to grasp absolute truth. In this light Kant wrote, *Religion Within the Limits of Reason Alone,* in which he dedogmatized religion but did not negate it.

The advent of Ibn Taimeya put an end to Ibn Rushd's understanding of interpretation and bracketed him and his philosophy between the ancestors and their followers, who both rejected him. In this sense, Ibn Rushd could be considered an exceptional, fleeting moment in the history of Arab philosophical thought or, to borrow the expression of Sami el-Nashar, Ibn Rushd is just an intellectual luxury, or, according to Henri Courbin, Ibn Rushd stands on the fringe of Islamic thought.

11

Ibn Rushd's Use of Allegory

Alfred Ivry
Professor of Judaic Studies,
New York University (USA)

The Greeks coined the word "allegory," which is derived in their language from *allos* and *agoreusis*, thus meaning literally "other speech," i.e., veiled or indirect language. The term "allegory" came to be used by them in both a broad sense, standing for figurative and metaphorical language in general; and in a narrow sense, denoting a particular literary form. In an allegory, the persons and events described stand for something else besides themselves, and are part of an extended narrative so construed. Allegory in this latter sense was not so much composed as it was superimposed upon stories of an earlier, and presumably simpler, time. Greek myths were treated by the Stoics as allegories, taking them thereby out of their original context and conceptualizing them in a manner compatible with the values and beliefs of the later period.

Allegorization as a hermeneutical technique has been as significant historically as the deliberate literary creation of allegories. Those who read earlier literature allegorically did not believe they were installing new meanings and values in the texts, any more than that they were writing a new story. The extended allegorical dimension of the texts was, in their eyes, no more arbitrary than the stylistically apt metaphors and similes found there. The allegorists thought that they were simply bringing out the inner meaning of the text, a meaning which it had always contained.

Philo Judaeus, living in Alexandria in the first century C.E., was the first person in the monotheistic tradition to treat the Bible systematically as an allegory. The Church Fathers followed him, accepting allegorical interpretation as one of the four ways Scripture could be understood, and the rabbis did likewise, within their own exegetical tradition. Significantly, the literal reading of Scripture retained a place of eminence among these complementary approaches, the words of revelation considered inherently sacred.

The Qur'an, with its ambiguous terms and verses[1] and its challenging similitudes[2] appeared to many Muslims to require interpretation, ta'wil, even while it cautioned against it.[3] Nevertheless, Qur'anic commentaries and other genres of Islamic literature abound in allegorical interpretations, understanding allegory here in the broad sense of metaphorical and figurative speech. Any term or action which is not to be taken literally is, in this construal, allegorical. The theologians of Islam, the mutakallimun, as well as the Sufi mystics, the Shi'i, and other groups within the Islamic community, all interpreted the Qur'an according to their conceptualization of God's nature and the nature of being. The philosophers followed in this path as well, construing the Qur'an as a philosophical document through the use of allegorical techniques. The main teachings of philosophy, however, were found articulated in other texts, the legacy of Greek philosophers, and the Qur'an was utilized mainly just to legitimate the teachings expounded elsewhere.

Allegoresis, the technique of interpreting a text allegorically, is thus not the preferred activity of the philosophers, and may be seen as a polemical and apologetic activity, undertaken mainly to defend philosophy against its critics, who were legion. Nor is the creation of allegories, as opposed to the philosophical allegorization of Scripture, much more popular among philosophers. There is, nevertheless, a number of significant allegories composed by the *falasifah* of Islam, and they are worth our consideration, however briefly.

Ibn Sina (Avicenna, 370–428 A.H., 980–1037 C.E.) is the philosopher who was most attracted to writing allegories, perhaps as an expression of his extraordinarily creative personality. He composed three allegories, *Hayy Ibn Yaqzan, Salaman and Absal,* and the *Recital of the Bird*, and wrote allegorical interpretations of varying length, including an extensive one in Persian, the *Mi'raj Nama*, which has recently been studied and translated.[4] His allegories made a significant impact upon later writers, particularly in Persia, and influenced the course of later Islamic philosophy. The peculiar brand of mysticism and philosophy which is characteristic of Persian theosophy may not represent Avicenna's own philosophy, but it was taken to be such by those impressed with his allegories.

In our day, Henri Corbin is the most forceful advocate for those who see Avicenna's allegories as representative of a distinctive mystical orientation. He regards this alleged "Eastern wisdom" (*al-hikmah al-mashriqiya*) as essentially different from the Western, Aristotelian kind of philosophy which Avicenna's other, more traditionally written philosophical works, offer.[5] Most Western scholars do not share Corbin's view, and believe the allegories are a representation in mythic or story form of the "logos" or rational account of Avicenna's philosophy.[6] That philosophy, while regarded by many as essentially Aristotelian, is yet heavily suffused with Neoplatonic themes and constructs, such that the allegorical presentation of it need not be seen as deviating radically from the more prosaically written treatises.

The interpretation or allegoresis of Avicenna's allegories may thus yield a more literary but essentially standard version of his philosophy, or lead into uncharted paths. The choice of which path to take depends on many factors, one being the facility with which correspondances can be assigned between the characters and events of Avicenna's allegories and the components or data of his philosophical constructs. The longer and more fantastic the allegory (as in his *Hayy Ibn Yaqzan*) the harder it is to establish these correspondances with confidence, the story line seeming to take wing on its own. The symbolism, however profuse, is not easily correlated with specific philosophical referents.

One of the striking differences between Avicenna's allegories and his "straight" philosophical compositions is that the allegories speak more to the passionate nature of the soul, be it the "warring" psychic faculties allegorized in *Salaman and Absal*, or the psychic desire for union with God, the source of all being, as allegorized in *Hayy Ibn Yaqzan* and the *Recital of the Bird*. Unlike his writings on the soul, which are part of the standard philosophical repertoire, rooted in Aristotle's and Alexander of Aphrodisias's respective *De anima* compositions, Avicenna's allegories emphasize the sense of loss and regret which follow the experience of conjunction, represented as encountering the king in his palace. We are not able to sustain conjunction, our physical natures draw us down and away from the world of truth and eternal being.

It is a similar sense of dissatisfaction with the world, with its political as well as physical and material structures, which comes to dominate the *Hayy Ibn Yaqzan* allegory of the Andalusian philosopher and courtier Abu Bakr Ibn Tufayl (died 1185).[7] The allegory here is of an autodidact on a deserted island who reaches full knowledge and gnosis. Hayy comes to believe in the essential unity of all being, and the essential unreality and worthlessness of physical existence. He practices Sufi techniques of abnegation and unification, longing for the release and fulfillment which death brings.

Ibn Tufayl's allegory has an even more explicit political dimension than that implicit in the mystic's path. Hayy wishes to bring his insights to society and benefit his fellow man, but he finds himself unwelcome. The truths which he expounds, though based on Qur'anic passages, do not appeal to them. Hayy concludes that most people require a literal presentation of their faith, and any attempt to interpret it in more universal and abstract terms is doomed to failure, and negative reaction.

Ibn Tufayl ends his allegory with Hayy returning to his island, resigned to the inadequacies of human beings en masse. They are not to be educated beyond the conventional wisdoms and practices necessary for society's welfare. One is to leave people with their popular religious conceptions and observances, and seek a personal salvation, ultimately to be found beyond science and philosophy, in mystical gnosis.

Avicenna and Ibn Tufayl are the main allegorists among the Muslim philosophers, and it is highly likely Abu 'l-Walid Muhammad Ibn Ahmad Ibn Rushd, known in the West as Averroës (1126–1198), was familiar with their allegorical compositions. It was Ibn Tufayl, after all, who introduced Averroës in 1169 to the Almohad caliph Abu Ya'qub Yusuf, and we know from Averroës's writings that he was a close reader of Avicenna's work.

Averroës was commissioned by the Prince of the Believers to comment on Aristotle's writings. This charge amounted to almost a life-long commission, in which Averroës wrote a total of thirty-eight commentaries of varying size and degree of detail.[8] Mostly all of Aristotle's philosophical corpus was commented upon, with the notable exception of the Stagirite's *Politics*, for which Plato's *Republic* was substituted. Averroës was following thereby the philosophical legacy of the Hellenistic world, utilizing also in his commentaries some of the major Peripatetic commentators of late antiquity who had also been translated into Arabic, notably Alexander of Aphrodisias and Themistius.

Averroës's creation of a philosophical oeuvre infused with Aristotelian thought could lead one to believe he worked in a philosophically sympathetic environment, and to some degree that is probably true. Certainly he had the backing and support of the caliph for his project, and there must have been an educated and interested circle at court, or in the kingdom, for whom he wrote. At the same time, it is worth remembering that in his old age Averroës fell victim to an antiscientific and antiphilosophical campaign instituted in 1194 by the caliph's son and successor, Abu Yusuf, Al-Mansur. It should be realized that the opposition to philosophy which surfaced then must have been present all along, and that Averroës had to have been aware of it.[9]

Elsewhere I have discussed the diverse ways in which Averroës presented Aristotle to the presumably different audiences for which he wrote his short, middle, and long commentaries; and have shown that he reserved the most rigorous exposition of Aristotelian teachings, those with the least concessions to Islamic beliefs, for his long commentaries, those which presumably none but philosophers would read.[10] Further proof of Averroës's political awareness may be found in his *Kitab fasl al-maqal wa taqrir ma bayn ash-shari'ah wa l-hikmah min al-ittisal*, which may be translated loosely as "On Distinguishing the Discourse and Establishing the Connection between Religion and Philosophy" (literally, "the law and wisdom"). As George Hourani has written, this work may be seen as a legal counterpart to Averroës's *Tahafut al-tahafut*, or *The Incoherence of the Incoherence*.[11] Whereas that work is a detailed philosophical rebuttal of al-Ghazali's earlier critique of philosophy, his *Tahafut al-falasifah*, or *The Incoherence of the Philosophers*, Averroës's *Fasl al-maqal* is a polemical, legalistic defense of the legitimacy of doing philosophy. Echoing Ibn Tufayl and other philosophers, however, Averroës also wishes to limit philosophical investigations to those qualified to pursue them, and he cautions against presenting philosophy's teachings to the broad public. The mass of people is to be left with the scriptural (that is, Qur'anic) presentation of the truth, uneducated as to its inner meaning.

In so limiting philosophy's public reach, Averroës may well have been trying to placate his political opponents, as Hourani has suggested.[12] These opponents came from two distinct groups, the lawyers, or *fuqaha* of Averroës's own legal school, the Maliki; and the Ash'ari theologians, represented by the formidable figure of al-Ghazali. Maliki law was extensive, and determinedly nontheological, dominating the intellectual climate of

Andalusia until the advent of the Almohad regime in 1146–47. Then a more tolerant attitude toward theology was shown, though Maliki lawyers were still present at court and elsewhere, opposed presumably to all forms of rationalizing, theological or philosophical.

Averroës had, in this respect, an ally among the *mutakallimun,* the theologians, who had been the first group in Islam to construct a nonliteral interpretation of the Qur'an. The reaction to this attempt had led the theologians into compromises of all sorts, including that of formulating controls on the use of allegory. Al-Ghazali composed rules to that purpose, which Averroës endorses in *Fasl al-maqal.* Averroës's quarrel with al-Ghazali and the theologians, therefore, is different in kind from his disagreement with the legal establishment. Yet his basic thesis is addressed to both groups, namely, that the practice of philosophy is commanded by the law, for those capable of pursuing it. Averroës's proof of this thesis, with which his book begins, is remarkably circular: the Qur'an obliges one to do philosophy, since a number of its verses refer to cognitive activities, which for Averroës must be philosophical in nature. The "reflection" (*al-i'tibar*) which the Qur'an urges upon believers is thereby given a patently tendentious reading.

> Since it has now been established that the Law has rendered obligatory the study of beings by the intellect, and reflection on them, and since reflection is nothing more than inference and drawing out of the unknown from the known, and since this is reasoning [*qiyas*] or at any rate done by reasoning, therefore we are under an obligation to carry on our study of beings by intellectual reasoning. It is further evident that this manner of study, to which the Law summons and urges, is the most perfect kind of study using the most perfect kind of reasoning; and this is the kind called "demonstration" [*burhan*].[13]

Averroës follows this statement by differentiating between demonstrative reasoning and the less "perfect" forms of dialectical, rhetorical, and fallacious, or sophistical, reasoning. "Demonstrative reasoning" could as well be rendered as the "demonstrative (or apodictic) syllogism," and this, for Averroës as for all other classical and medieval philosophers, is the acme of philosophical argument, that type of reasoning which leads to incontrovertible and necessary truth. Averroës understands that a proper understanding of this syllogism requires appreciation of the other, less certain, since unneccesary, forms of argumentation.

By inference, then, the Qur'an is seen to command the study of logic in all its divisions, as a necessary prelude to the demonstrative study of being in all its forms, itself a way of approaching demonstrative knowledge of God. The emphasis on demonstrative knowledge is crucial for Averroës, for it is that which will distinguish the philosopher from all others. Averroës recognizes that dialectical and rhetorical argument play an important role in bringing most people to assent to the truths which religion conveys; indeed, that Scripture itself uses all three kinds of arguments, corresponding to the three classes of people in society.[14]

The presumed challenge of the lawyers to Averroës's thesis, viewing philosophy as *bid'ah*, heretical innovation, is met squarely with the response that philosophical interpretation is no more of an innovation than the developed study of the *shari'ah* itself. Indeed, for Averroës the pursuit of philosophy is superior to that of the law, since the lawyer must make do with "reasoning based on opinion," that is, conjecturally based syllogisms (*qiyas zanni*), while the philosopher argues from necessary premises, his reasoning "based on certainty."[15]

Averroës takes on the *fuqaha* again in the second chapter of this work on the issue of *ijma'*, consensus, understood in the sense of unanimity. The question is whether philosophy, despite its demonstrative method, is permitted to differ with the unanimous interpretation of the scholarly community on the way in which to understand a given Qur'anic verse, whether allegorically or literally. Underlying this question is the religious dogma that a doctrine held by consensus of the community cannot be wrong, thereby privileging traditional and not philosophical perspectives. Averroës's response to this challenge is in effect to deny its premise, and with that to shatter the myth of religious and hence cultural uniformity. He contends that there is no demonstrable certainty that unanimity ever obtains in theoretical matters.[16] One can never be sure that all the authorities of a given period and place have been polled, or that they have been fully candid as to their views. As with the Qur'an itself, scholars are likely to have esoteric interpretations which they keep from the public.

There are certain fundamental beliefs in Islam which Averroës nevertheless accepts, defending himself and philosophers from the charge of unbelief that al-Ghazali and others levelled against them. These beliefs are central to the faith: creationism, divine omniscience, and immortality. Averroës's understanding of these notions, it quickly emerges, is quite different from traditional views, putting in question his seeming agreement with the community's understanding of them.[17] He is in effect illustrating his point regarding the variety of ways in which a concept may be understood. Averroës's real difference with al-Ghazali, and with the theologians in general, emerges gradually and rather obliquely in his work. As stated, both he and they recognize the legitimacy of allegorical interpetation when the apparent or literal meaning in the Qur'anic text conflicts with a rational understanding of it (understanding "rational understanding" in the most basic sense); and they both recognize the need to use allegory only where necessary. However, Averroës defines *ta'wil*, which Hourani translates as "allegorical interpretation," in a way which signals his differences with al-Ghazali. It is for Averroës the "extension of the significance of an expression from real to metaphorical significance, without forsaking therein the standard metaphorical practices of Arabic, such as calling a thing by the name of something resembling it or a cause or consequence or accompaniment of it, or other things such as are enumerated in accounts of the kinds of metaphorical speech."[18]

This definition brings allegory down to earth, treating it as equivalent to metaphors of the physical properties of an object, be it a resemblance (*shabih*), cause (*sabab*), consequent or effect (*lahiq*), or accidental concomitant (*muqarin*). An allegory/metaphor thus has physical correlatives, and refers to them. The controlling feature is the physical object, the world as given initially to sensory experience, and to which all our imaginative and intellectual constructs revert.[19] It is this reality, the natural world, which al-Ghazali and the theologians of Islam, his fellow Ash'arites, rejected in principle. As Averroës says, "Many of the principles on which the Ash'arites based their knowledge are sophistical, for they deny many necessary truths such as the permanence of accidents, the action of things on other things, the existence of necessary causes for effects, of substantial forms, and of secondary causes."

For Averroës, then, the allegories of the *mutakallimun* must be wrong, having a mistaken referent to begin with, a false philosophy. This view informs his earlier statement that allegorical interpetations, *al-ta'wilat*, ought to appear only in "demonstrative books," where philosophers alone will read them, only they capable of fully understanding them. He views the presence of allegory in nondemonstrative books, and the interpretation of them by poetical, rhetorical, or dialectical means, as a grave error, leading to religious and political dissension. Averroës faults al-Ghazali and the Ash'arites in general for this. Beyond the polemical note lies the basic disagreement he has with the theologians: they have a false concept of reality, and therefore their figurative representations of it are unreliable and misleading.

By this narrow and physical construal of allegory, Averroës tries to rein in imaginative configurations, making the imaginative faculty itself conform to the dictates of the intellect, obedient to what was taken to be the experience and comprehension of a natural world. The esoteric interpetation of Scripture is thereby made to reveal a scientific world view, both a natural physics and metaphysics as well as a political philosophy. Averroës's attitude to allegory is thus the opposite of his philosophical predecessors, particularly Avicenna. For Avicenna, as we have noted, wrote extensive allegorical tales the exact meaning of which is often elusive. Avicenna's approach to allegory thus reflects a more appreciative attitude to the power of the imaginative faculty than that held by Averroës, as well as a greater inclination towards mystical experience, strengthened by his greater use of Neoplatonic constructs. Averroës, on the other hand, preferred allegoresis to the writing of allegory, and used it to direct attention toward Aristotelian physics and metaphysics, and not away from them.

Averroës's political philosophy, however, is not all that different from the pessimistic views expressed by Ibn Tufayl. Both men write openly about the need not to teach their ideas openly, and it is likely that Averroës would have been sympathetic to Ibn Tufayl's use of allegory for political purposes. It may well be that Averroës's commentary on Plato's *Republic* should be looked at in this light, and that Averroës understood the *Republic* as an allegory. His commentary on this work, which falls between his short and middle style of commentaries, is not so much of an allegoresis of the *Republic* as a paraphrase of it, a retelling intended as an allegory. Understanding his "commentary" in this light will help explain his seeming endorsement of much in the *Republic* which flaunts Islamic mores and law. Averroës could have accepted Plato's work more as an allegory of the ideal state than as a model of one.

Allegory for Averroës, accordingly, is more akin to political philosophy than it is to metaphysics. Philosophy for him should point towards science and away from theology and mysticism. Religion need not be in conflict with philosophy when properly understood, but it is best not to mix—and mix up—the two. Sound advice then—and now.

Postscript

Many speakers at the conference for which I prepared the above paper presented Averroës as a figure of contemporary significance, emphasizing his dedication to scientific pursuits, philosophy, and democratic values. As my paper has attempted to show, Averroës was for the most part a champion of science as then understood, and of a naturalistic, even nominalistic philosophy. It is also clear, I hope, that Averroës had a political philosophy which, in its rejection of *ijma'*, was antiauthoritarian, and to that degree, democratic in spirit. His use of allegory was essentially political, to legitimize scientific and philosophical pursuits.

Averroës was not, however, truly democratic in spirit, and had, with Plato, little regard for that form of government. It is anachronistic, to say the least, to impute democratic ideals to any twelfth-century figure, be he Muslim, Jewish, or Christian. Though Averroës wished to distance philosophy and science from theology and the law, he had no fundamental objection to a theocratic government; as a *qadi* and authority on religious law, the *shari'ah*, he was instrumental in implementing it, as far as circumstances permitted. Adopting Averroës for contemporary liberal political purposes is therefore problematic, and threatens to distort his life and work.

It is of course possible to "allegorize" Averroës and thereby create a person with modern sensibilities. Given the bold metaphysical positions he took in his lifetime, and those which were later attributed to him, Averroës, with a little creative ingenuity, can be reconstructed along liberal lines. Actually, this would be furthering a transformation begun already in the Middle Ages, when the original Ibn Rushd was transformed to the Latin Averroës, the putative champion of the "double truth" of Averroism.[20]

Is this construction/deconstruction a task for contemporary philosophers and scholars, however? Are we to create myths and invent the past for political purposes? The traditional definition of philosophy as the love of truth argues against this. It should be admitted, however, that the Platonic tradition of political philosophy, both classical and medieval, is more sympathetic to such an orientation. Moreover, it could be argued that in societies struggling to secure democratic rights (and which society is entirely free of such a struggle?) the latter approach is still required.

It is significant, for us, that Averroës, following al-Farabi in a tradition which goes back to Plato, believed the people needed fictions and imitations of the truth to sustain themselves and preserve the society in which they lived.[21] It is likely that Averroës's allegorization of the Qur'an in the *Fasl al-maqal* for philosophical purposes was a deliberate act of mytho-poesis, a hermeneutical strategy dictated by personal and political convictions. This, however, does not preclude the view that Averroës sincerely believed in his philosophical reading of the word of God, since he, together with all other philosophers, believed truth is one.

If, then, Averroës could allegorize the religious tradition to suit philosophy, why should we not rise to the challenge of the times and do something similar, namely, allegorize Averroës himself? As he invented the past in interpreting it, so may we reinvent it, in interpreting him. This argument may, in addition, receive philosophical support of a kind by postmodernists who believe that all knowledge, past and present, is an invention or construction by the writer(s) involved, and hence that all interpretations are equally valid. Refuting this argument is difficult if not impossible, since the premises of such a refutation are just those which are denied, namely, that there is a substantial core of factual history which we may know, and there are primary significations in texts which we can identify.

Rejecting these assumptions may free one from historical constraints, and from the tyranny of the text, but this path leads to scholarly anarchy and its own kind of political manipulation. The text becomes what you wish it to be, the philosopher your servant. This is all too often the fate of persons and texts in authoritarian societies, but should not be emulated in societies which strive to be free. Philosophers must be wary of lending themselves to such methods. Today the past is altered to fit a liberal agenda; tomorrow, a conservative one; and the next day? One may say that this is what goes on anyway in the political arena, and that the philosopher should not retreat from the problems of society to an ivory tower. It is, however, shortsighted to believe that the scholar or philosopher will maintain credibility and influence once he or she is perceived to be a propagandist for a particular political view. The philosopher particularly must remain, like Socrates, the gadfly of society, questioning and challenging accepted truths.

The medieval philosophical tradition maintained this Socratic posture, albeit discreetly, and not for the most part in a direct confrontational mode. It was transparently clear, however, that philosophy offered an alternate perspective on the world from that of traditional religion and the various traditional "sciences." However obliquely critical of the institutions of their society, medieval philosophers, including Averroës, conformed to them. Though close to the centers of power on occasion, our Muslim philosophers did not become spokesmen for particular regimes. We should not turn them into such today, or become such ourselves.

Notes

1. Arabic: A*l-ayat al-mutashabihat.* Compare Qur'an, Surah 3, verse 7.

2. *Amthal,* said to be struck by God himself; see, for example, Qur'an 14:28, and compare J. Wansbrough, *Quranic Studies* (Oxford, 1977), pp. 239–44.

3. Qur'an 3:6, 25:33.

4. Compare P. Heath, *Allegory and Philosophy in Avicenna (Ibn Sina)* (Philadelphia, 1992), pp. 109–43.

5. Compare H. Corbin, *Avicenna and the Visionary Recital,* W. R. Trask, trans. (New York, 1960), pp. 3–16 et passim. This latter work contains translations of the three Avicennian allegories mentioned above.

6. Compare Heath, *Allegory,* pp. 8–10 and 149–55, and see D. Gutas, *Avicenna and the Aristotelian Tradition: Introduction to Reading Avicenna's Philosophical Works* (Leiden, 1988), pp. 299–307.

7. Compare L. E. Goodman, trans., *Ibn Tufayl's Hayy ibn Yaqzan: A Philosophical Tale* (New York, 1972), and compare R. Kocache, trans., *The Journey of the Soul: The Story of Hai bin Yaqzan* (London, 1982). See too the recent collection of studies, *The World of Interdisciplinary Studies on Hayy ibn Yaqzan.,* L. Conrad, ed. (Leiden, 1995).

8. Compare H. A. Wolfson, "Inventory of Averroës' Commentaries," *Studies in the History of Philosophy and Religion,* I. Twersky and G. H. Williams, eds. (Cambridge, Mass., and London, 1973), 1:433–40. The current state of publication of these commentaries is summarized in J. Puig in the introduction to his translation of *Averroës' Epitome De Fisica* (Madrid, 1987), pp. 20–24.

9. Compare M. Cruz Hernandez, *Abu-l-Walid ibn Rušd (Averroës). Vida, obra, pensamiento, influencia* (Cordoba, 1986), pp. 23-40.

10. Compare Ivry, "Averroës' *Short Commentary* on Aristotle's *De anima,*" *Documenti e Studi* 7:1 (forthcoming); and see Ivry's "Averroës' Middle and Long Commentaries on the *De anima,*" *Arabic Sciences and Philosophy* 5:1 (1995), 75–92.

11. Compare G. Hourani, trans., *Averroës: On the Harmony of Religion and Philosophy* (London, 1967), p. 5. Specifically, Averroës is responding in this work to al-Ghazali's *Faysal al-tafriqa bayn al-islam wa 'l-zandaqah,* R. J. McCarthy, trans., *Freedom and Fulfillment* (Boston, 1980), app. 1.

12. Ibid., p. 35.

13. Ibid., p. 45.

14. Ibid., pp. 45 and 64.

15. Ibid., p. 51.

16. Ibid., p. 52.

17. These issues have been examined in detail in I. A. Bello, *The Medieval Islamic Controversy Between Philosophy and Othodoxy* (Leiden, 1989), pp. 83–141.

18. *On Harmony*, p. 50, and see Hourani's note 62.

19. Ibid., pp. 61 and 68.

20. The transformation of Averroës may be traced to the introduction of his writings to the Latin West. Compare A. Ivry, "Averroës and the West: The First Encounter/Nonencounter," *A Straight Path*, R. Link-Salinger et al., eds. (Washington, D.C., 1988), pp. 142–58.

21. Compare Plato's *Republic*, 3:389B, and compare *Averroës' Commentary on Plato's Republic*, E. I. J. Rosenthal, ed. (Cambridge, 1979), p. 32 Hebrew, 129 English; see too Alfarabi's *The Attainment of Happiness*, M. Mahdi, trans., in R. Lerner and M. Mahdi, eds., *Medieval Political Philosophy* (New York, 1963), pp. 77–79; and compare the reference in note 6 above for Avicenna's similar view.

12

Reason and Action in Africa

Odera Oruka
Professor of Philosophy,
University of Nairobi (Kenya)

W hat most people know as the Enlightenment, at least in historical context, is the awakening which had its most dominant period in seventeenth- and eighteenth-century Western thought. This is a period which Thomas Paine termed the "Age of Reason." It was conceived that, given the right reason, all truth is ultimately knowable. The world, it was taken, is governed by a natural law which ensures that each stage is a development of the overall universal progress.

The German philosopher Leibniz (1646–1716) postulated the "principle of sufficient reason": everything has a reason why it is as it is. Isaac Newton propounded the law of universal gravitation (1686). Enlightenment in this period then was an era in which reason and rational investigation became universal methods of all objective knowledge. It was therefore not surprising that enlightenment would frighten religious and political orthodoxies. Right reason and natural law were seen as independent of Christian religion (Hugo Grotius), and rigorous intellectual-cum-mathematical reasoning was the means for establishing truth. Religious revelation became noticeable but not the standard.

Enlightenment in a political world distinguished the natural law operating in nature as it is and the natural law operating for persons and human society. In the one case the law explains things as they merely are, in the second case it prescribes to humans what ought to be. But as most human beings are far from what they ought to be, enlightenment applied to politics became critical and revolutionary.

Enlightenment in the West and East has had its latest development in the Marxist revolutions. Would the end of Marxism (if at all) mean the death of enlightenment in those regions? It is, however, important to note that the modern alternative to Marxism, that is, free enterprise and market economy, offer a classical case of inhuman exploitation and economic anarchy. And these two are each or together a negation of the culture of right reason.

Ibn Rushd—Averroës (1126–98)

Ibn Rushd, or Averroës, is one of the most outstanding thinkers and scientists in the Islamic world. Enlightenment, the way it came to be in seventeenth- and eighteenth-century Europe, was not really a creation of its proponents. It was an attempt to recapture the lost philosophic glory and practice of ancient Greece.

Coming between ancient Greece and the Enlightenment of the seventeenth century, Averroës, reformulating Aristotle, postulated that the individual soul is not immortal while the active intellect is. Averroës was for enlightenment and against all unjustifiable orthodoxies.

It is no wonder then that he was excommunicated by the religious orthodoxy of his time. A contemporary of his, al-Ghazali, wrote *The Destruction of Philosophy*, since all truth was in the Qu'ran and there was no need for speculation. Ibn Rushd responded with *The Destruction of the Destruction*, since for him religion is only an allegorical form of philosophic truth, a fact which the mainstream orthodox believers do not grasp.

Reason and Action in Africa

One relevant historical question is, to what extent was there or is there an age of reason (enlightenment) in Africa? I wish to leave this question to the historians because I want to concentrate on a question which is of most immediate significance: To what extent did reason succeed or fail to liberate Africa after the collapse of physical colonialism?

In a paper which was presented to the First Afro-Asian Philosophy

Conference here in Cairo in 1978, entitled "Philosophy and Humanism in Africa"[1] I wrote,

> In ARID (African Republic of Inhumanity and Death) the group that has the political power identifies itself and its power with the moral law and moral good. Truth is recognized to be nothing but the expression of the will of and interest of supreme political personality. Opposition parties, institutions and personalities are branded as the very opposite of the truth and good of the nation. Opposition in ARID is treated as nothing but the incarnation of falsehood and evil. Its existence is supposed to spell doom for the Republic. It must then be wiped out; and it is indeed ruthlessly wiped out.

THE OPPOSITION

These were lines read over sixteen years ago. Since then the situation has worsened, culminating even in the collapse of the reality of a state in some countries: by the 1990s Liberia, Somalia, Chad, Rwanda, Burundi, and to some extent the Sudan have literally collapsed as states. The wiping out of any opposition resulted in national self-destruction.

In Nigeria, Zaire, Algeria, Zambia, Malawi, Kenya, and a number of others countries opposition suffered irreparably in the 1980s, and even in the 1990s most opposition forces have not found their grounds. The reality is that truth and right are with the supreme political authority, and both reason and opposition are evil that must keep nursing themselves in the intensive care units.

After about three decades of postindependence disenlightenment in Africa and the decline of the Cold War, a new glimmer of hope appeared on the scene: Africa all over was to democratize and opposition parties were receiving their legitimation. This heralded a new age of some sort of enlightenment, an age in which human authority and will are to dialogue with reason and natural law. Will this succeed? Only the future can tell, though in our continent brute action and dogmas are often stronger than reason and enlightenment.

ACADEMIA

One aspect of any nation that is the real custodian of reason and enlightenment is academia. But experience in three decades of postcolonial Africa shows that university academic institutions that have not collapsed remain centers of learning that are run by the whims of those in political authority; the resident academic administrators in these institutions are merely fearful, subordinate standbys for the supreme political personality. They are appointed and dismissed at will and through radio messages, not through formal letters. They are ignorant even of their own terms and conditions of service. And they cannot even ask for clarification from the relevant bodies. They cannot do so because their own will is totally subdued by the authority and whims of those in political power. And so they endorse and try to implement directives which any right reason would dismiss as absurdities.

The scholars who find themselves subjects of this sort of academic administration became demoralized. Some quit for greener patches abroad while others stay on as demoralized subjects waiting for the days of their death.

THE MASSES

If opposition and academia currently offer no hope for an age of reason in Africa, where else can we turn for hope? Perhaps to the masses. Perhaps women's liberation movements or the youth can offer hope. The masses usually are the most authentic and enduring aspect of every nation. But the masses are never the imitators or protectors of enlightenment. As my friend Mourad Wahba has observed, since 399 B.C.E., when Socrates was condemned to death, there was a rupture between philosophy and the masses. He refers to this as the "rupture in history":[2]

> This event happened in the year 399 B.C. on the occasion of Socrates'
> condemnation to death owing to "impiety," corrupting young men and
> denying the gods. This was the apparent cause of his death. But what was
> behind it? It was Socrates' endeavors to unmask the roots of the illusions
> of the pseudo-absolute, blazing the trial for the passage to the total de-
> velopment of man. Socrates was trying to achieve this task within the
> mass-man and that is why he was dangerous.

Wahba finds two types of reason embedded in the *Euthyphro*: "Official reason" (for the rulers) and "mass-reason" (for the mass culture). Nietzsche had advised higher men to depart from preaching in the marketplace because it is infested with the masses, who cannot but misunderstand the preaching. In spite of all these, Wahba still returns philosophy to Socrates: "It will be Socratic in a modernized way."[3]

Yes, but before we come to this we shall need a thorough overhaul in the current political, academic and traditional cultures in Africa. The intelligentsia and the masses must enter into a dialogue. This is one way to ensure the abolition of official reason, which today in Africa is the most formidable stone against enlightenment.

In her paper titled "Absolutes and Development in Contemporary Arab Thought" Prof. Mona Abousenna competently explains the "oppressor/oppressed dichotomy." This is the ruler/masses dichotomy. The ruler has absolutized himself and stolen God's identity card. He becomes a tyrant wearing the mask of God. The masses see no legitimacy in liberating themselves. And in this sense "the masses are doomed to be eternally trapped in the illusion, since within totalitarian systems, the prosecutor and the judge are always one and the same person."[4]

Most of the leaders who pioneered Africa to independence or the military upstarts who removed the pioneers saw themselves as President. Mobuto recently puts it as the "Patriarchs of Society."[5] As patriarchs they are not to be subjected to the routine rule of law. They are the embodiment of national justice, and both the constitution and the judiciary are mere functions of the national justice. And this in reality is no more than a manifestation of the dialectics of the whims of the supreme political personality.

WOMEN'S LIBERATION

To what extent are the institutions of women's liberation insurance for the age of reason and enlightenment in Africa?

Various donors have rightly established that "woman" is a suppressed personality in Africa as elsewhere. Their calculation is that by liberating the African woman, we shall be liberating the home, the youth, the masses, and indeed the society. This is also what we who are for the age of reason hope for.

There is, however, a risk that an aspect of women's liberation will turn out (unexpectedly) to be the occasion of the creation of an elite of dominant and dominating females who have no taste for the masses (male or female) and who prefer to entertain themselves at the high tables with the perennial male autocrats. We wish that this will not be so but let us take the precaution.

In Africa the programs for gender equality and women's liberation remain a compromise between the male-dominated governing elites, the donor communities, and the elite women who lead such programs. There is no clear indication that the programs are worked out between the leaders and the suffering masses and rural women and youth. This could end up as representation without consultation.

To ensure the age of reason the women's liberation movements should ensure that the right reason is not just for the female gender, it must be for all the oppressed and ultimately for humanity in general. The formerly oppressed who now wish to oppress negate the culture of right reason. Perhaps this was the pitfall of Soviet-bloc Marxism blazing the banner of the dictatorship of the proletarians.

Notes

1. See Mourad Wahba, ed., *Philosophy and Civilization* (Cairo, 1978), p. 121.

2. Mourad Wahba, "A Case of Rupture in History," in *Philosophy and the Mass-Man* (Cairo, 1983), p. 17.

3. Ibid., p. 21.

4. In H. Odera Oruka and D. A. Masolo, *Philosophy and Culture* (Nairobi, 1983), p. 54, and Proceedings of the 2nd Afro-Asian Philosophy Conference (Nairobi, 1981).

5. I have given some more explanation about African patriarchs in "What Is Justice?" chapter 14 of my book *Ethics* (Nairobi, Kenya: University of Nairobi Press, 1990).

13

Ibn Rushd, European Enlightenment, Africa, and African Philosophy

Ernest K. Beyaraza
Professor of Philosophy,
Makerere University (Uganda)

The conference idea that "the present stage of development in the world . . . is characterized by the predominance of factors of disintegration" sounds rather alarming, but can be substantiated in many ways. It is a fact that the long "cold war" has left the former Soviet Union a broken-up empire. The former socialist system appears to have completely broken down, too, after having spread to about three-fourths of the world. Mysterious wars in Eastern Europe and Africa are still raging. Greed has hit the world so hard that unnecessary wars have been created and fought not only to sell the war equipment, but also to loot raw materials like oil. The former socialist states which had hoped to enter the paradise of communism are so hard hit that recently a journalist claimed to have witnessed Charles Dickens's characters like the Artful Dodger in great Moscow. After Africa had changed hands from colonial masters to multinational corporations, exploitation has increased so much that one wonders whether the current African economic trend can even be estimated. The drug scandal from which great world leaders have minted their fortune has left many societies confused as the effects of drug addiction and associated crime could be comparable to war and poverty in many ways. As if these were not enough, AIDS is threatening to wipe out certain generations in various societies.

For Africa, the effects of this scourge could easily have worse disastrous effects than the slave trade. For the whole world, perhaps the global warming, as the result of the greedy and inconsiderate exploitation of natural resources together with pollution, may be the biggest threat, if we survive the still-possible nuclear war.

Against this background, our next conference idea, namely that "the only means of overcoming disintegration and achieving integration, from a philosophical perspective, is critical reason," can also be substantiated. It is undoubtedly true, *from a philosophical perspective,* that critical reason is the means of overcoming disintegration. Many of our problems arise from our emotional feelings and desires like greed, anger, racism, tribalism, and religious sectarianism among other evils. If some people thought beyond profit, for example, they could realize that their dumping of toxic materials in poor countries immediately adversely affects those countries, but ultimately these effects spread to the rest of the world. If such people could overcome their greed, then they would stop sponsoring such evils as academic cheats who deceive the world, for example, that equatorial forests are actually no longer the lungs of the earth. If these people could think more seriously, then they would see serious symptoms of things to come in such recent floods as those in northern Germany and Italy. The world badly needs critical reasoning. Unfortunately, while we are here deliberating on these serious issues, those who matter in our contemporary world are using computers to calculate how much profit they have gained from the ongoing wars, from the spreading desert in Africa due to deforestation, from refugee-associated problems, and even from AIDS. Every evil appears to be real good business.

This paper, however, is of the view that nonphilosophical means to the solution of the current disintegration in the world should also be sought and implemented to complement the efforts of critical reasoning. Unless we unqualifyingly adopt Plato's view that truth is knowledge and ignorance vice, we are bound to accept that many who know misuse their knowledge to commit evil deeds. It seems that we need the humility to understand our limitations at all levels including the philosophical ones. We recall how long it took thinkers to realize that the earth is not flat. We are also aware of the dominance of extreme rationalism and a priorism and how long it took to change from Absolute Truth to mere truths which change and improve with various methods. When the Reformation took place, those who expected a better quality of life were taken aback by the subsequent religious wars and almost incurable sectarianism. The Marxists, today, are trying to find out where they went wrong, after the expected next stage to socialism, that is, that communism has been so unbelievably reversed. Similarly adherents of the Enlightenment got the shock of their lives when science, instead of leading society to heaven as was expected, led people to the hell of war. The effects of this shock are still with us in contemporary philosophies like existentialism, for example, so there is a need to talk and listen even to fundamentalists. They, too, have their story to tell. Above all, if we do not talk and listen to others, how do we expect them to listen to us? And if we are not listened to, how can we change, or at least influence the world? We certainly need unity in the world, and one of the means to arrive at it is through dialogue.

The Role of Philosophy During Historical Upheavals

It is undisputable that the present stage of development in the whole world is characterized by the predominance of factors of disintegration. The role of philosophy at such a crucial moment in human development may be exemplified by Rene Descartes' philosophical thought at a time when the traditional source of authority, that is, the church, was fast dwindling, and when the new authority, that is, science, was too young to take over the government of European societies.

Descartes' contribution was to replace the two ineffective authorities with critical reason. This may be justified by the following observations: The dictatorial tendency is to force man to follow things dogmatically. This requires constant, strong, and effective leadership. However, this is inhuman as man by nature wants to participate in everything including his government. Thus, dictatorship always survives on force and not on acceptance. A healthy society discusses issues, and this leads to the rule of law. In the case of a social crisis, man has no alternative to his own reason, which he must apply to discover the real problems before they can be solved. This rational approach to issues is the philosophical role during upheavals, and we may be thankful to Descartes for his contribution.

At the time of Descartes, not only the church and its authority had disintegrated but also a number of human values, if not the whole value system. The issue of value neutrality had been concomitant to the mechanical picture of the world, as had been emphasized by classical Newtonian science. It became even more concrete through the subsequent scientific revolution, particularly the epistemological and methodological revolution in science and philosophy inspired by Descartes.

This led to a sharp distinction between what is objective and what is subjective in the acquisition of reliable knowledge. According to the mechanical world picture, nature is a vast machine governed by qualitative laws and relationships. Nature is written in the language of mathematics. Its features, that is, matter, motion, and physical magnitudes, are objective. The methodology to know these objective realities must take wide account only of those features which can be quantified, or written in nature's language. The very essence of the world is given by these objective properties together with the mechanical laws that govern them. According to Galileo and Locke, these essential features of the world are "primary qualities." The rest, for example, colors, values, interpretations, purpose, theories, and so on, are not objective *realities* as they do not explain the world, but can only be reduced to objective *terms*.

Consequently, objectivity is limited to objective entities and truths. While the entities are the objective elements of reality, the truths are arrived at through methods that take no account of anything subjective, that is, methods which are unbiased. The search for mechanical "proof" methods, for example, computer algorithms and cost-benefit decisionmaking, is the ultimate outcome of the ideal of rational, objective method.[1]

The eighteenth-century Age of Enlightenment was the climax of this scientific revolution. The key idea here is light vis-à-vis darkness, and pertains to understanding, or having knowledge, vis-à-vis being ignorant. This may be supported by Kant's subjective explanation of "enlightenment" as man's coming of age from the state of infancy which rendered him incapable of using reason without the aid of others.[2] It may also be reflected in the slow growth of science itself right from the Renaissance period to its maturity in the eighteenth century. Along the line of this development we come across a witty attack on medieval religiosity and praise for the scientific achievements in the new belief that "God said, Let Newton be, and there was light"! That the Age of Enlightenment is the climax of the Renaissance revolution is further demonstrated by Runes in the following words: "The ideals of the enlightenment period, the impassioned zeal for the materialization of the ideal man in an ideal society show clearly that it was basically related to the Renaissance and its continuation."[3]

This paper joins the rest in singing songs of praise to the eighteenth-century Age of Enlightenment. That science, whose maturity characterizes this age, currently rules the world may be undisputable. The scientific contribution to modern technology, medicine, communication, research, and health, together with such systems as the social, political, educational, and economic, are clear examples or testimonies to scientific achievement. Thus, the results of enlightenment in liberal humanists and rationalists in the West, together with other people who have been influenced by the West, are tangible. The eighteenth-century Age of Enlightenment thinkers are so "unparalleled for their lucidity, courage, hatred of darkness, and love of truth that they are of vital interest to all men and women today."[4]

This paper also recognizes and celebrates Ibn Rushd, or Averroës (1126–98), for his significant contribution to this great revolution in our thought system. It is a pity that this great thinker was persecuted and his books burned. It is lamentable that it is only today, at the close of the twentieth century, that we are wondering how enlightenment can be a factor of alleviating, or even overcoming, cultural stagnation and disintegration in the Arab-Islamic world, and how Ibn Rushd's philosophy can help in breeding enlightenment in the Arab-Islamic world, which could be the basis of establishing a cultural bridge between Arab-Islamic, Afro-Asian, and European cultures.

Ibn Rushd and the European Enlightenment

Runes divides enlightenment into two parts.[5] The first part has a subjective meaning, as we have seen in Kant's concept of enlightenment. The second part has an objective meaning that refers to a cultural period distinguished by the fervent efforts of leading personalities to make reason the absolute ruler of human life, and to shed the light of knowledge upon the mind and science of any individual.

While the term is generally applied to the European Enlightenment stretching from the early seventeenth to the beginning of the nineteenth century, the above-mentioned efforts cannot be confined to a particular time, or nation, as we can learn from history.

So Ibn Rushd is viewed as one of the thinkers who contributed to the development of the concept of enlightenment, just as the much later or subsequent thinkers like the English empiricists, Bacon, Hobbes, and Locke. This includes many "free thinkers," moralists who believed in the "light of reason," and radical French enlighteners who were sarcastic and critical of the past, showing that their philosophy got its momentum from the moral corruption at the royal court and the abuse of kingly power in France.

Also included are such ideas as Descartes's doctrine of "clear and perspicuous ideas," Spinoza's critical attitude toward religion, and Leibniz together with Wolff's "reasonable thinking," which prepared the philosophy of Bayle, Montesquieu, and Rousseau.

What in England and France remained on the stage of mere ideas and utopian dreams became reality in the new commonwealth of the United States of America. Thus the "fathers of the Constitution" were enlightened, for example, Franklin, Jefferson, Adams, Hamilton, and Paine, who was their foremost literary propagandist.

In Germany we have examples in Leibniz, whose interest was in the cult of pure reason, disappointed by the Reformation and the bloody religious wars among Christians; the philosophers of natural law, such as Grotius; and Schiller, whose lyric and drama served as a powerful commendation of ideal freedom, liberty, justice, and humanity. Kant's celebrated critiques were partly the result of his attempts to reconcile English sensism, as advocated by thinkers like Hume, and French skepticism as exemplified in Descartes. However, this enlightenment, characterized by the radical rationalism and the animosity against religion, gave rise to strong philosophical, theological, and literary opposition, as evidenced in Hamann, Jacobi, and Laveter, who appear to have triumphed over the advocates of the above type of enlightenment.

This last part may serve as a good introduction to Ibn Rushd's contribution to the Enlightenment. Ibn Rushd was all round, having studied theology, law, medicine, mathematics, and philosophy, and having worked as judge, physician, and writer. His commentary on the works of Aristotle influenced Thomas Aquinas. However, his theories of human nature and the nature of truth gave rise to two camps comparable to those cited above. According to Ibn Rushd, man possesses only a disposition for receiving the intellect coming from without. Besides, Ibn Rushd believed in "two-fold truth," that is, that a proposition may be theologically true and philosophically false and vice versa.[6]

While the latter belief is nowadays commonly shared, as evidenced by the "explosion of knowledge" that has led to the worrying situation of specialization in our contemporary educational systems, the former doctrine underlines human individualism, or conceiving each person as an individual being. Those who underline shared humanity do not accept this position. Yet both views claim to be Aristotelian. From the expertise of Roland Teske we learn that several texts in the commentary of Averroës on Plato's *Republic* regarding the end of man point to a difficulty latent in the moral philosophy of Aristotle.[7] This is because in the *Nicomachean Ethics* Aristotle argues that the ultimate end of man is happiness and that happiness consists in intellectual contemplation or wisdom.[8] The difficulty with intellectual contemplation as the ultimate end of man in a this-worldly ethics is that it would seem impossible for the majority of mankind to attain such an end. This difficulty, to the best of Teske's knowledge, is never made explicit in the text of Aristotle. In Averroës, however, the question becomes explicit and crucial.

The end of man in the moral philosophy of Averroës based on that of Aristotle is happiness—an action of the rational soul in accordance with virtue.[9] According to Averroës, however, human perfection is not simply one; rather there are many types of human perfection, although wisdom continues to hold the highest rank. Different people achieve human perfection at different levels. Some do not have the potential to achieve the ultimate perfection.

We may then conclude that this leaves plenty of room for those who can to struggle as much as possible to improve themselves towards perfection. This upward mobility in which everyone is a candidate to participate in his own way, according to his disposition or ability, stresses the type of enlightenment whereby everybody is invited to participate in self improvement, and whereby those who excel are requested to enlighten those who are lagging behind. It appears, therefore, to be clear that the European Enlightenment has some roots in the philosophy of Ibn Rushd. With this, we may examine other types of enlightenment.

A Broad View of Enlightenment

"Enlightenment" can neither have one meaning, nor be limited to one person or group in space and time. Thus it is said that Siddhartha Gautama, circa 563–483 B.C.E., son of a ruler in North Benares, India, renounced luxury and became an ascetic at the age of twenty-nine, having achieved "enlightenment" under a *bo* tree in Buddh Gaya, or Bodh Gaya village. It is due to this that he was given the title "Buddha," a Sanskrit word for "the enlightened one."[10] The great "enlightenment" gave him the principles of Buddhism.

Everywhere man finds himself in a complex situation from which he needs means of liberation, or salvation. In the case of India, at that time, Buddha taught four noble truths: existence is suffering, the origin of suffering is desire, suffering ceases when desire ceases, and, finally, the way to reach the end of desire is by following the "noble eightfold path," which comprises right belief; right resolve, that is, to renounce carnal pleasure, harming no living creature, and so on; right speech; right conduct; right occupation or liking; right effort; right contemplation or right mindedness; and right ecstasy. Unfortunately, such "enlightenment" often ends up in dogmatism, when, instead of making personal efforts to understand, people become indoctrinated. This can be said to be characteristic of all religions. Hence, fundamentalism is the logical consequence.

It is the contention of this paper that everywhere man is face to face with nature. At this level, human needs and problems are similar. The natural causes, such as natural catastrophes, and human causes, such as greed and selfishness, are similar. Some of the solutions, such as self-restraint, are also similar. What tends to differ radically are the metaphysical additions. In the case of Buddhism, the final goal is to escape from existence into blissful nonexistence, *nirvana,* a Sanskrit word for annihilation. Besides this ultimate end, an individual person is assumed to comprise preexistent elements that disintegrate at his death. These are considered to be recombined in a similar fashion. Finally, any metaphysical position tends to start at the natural level with the intention of explaining natural realities. Thus, the Buddhist "salvation" doctrines, like any other, are intended to guide everyday human life. In the case of Buddhism, by religious living, man seeks to escape from the above-mentioned chain. With this, there is no need to look for similar concepts of "enlightenment" in other societies, for example, in Africa. What is being contended is that this is not a peculiarity of one society that is totally absent in other societies.

Similarly, the reaction of ancient Greek philosophers, that is, the cosmologists, is another interesting level of "enlightenment." Here the point is that there is a natural desire by all people to explain things rationally, that is, to have personal reasons for believing and accepting things. While there is no society where individuals are free of religious and other worldviews, particularly when they are young, there is likewise no society where individuals do not question their traditional beliefs. Consequently, the Greek demythologization of the universe is a mere example of so many others. Creators of myths can uncreate them. This has taken place in all human societies, but at different places and for different reasons.

Within the recorded history of Western philosophy, we witness a pattern whereby the ancient Greeks' search for natural laws is submerged by theology in the Middle Ages. But underneath this general umbrella we come across individual thinkers who were both theologians and natural scientists, such as St. Albert Magnus, the teacher of St. Thomas Aquinas. We have already seen how Aquinas was influenced by Ibn Rushd. At this juncture, we may turn to the general situation which was characterized by Plato, whose dualism was adopted by St. Augustine, and then Aristotle, whose natural tendencies were adopted by Aquinas. However, for both Augustine and Aquinas, philosophy remained the handmaid of theology. Both maintained "enlightenment" as the illumination of the human soul, or introspection. So the novelty may be Ibn Rushd's course, which eventually links up with extremists like William of Ockham at the time when medievalism was giving way to the Renaissance period. The new tendency was toward natural laws instead of theology and spirituality. Thus, when thinkers like Dante ridiculed the medieval Catholic worldview, which was based on Aristolelianism, a new type of "enlightenment" was emerging. It is this type which may be correctly dubbed "European Enlightenment" because it was characterized by the European scientific outlook on life, which was and still is anti-Aristotelian. Since the European worldview, during the medieval period, or the Christian era, was basically Aristotelian, many Europeans struggled to "enlighten" their fellow Europeans against this falsehood. In certain cases, the struggle still continues today.

The struggle, however, takes a different shape when "enlightened" Europe meets Africa. If we examine European revolutions, for example, the Glorious Revolution in seventeenth-century England (1688) and the French Revolution in the eighteenth century (1789), we find that the basic characteristics of this type of "enlightenment" hinged upon the absolutely inalienable rights of the individual, upon freedom of speech and of thought, and upon the moral rights of any people to revolt against any form of government that suppresses their liberties.[11] It is these ideas which subsequently influenced such European thinkers as Bentham and Austin, who challenged the medieval concept of law that protected medieval feudalism. They established positive law, that is, manmade law, or law as it is vis-a-vis law as it ought to be. These liberating ideals spread to other thinkers, like Locke, Rousseau, Montesquieu, and eventually to the American writers of the Constitution, among other thinkers.

European Enlightenment and Africa

The problem that arises here is that when we turn to Africa, we find that the same Europe and America which have been fighting for human rights at home unleash inhuman brutality on the African people. Hence, at this juncture, this paper examines Western hypocrisy in Africa. Secondly, this paper emphasizes the need for Africa to be aware of this hypocrisy, which currently entails a number of hidden agendas. In the spirit of this conference, this paper contends that such awareness is the type of "enlightenment" that Africa badly needs today. If Europeans and Americans who fought for their independence and for human rights as a whole are known as "enlightened" thinkers, there is no reason why Africans who are doing exactly the same should not be seen in the same light. However, while Europeans fought their own dictators, Africa has an added problem of fighting both African dictators at home and their masters abroad. Many dictators have been overthrown by Africans only to be reinstated by their foreign masters the following day. It is for this reason that this paper recommends combined efforts by world peace lovers to fight for the independence of Africa. This paper has respect for those who believe that Africa can manage on her own. However, the truth remains that Africa needs the rest of the world to check the greed that has been unleashed on her by unscrupulous Africans and foreigners alike. The problem of consumerism appears to be employing scientific and technological means to destroy weak, helpless, and unsuspicious areas like Africa. But, as a result, the whole world is likely to suffer. Heaps of lies and myths are also being used to achieve the selfish objectives of consumerism. We need enlightenment to blow these myths up before they blow us up.

Despite the bright, and sometimes even hot sun ever shimmering over Africa, Africa has been dubbed the "Dark Continent." So, when it came to "enlightenment," or supplying some badly needed light, Africa was the candidate with the biggest demand! The black people were regarded as inferior just because of their color.

However, given the fact that people have moved freely and in mixed groups from time immemorial, and that civilizations have developed at different times on all continents, one wonders whether racism is not a mere creation for political and economic strategies. Today, for example, excavations reveal that objects from distant places like China were available on the East African coast long before the various racial stories were concocted. We know that the Middle East was highly connected with Africa, not only through trade, but also through religion. That Jewish relations extended to Africa is even proved by the fact that only recently some Jews were repatriated from Ethiopia to Israel. Perhaps, the *King Solomon's Mines* story may not be merely creative. The connection between Africa and the Arab world is another piece of evidence that it is not easy to determine how Africa first met the rest of the world, and how civilizations involved Africa, long before many European societies were established. It appears that the colonial era is responsible for categorizing and dividing people who had long cordially lived together free of racism.

Hundreds of years before the eighteenth-century Age of Enlightenment, Europe and Africa had met in many different ways. St. Augustine of Hippo took civilization from Africa to Europe through Christianity in the early medieval period. Right now we are celebrating Ibn Rushd, who was born at Cordoba and died in Morocco as far back as the twelfth century. Despite his being non-European, it is Europe which has benefited from the enlightenment he initiated. Did he consider himself a European, an Arab, or an African? Did the area around the Mediterranean Sea view itself as partly Europe and partly Africa? It is the view of this paper that we are looking at that former united area through our current divided eyes. Our modern racism, which did not exist then, makes us misinterpret certain issues. It is with such bias that Europe later on wanted to convince the world that it was Europe itself which owned civilization and enlightenment, and that it had the duty to spread it to the rest of the world. Only recently we celebrated Amo, a Ghanian who lived in Germany and became a professor of philosophy there hundreds of years before the Age of Enlightenment. Yet, Ibn Rushd and Amo are merely those who are known to us. This writer has just returned from the University of Bayreuth, which is situated in the city where black people were once washed. Where were they coming from? Were they the first ones to go to Germany? What became of them? Does it make sense when we later on read that it is Europeans who discovered other peoples in their respective areas, as if they were part of nature?

The point being argued here is that it was extremely hypocritical of the eighteenth-century Europeans of the Age of Enlightenment to turn them-

selves into the origin and center of human civilization. It was unfair of them
to think of "other cultures" and "other minds" as being inferior to European
ones. As we have just seen, there was a lot of unity in the world whereby
people of different races had met and cordially worked together long before the eighteenth century. How could then the nineteenth-century theorists underline such theories as that of evolution which classified people
into *races* and categorized them into different *species* due to *color* alone?
It was not the first time that the world had discovered that the people who
populated it were of different colors. The different races had long thought
and worked together. What, then, were some Europeans trying to prove
when they strutted around with tape measures and started measuring
African people's skulls? After all, this is the time when these very Europeans were seriously fighting with the Africans, whom they were invading!
How could people organize themselves to fight you so effectively and then
you pretended to wonder whether they were people, or not? Was anybody
really wondering whether Africans were human beings or not? Did these
theorists and architects of chaos take racism seriously? Did the colonists
mean what they said when they told such people as the Rwandan Tutsis that
they were superior to Hutus? Is it fair that the world should look at Africa
as a chaotic continent after such colonists made sure that "things fall
apart"? If anybody took racism seriously, this paper is of the view that such
a person was indeed the victim of the theorists. Unfortunately, later on the
Africans themselves were victims. Up to now, there are some who still believe that they are inferior beings just because of color.

The eighteenth-century Age of Enlightenment mood arose as the result
of the maturity of science. It was believed that through the understanding
of physical laws, man could understand nature better. Man could also use
these laws to predict and then control nature. As we have seen before, no-
body should be against the rise of science, which is the ruler of the world
today. Above all, we should realize that science as such has never attacked
any race. It merely attacks wrong ideas and practices. Actually, the war of
science was waged in Europe itself, where it sought to topple religious
ideas and then take control of Europe.

The real problem is that some Europeans have misused science and the
Age of Enlightenment for their own benefit. Ironically, some believers
who were being harassed in Europe for their religious ideas used scientific
means to retain and even spread these ideas in Africa. The colonists who
wanted to exploit other lands used science to achieve their objectives. The

settlers used science to discover new lands and to kill off their owners before they appropriated them. They are still using science to develop them. In short, science in itself is excellent, but many opportunists have misused it to the detriment of Africa.

Consequently, Africa regards the eighteenth-century Age of Enlightenment with mixed feelings. While this age should be regarded as a human achievement, Africa has been so unfortunate as to suffer so greatly from it that some African thinkers have openly attacked "reason."[12] Surely reason is a human tool. Whoever attacks it uses it in doing so. As for science, Europe has used it in controlling and exploiting Africa so much that there are many ways in which some consider science as a European thing. This is false. As we have seen, European civilization emerged from earlier civilizations. Besides, while Europe or the West has admittedly developed science the most, scientific know-how has nothing to do with race. There are many whites who simply cannot do science. They do not have enough brains for it. If science were a "white" thing, all whites would do it, and the rest of the world would just watch in admiration. However, the story of "brain drain" is enough to demonstrate to us that all races are both capable and incapable of mental work.

While there is a dire need for all races to participate in the scientific revolution and to develop technologically, there is an equal need to persuade Europe or the West to stop using science selfishly. Such selfishness is evident, for example, in the fact that colonialism made efforts to destroy African skills but did not want to replace these skills with European ones. This is not surprising, since many came to Africa to exploit and not to develop. Such an argument has been successfully developed by Walter Rodney in his book *How Europe Underdeveloped Africa.*[13] The selfishness is still evident not only on the African continent, but also in America, where the African Americans are living like second-class citizens. Perhaps the world has or will learn positive lessons from uprisings like the recent one in Los Angeles, and will make sure that similar ugly scenes are not repeated.

In addition to this, it is really surprising that when the West talks of disarmament, the message is directed to the so-called Third World countries, instead of the real threat. When we use examples only from non-Western thinkers to criticize, the criticism may appear to be biased. So we shall conclude this part by looking at some theories of conquest from the point of view of European thinkers or critics. We shall take examples from Spain, one of the early large empires, and then Britain, over whose empire the sun never set.

In the case of Spain, it was believed that the Spanish emperor was lord of the earth and could subjugate anyone at will; that the pope could grant territory to a ruler anywhere he wished; that the fact of "discovery" in itself constituted a sufficient reason for the exploring power to assume rulership over primitive peoples; that refusal to accept Christianity, or the existence of immortality against nature, could cause a people to forfeit the right to self-government and, finally, that the Spanish nation had a right to conquest by virtue of a special grant from God. It is with such mentality that the Spanish conquest of Mexico was carried out.

Even Vittoria (1480–1546),[14] who is regarded as the founder of international law, could not stomach this attitude. He himself was Spanish and lived during the heyday of the Spanish conquests in the New World. His theory is that the only just conquest is conquest because of some necessity. In the case of Spanish conquests in the Americas, he established the following titles, or conditions for it: if the Americas violated the Spaniards' right to travel there, if they refused Christian missionaries to preach the Gospel, if there was a forceful proselytism of native Christians by the Indians, if there was need to have a Christian government for converted natives and, in general, to stamp out tyranny and introduce progressive government. Subsequently, the idea of "civilization" took root, and no society was allowed to live outside this so-called mainstream. Even today when "tribal clashes" take place in some countries the tendency is to favor the "tribe" which is considered the more "developed" of the two.

While these medieval ideas still affect us, those which do so even more are those which stem from the eighteenth-century European Age of Enlightenment. Physical science had become so successful that its method was applied to man and society. Hence, the nineteenth-century development of anthropology, sociology, and related social sciences. Africa has directly suffered from these new sciences partly because many theories which were developed in Europe were proved wrong or right in Africa. Up to now, Africa is the experimental field for all sorts of theories, ranging from economic to medical ones. It is possible that the current spread of sicknesses like strange malaria and AIDS is the result of such experimentation with human beings. The experiments with such systems as the educational and the economic systems are also still current. The dumping of banned commodities and toxic waste products is still going on. Some have gone as far as suggesting that instead of meeting so much trouble in transporting these waste products they had better build the dangerous factories in Africa! Our contemporary enlightenment must entail such awareness and the subsequent resistance to fight for our rights and survival.

The fact that there was malice in conquests is evident in Lord Morley's story of conquest as practiced by the British. Like Vittoria, who was bothered by his country's conquest of Mexico, Morley was bothered by the British conquest of Chitral in what is now Pakistan in 1895. The following is his frank description:

> First, you push your territories where you have no business to be, and where you had promised not to go; secondly your intrusion provokes resentment, and in these wild countries resentment means resistance; thirdly, you instantly cry out that the peoples are rebellious and that their act is rebellion (this in spite of your assurance that you have no intention of setting up a permanent sovereignty over them); fourthly, you send a force to stamp out the rebellion; and fifthly, having spread bloodshed, confusion and anarchy, you declare with uplifted hands that moral reasons force you to stay; for if you were to leave, this territory would be left in a condition which no civilised power could contemplate with equanimity or composure.[15]

While the West has worked so hard to influence Africa for Western benefit, it is the duty of Africa to liberate itself. One of the ways out of such a situation is through "enlightenment" in the sense of awareness. For this, Africa needs a lot of things, including philosophy. Above all, one of the effective colonial methods has been the mental one. It involves killing enlightenment. The Chinese saying that a protruding nail must be hammered back has been efficiently used to take care of those who resist. To regain independence, we need mental decolonization. This entails enlightenment. Philosophy contributes to this particularly in the form of critical thinking.

European Enlightenment and African Philosophy

When it comes to African thought and practice there are many scholars who falsely believe that there is no such thing as African philosophy. According to them, what actually exists is philosophy in Africa. They look at philosophy as a subject taught at a university, just like mathematics, and argue, even using the terminologies of philosophy itself, that logic, epistemology, ethics, aesthetics, and so on, are all Greek inventions. After all, school education is of European origin. So also philosophy as a subject is foreign to Africa. As for doctrines, they think that both idealism and materialism are strictly European. They seem to see no other way of conceiving philosophy.

However, the truth is that philosophy is human. All people philosophize. While they may not use the same terminology, the concepts remain the same. All people wonder about things, and look for their explanations, even ultimate ones. Out of this, they build values and systems of thought and belief on which they anchor their practical life. Without philosophy, societies would be chaotic. Even the malicious colonists and imperialists have admitted the order and social justice which they first witnessed when they arrived to carry out their duty of "civilization."

Another falsehood which one comes across in African philosophy is that it starts with Rev. Fr. Placid Tempels's small book of yesterday, *Bantu Philosophy*. If philosophy is human, how can it begin with a small man like Tempels? The story of Tempels is simple. As a missionary, his concern was conversion. At first he, and his fellow missionaries, thought they had succeeded when they gathered a few black people, taught them Christian practices, dressed them in European clothes, and even gave them European names. However, the truth dawned on them when they discovered that in serious matters like life and death, the "Christians" went back to their traditional practices, for example, consulting their traditional medicine men. This created the impression that there was some deep African conception of life which the missionaries had not understood. Tempels, who had been brought up under the influence of systematic philosophy, sought for this explanation in terms of what he understood philosophy to be, that is, the fundamental explanation of things, or the underlying principle or issue which explains other issues. After Tempels, a host of thinkers tried to establish African philosophy along these lines, as if Hegel's concept of philosophy, that is, an external reality that accounts for all the rest, really held some water. It is in this category that we meet current African scholars like Rev. Mbiti, who explains the African failure to convert by theorizing that while Christianity has a three-dimensional concept of time, and while it believes in eschatology, the Africans have only a two-dimensional concept of time. They believe in a short present (*saasa*) and a long past (*zamani*). Consequently, while European culture tends to look toward the future, African culture looks toward the opposite direction, that is, the past, and that is why they could not understand what the white man was talking about! This appears to be one of the worst attacks on the Africans by an African, since a person devoid of the concept of the future is incapable of planning. Indeed, Mbiti thanks Europe for teaching Africa how to plan![16]

This paper does not consider philosophy as a reality beyond man that man has the duty to look for. Philosophy is simply the human act of using mental powers vigorously. In this process, man identifies basic problems which also make philosophy what it is. Thus, our simple act of thinking, and the simple subject matter of our thought, for example, where to get the next drink, cannot constitute philosophy. Consequently, philosophy is a mental activity on issues or principles. As a mental activity, philosophy belongs to man as man, and not to man as African, European, Arab, Asian, or for that matter, woman or man. It is a mere mental process.

However, people do not simply philosophize. They also establish problems, issues, views, doctrines, and schools of thought, among other things which we generally consider a philosophical product. In this sense, one can identify doctrines as African, European, Arab, Asian, and so on. These views must be created by individual thinkers. As such, they are not African, European, Arab, or Asian from the racist point of view. Thinkers from these races are free to agree or disagree with thinkers from races other than their own.

On the other hand, there are some fundamental ideals which were established from time immemorial, and which hold peoples together. On the surface, we see a people with a common culture behaving according to certain peculiar beliefs. These beliefs are explainable by fundamental ideas which may be called philosophy. This cannot be what thinkers like Tempels were looking for. Tempels tells us that the African philosophy he had in mind could only be established by Europeans. After the European had explained, the Africans would turn round and say, in admiration, "Oh Mzungu! You really understand us!" Above all, Tempels and his group held that such philosophy explained the thinking of all Africans! This paper argues that since philosophy is human, ideas are relative and historical. They must have meaning to the people who think them. If they lose meaning, the people are free to throw them out, and to think anew, in order to create better ones.

At this juncture this paper praises Kant's concept of enlightenment, which underlines subjectivity. The maturity of each individual is the meaning of life. A society which does not want its people to grow mentally commits a crime against being. It is this very crime which Europe has committed in Africa by removing African skills and systems without really replacing them, in order to control Africa in every way. The case of apartheid in South Africa, where blacks were denied proper education, among other means of human development, serves as an example of strategies for dependence. This total dependence was calculated to empower Europe, or the West. With independence, therefore, Africa must underline philosophy, without which education is indoctrination, politics is dictatorship, work is slavery, among other limitations.

Philosophy means many different things to many different thinkers. There are those who confuse philosophy and a philosophy. It is true that many philosophers are identified with their points of view, or doctrines which they have both articulated and lived. Consequently, we have clear systems or schools of thought within which we locate and understand these thinkers.

Despite the obvious past and present European destructive tendencies in Africa, it is only fair to recognize the positive aspects of the European and African encounter. First on the list is the human ability to overcome indoctrination and other methods of subjugation. One of the methods used to dissuade people away from "enlightenment" was to build churches and bars instead of schools in their localities. This method was used in both America and South Africa, together with other places where deliberate attempts to keep certain communities backward have existed. That the same communities looked through such evil tricks demonstrates the innate human ability to analyze and understand issues. However, we must also recognize the fact that it is not all the Europeans, or the Westerners, who have been against "other cultures." It is not all whites who are greedy. Very many of them have tried hard to help the marginalized people. That is why Africa distinguishes between the "bad whites" who looted land among other types of property, enslaved the people, and mistreated them in all ways, and the "good whites," who built schools, hospitals, and means of communication, among other things. There are those who have often hidden behind good-sounding ideas like religion, civilization, development, and so on to carry out evil hidden agendas. But many others have sacrificed a lot, including life, to liberate Africa. Yet there are many Africans who have knowingly or unwittingly co-operated with evil foreigners to sell off their countries.

Philosophy should help individuals to analyze issues objectively. Africa needs philosophy for this purpose. Africans should be encouraged and assisted to be critical thinkers. Thus, there is a sense in which philosophy is an individual affair. One of the ways of stopping people from being philosophical in this sense is to tell them lies that there is something called philosophy out there which they should look for and then utilize. We have seen that this is the mistake which Tempels and his followers made.

We are returning to it because a similar mistake was made by some nationalists, and it is still being made today.

At the 1959 Congress of Black Writers and Artists held in Rome, the subcommission on philosophy, clearly conscious of the role of philosophy in the promotion of a truly African culture, suggested to the modern African thinker that he identify the elements of a genuine African wisdom, complementary to other human wisdom, and that he express the specific categories of African thought. The African philosopher, concluded the members of this commission, should safeguard the unitary vision of cosmic reality which characterizes the wise men of traditional Africa.[17]

It is true that during this period, when Africa was fighting for independence, Africa needed such a common front. It is also true that until today, when the war is continuing in an even more sophisticated way, Africa needs unity, as well as ideologies, or an ideology. However, there is reason to safeguard against the possibilities of such needs killing personal initiatives and independent thinking. Such possibilities are so easy to come across that some people are beginning to complain about the "diploma disease" which has found its way into human society through academic dictatorship. It is possible to have academic dictators who hardly think beyond the theories that were forced down their throats before being crowned doctors. They cannot cure ignorance. Similarly, it is possible to come across ideological demagogues who cannot think beyond their ideologies. The only way out of such situations is freedom of thought and critical thinking.

When such freedom is carried out in the proper direction, with correct methods, and to the desirable levels, it becomes an important ingredient of the type of philosophy that this paper advocates, whether such philosophy is carried out in Africa or elsewhere in the world. Philosophy is unlimited human participation to identify life problems and issues and to deal with them rationally.

With this, we may conclude by once more celebrating thinkers like Ibn Rushd, who set the pace for the promotion of enlightenment. We celebrate Kant as the theorist of human maturity. His subjectivism is the liberation of each individual person. It is actually the meaning of life. The development of a society and of mankind as a whole depends on that of the individual. So, anyone who is against the development of individuals is against the development of society and mankind as a whole. That enlightenment in this sense has taken root in Africa is evident in various ways. The following are only some examples. First, Africa has been able to fight for her independence both from colonialism and neocolonialism. While the independence war is still raging on many fronts, what is important is that awareness has taken place. For any type of liberation to succeed, mental liberation comes first. Second, Africa is undergoing a cultural revolution. The idea that is in vogue is inculturation. When Europe first met with Africa, what took place was acculturation. The two cultures simply collided with each other. Now, efforts are being made to sort out which African traditional values and which foreign ones are good for the new Africa. Hence, inculturation. If this succeeds, the new culture will be the peoples' culture, intended to meet the people's needs. Their values will be truly theirs, not inherited for the sake of it, even when they are meaningless, and not imposed on them through cultural imperialism. Thirdly, Africa is working hard to establish the rule of law. This is evident in the efforts to establish democracies by fighting dictatorships and writing constitutions, among other things. Fourthly, nongovernmental organizations are mushrooming to enlighten the people about their human rights and to help them fight for them.

In the general field of education, the teaching of philosophy is gaining currency. The traditional methods of teaching are giving way to modern ones whereby individual participation is highly encouraged. Critical and creative thinking is given priority. Above all, in the inherited system which has been tending towards specialization, interdisciplinary teaching is being introduced to stop individuals from ending up as mere cogs in the wheel of society. In a nutshell, the possibility of education ending up in indoctrination is being radically changed.

This paper ends by adding that Africa cannot afford examining the concept of enlightenment as a mere academic exercise. Africa concretely needs enlightenment. A lot of things have gone wrong. Despite the presence of enlightenment as elaborated above, there is still a lot to be done. The problem of what, how, and why things have gone wrong still exists. We may see this problem in those Africans who still participate in unthinkingly destroying mother Africa. Some are even seriously destroying the few thinkers who are capable of saving the situation. Many have forgotten colonial evils to the extent that they are consulting colonial masters on how to solve problems that were deliberately created by those colonists. Many trust greedy and destructive foreigners more than their countrymen, and even sensible leaders do so.

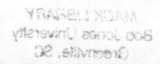

Furthermore, Africa needs enlightenment to formulate more viable policies and strategies for recovery and development. We need enlightenment to develop scientifically and technologically. We need enlightenment to develop socially, religiously, politically, economically, and in all other areas. We cannot get anywhere through remaining at the receiving end, or even copying. We must be creative.

Notes

1. E. D. Klemke, Robert Hellinger, A. David Kline, eds., *Introductory Reading in the Philosophy of Science* (Amherst, N.Y.: Prometheus Books, 1980), p. 226.

2. D. Dagobert Runes, ed., *Dictionary of Philosophy*, 15th ed. (New Jersey: Littefield, Adams, 1964), p. 92.

3. Ibid.

4. Isaiah Berlin, *The Age of Enlightenment* (New York: Mentor Books, 1963), back page.

5. Runes, *Dictionary of Philosophy*, p. 92.

6. Ibid., p. 30.

7. Roland J. Teske, "Averroës on Man's End," in *The New Scholasticism* (1963), p. 437.

8. Aristotle, *Nicomachean Ethics*, 1097, pp. 20–21.

9. *Aristotelis omnia quae extant opera . . . Averroës Cordubensis in ae . . . Omnes Commentarii, Venetiis apud Juntas, 1573–75,* vol. 3, fol. (16M).

10. James Mark Baldwin, ed., *Dictionary of Philosophy and Psychology*, vol. 1 (Gloucester, Mass.: Peter Smith, 1960), p. 326.

11. Henry D. Aiken, *The Age of Ideology* (New York: New American Library, 1956), p. 53.

12. For further information on such an attack, see Prof. Outlaw, *Philosophy Made Out of Struggle.* His argument is that whites have used reason to attack blacks, and that reason is not the only important aspect of human life. See also Negritude thinkers like Senghor who were so confused by the racist thinkers as to accept that while Europeans reason and Asians meditate, blacks use their emotions.

13. Walter Rodney, *How Europe Underdeveloped Africa* (Nairobi: Heinemann, 1972).

14. For the traditional views on Spain and the new theory by Vottoria, see Jeremiah Newman, *Studies in Political Morality* (Dublin: Scepter, 1963).

15. For further information on how Britain maliciously created her empire, read Raymond de Martini, *The Right of Nations to Expand by Conquest* (Washington, 1955). See also Newman, *Studies*, p. 119.

16. S. J. Mbiti, *African Philosophy and Religions* (Nairobi: Heinemann, 1969).

17. See Claude Sumner, "The Rise of Philosophical Thought Within Black Africa," in Mourad Wahba, ed., *Philosophy and Civilization*. Proceedings of the First Afro-Asian Philosophy Conference, Cairo, 1978.

14

Between Ernest Renan and Ernst Bloch: Averroës Remembered, Discovered, and Invented. The European Reception Since the Nineteenth Century

Stefan Wild
Professor of Oriental Studies,
University of Bonn (Germany)

Mourad Wahba has coined the term "the paradox of Averroës." This paradox consists in the fact that the "Latin" Averroës played a generally acknowledged role for the philosophy of European enlightenment, whereas the Arab Ibn Rushd and his work were neglected and disavowed by Islamic culture, the very culture which had produced him. There was a Latin Averroism as an important intellectual movement, but there never was an Arabic or an Islamic *Rushdiyya* to match it. According to Mourad Wahba, the absence of renaissance and enlightenment in the Muslim world corresponds to the absence of such a *Rushdiyya*. Anke von Kügelgen has, in her monumental study *Averroës and Arab Modernity,* exhaustively demonstrated which new role Ibn Rushd played in Arab intellectual life since the end of the nineteenth century.[1] The reader cannot be but amazed by the variety of learned interpretations which have been offered since the famous public debate between Farah Antun and Muhammad 'Abduh in the years 1902–3. Muhammad 'Abduh sees in Ibn Rushd a brilliant historical example of a Muslim philosopher and scholar embodying the highest ideals of Islamic tolerance. Since then, Ibn Rushd has been seen variously as a neo-Mu'tazilite

155

who was more or less plagiarized by Thomas Aquinas (Mahmud Qasim, 1913–1973), as a representative of a specifically Maghribi brand of rationalism (Muhammad 'Abid al-Jabiri, born 1936), or as an early proponent of materialism (Tayyib Tizini, born 1938), to name but a few interpretations.

Anke von Kügelgen has shown beyond a doubt what role the European reception of the Arab Ibn Rushd in the form of Averroism played in this inter-Arab debate, and particularly what part the nineteenth-century French philosopher Ernest Renan had in it. Until deep into the twentieth century, Ibn Rushd was often either a Maliki *faqih* of distinction, equally well versed in natural sciences with a more or less suspicious leaning toward antique philosophy, or he was Ibn Rushd as seen by Renan.

My own contribution will analyze some important European interpretations of the role of Ibn Rushd's teachings in the Arabic and the Islamic world and then focus on two issues: (1) the part played by the image of Ibn Rushd/Averroës as constructed by Renan and others in the formation of the idea of a specifically Oriental and Islamic form of enlightenment and the idea of a specifically "Oriental" form of decadence and decay; (2) the perspective within which European intellectuals after Ernest Renan saw the Arab Ibn Rushd. These two topics are interrelated but not identical.

Thomas van Erpe

One of the first scholars to recommend the study of Ibn Rushd's original works in Arabic to European students of philosophy was one of the eminent figures of oriental studies in the late sixteenth and early seventeenth centuries: the Dutch Thomas van Erpe (1584–1624, latinized as Thomas Erpenius), well known as the author of the first scholarly grammar of Arabic in any European language.[2] In an appeal to the students of philosophy, he exclaimed: "Keep in mind, you students of philosophy, how important it is, to hear the second Aristotle—and I mean Ibn Rushd—teaching in his own language in the most distinct manner. You call him wrongly Averroës, who stammers in Latin to a degree that you complain justly to be hardly able to understand him and to need an interpreter for the interpreter."[3]

M. J. Müller

Marcus Joseph Müller (1809–1874) deserves credit for the first Arabic edition of three of the main philosophical texts of Ibn Rushd (*Fasl al-maqal, al-*

Damima, and *Kashf al-adilla fi 'aqa 'id al-milla*)[4] and the first translation of them into a modern European language. His edition was based upon a single Arabic manuscript of the Escorial. Until 1935, all editions, including those made by Arabs, depended directly or indirectly on Müller's edition.[5]

Ernest Renan

In many ways, the modern picture of Ibn Rushd inside and outside the Arabic and the Islamic world is still largely determined by Ernest Renan (1823–1892). Renan is said to be the first scholar to introduce critical historicism and a certain positivism into oriental studies. Under the influence of the Protestant Tübingen school of biblical studies he distanced himself from dogmatism. One of his early works is a *Histoire générale et système comparé des langues sémitiques* (1863), and he initiated the project *Corpus Inscriptionum Semiticarum.* In his *Vie de Jésus* (1863), he wrote, under the influence of the Leben-Jesu-Forschung a novel-like biography of Jesus Christ which cost him his chair at the Collège de France. And if Renan has dominated the reception of Ibn Rushd in Europe he has been possibly even more important for his reception in the modern Arab world. This was the result of his monumental study *Averroës et l'averroisme—Essai historique.*[6] Renan based his interpretation of Ibn Rushd's philosophy mainly on Hebrew and Latin translations, a fact which was duly noted and criticized by Max Horten (see below). He was, however, the first to collect the most important biographical material from the Arabic sources (Ibn 'Abbar, al-Ansari, Ibn Abi Usaibi'a, al-Dhahabi) and attempt a critical edition of these texts.

Renan was the loudest voice to proclaim that in Arabic philosophy as shown by Ibn Rushd the Aristotelian tradition had eliminated Islam and put itself at its place: "What is Arabic in this so-called Arab science? The language, nothing but the language. . . . Is it at least Muhammadan? Has Muhammadanism been in any way a support for those rational studies? In no way." This quotation comes from the well-known lecture published in the Parisian *Journal des Débats* of March 29, 1883.[7] It is well known that Renan thought he was paying Jamalaldin al-Afghani a high compliment when he said of him, "The freedom of his thought, his noble and loyal character, gave me the impression, while talking to him, that I had in front of me one of my ancient acquaintances, such as Avicenna or Averroës, or some other one of those great unbelievers who, for five centuries, upheld the tradition of the human spirit."[8]

It is understandable that more traditionally minded scholars resented this approach and objected to this view. According to Ignaz Goldziher, Renan's lecture was translated into Arabic and refuted by a certain "Hasan Efendi 'Asim" in a lithographed and undated edition.[9] And it is remarkable that in 1923, the Egyptian University of Cairo organized a celebration in honor of Ernest Renan's memory.[10] I do not know whether the proceedings of this celebration have ever been published completely. Mustafa 'Abdalraziq (1885–1947) delivered a lecture on the exchange between Renan and Jamaldaldin al-Afghani, a lecture which was then unfavorably commented upon by Rashid Rida in *al-Manar*.[11] Hourani comments on Mustafa 'Abdalraziq's book *Tamhid li-tarikh al-falsafa al-islamiyya*[12] by saying: "His book . . . is written within the context of nineteenth century rationalism. It is the ghost of Renan which haunts it."[13]

The "ghost of Renan" is at the same time one of the main protagonists of a specific dating of what Renan saw as the decline of rational culture in the Islamic world. In that he was not alone. There was almost unanimous agreement among scholars in nineteenth-century Europe that at some time in the twelfth or thirteenth century something irreversible had happened in the Islamic world, an event which was to lead to universal decay and decline causing a general torpor of any but the most repetitive intellectual activites. The crucial date set by Ernest Renan to mark this change of eras was Averroës's death in 1198. Since then a general state of *inhitat* was to be deplored. It was only in the nineteenth century that this era of *inhitat* was overcome—when the era of the *nahda* (renaissance) dawned. Without *inhitat* no *nahda*. And the *nahda* owed its existence to the influx of European ideas. So, in the eyes of many European scholars, the burning of Averroës's books, his exile, and his fall into oblivion are so many signals for what only later came to be termed decadence. The counter-movement was the Arab renaissance (*nahda*) of the nineteenth century, which has been declared a cornerstone of modern Arab intellectual history.

Like many French intellectuals of the nineteenth century who have often had a refreshingly blunt attitude toward complicated problems, Renan is not averse to sweeping statements. In the first two sentences of his crucial study *Averroës et l'Averroisme,* he states:

Averroës life occupies almost the whole twelfth century and is linked to all events of this decisive era for the history of Muslim civilization. The twelfth century saw the definitive failure of the attempt made by the Abbasids of the Orient and the Umayyads of Spain to create in Islam a rationalist and scientific development. When Ibn Rushd died in 1198 Arab philosophy lost in him its last representative, and the triumph of the Qur'an over free thought was assured for at least six hundred years.[14]

Is there anything historically verifiable in this statement, except for the dates? Is it true that the Abbasids and the Umayyads in al-Andalus wanted to create together a "rationalist and scientific" Islamism? It seems to me almost inconceivable that such a joint political effort existed at all. Did Arabic philosophy lose with Averroës's death its last representative? Only if we forget everyone between al-Iji (died 1355) and al-Bajuri (died 1861), who kept up the scholarly philosophical tradition. Finally: did in fact the Qur'an triumph over free thinking "for at least six hundred years"? We have only to remember Ibn Khaldun, who, after all, lived and worked in the thirteenth century, to see the fallacy of this argument. In an unobtrusive and suggestive way, Renan speaks first of "Muslim civilization" and "Islam," then of "Arabaic philosophy," and it is not very evident that he distinguishes between them.

But perhaps we should pay attention to the date 1198—the date of Ibn Rushd's death and what Renan makes of it. Renan tells us that "at least for six hundred years" since then free thought had been vanquished by the Qur'an. Adding six hundred years to 1198, we arrive at 1798—the exact date of the French "expedition" to Egypt. And I think that this was exactly what Renan had in mind. Since Averroës's death, Islam had been—if we take Renan seriously—under the "Qur'anic yoke" until Europe, or, to put it more exactly, Napoléon Bonaparte and his troops, brought enlightenment. The year 1798, the year of what was later called "la rupture coloniale," has been an almost magic date for the historiography of the Arabic and/or Islamic Middle East ever since. Then and only then, with the French army, modernity arrived, so claims Renan.

The period between 1198 and 1798 is for most historians of intellectual history in the Islamic East an epoch of darkness and asphyxiation. And it does not matter greatly whether one takes 1198 (Averroës's death) or 1258 (the Mongol capture of Baghdad) as the point of no return. The rise of the Ottoman Empire, the flourishing of the Moghul courts stand, of course, in strange opposition to this line of thought.

Renan did not completely overlook this point. But his explanation was of racist inadequacy:

> Arab philosophy offers the almost unique example of a very high culture
> which was almost immediately suppressed without leaving a trace and al-
> most forgotten by the people who created it. Islam revealed at this junc-
> ture what is incurably narrow in its genius. . . . Incapable of transform-
> ing itself and of admitting any element of civil or secular life, Islam tore
> out of its bosom any germ of rational culture. This fatal tendency was
> fought while the hegemony of Islam stayed in the hands of the Arabs, a
> race so fine and spiritual, or of the Persians, a race much given to spec-
> ulation, but it reigned without counter-weight since the barbarians (Turks,
> Berbers) took the rule of Islam.[15]

Renan's dating of Arab-Islamic intellectual history by making Averroës's death the beginning of a long era of universal decay was almost unbeliev-ably fashionable and is still dominating East and West. In the words of von Kügelgen, "Averroës's death becomes the turning point for European as well as Islamic intellectual history. Averroës becomes the symbol of the rise of European culture; to neglect him stands for the downfall of Islamic culture. As an Arabic Muslim philosopher he guarantees modernity."[16] Renan presented a historical vision which was shared by many if not most scholars. T. J. de Boer, author of the short and influential *History of Philosophy in Islam,* echoes Renan by saying about Averroës: "It looks as if the philosophy of the Muslims achieved in him the understanding of Aristotle only in order to die after having completed its course."[17]

An important school of thought has tried to revise this historical model. According to this "revisionist" school (Peter Gran, Reinhard Schulze, and others), there was an "Islamic eighteenth century," an intellectual movement toward modernity and enlightenment in the Ottoman Empire and elsewhere in the seventeenth and eighteenth centuries which corresponded to the European era of enlightenment but was independent of it.[18]

Max Horten

Max Horten (1874–1945) devoted his whole scholarly life to make Arabo-Islamic philosophy accessible to the Western reader.[19] His studies of Ibn Sina, Al-Farabi, al-Shirazi, Abu Hashim, al-Razi, al-Tusi, Abu Rashid go up to Muhammad 'Abduh. Next to Ibn Sina, the man he devoted most of his interest to was Ibn Rushd. Horten gave a condensed translation of the *Tahafut al-tahafut* into German[20] and attempted to sum up Ibn Rushd's system of metaphysics in *Die Metaphysik des Averroes.*[21] His general approach tries to show the main topics, the way of reasoning for each of these personalities from inside the texts, as it were. There is a lot of translation in each of these studies, and a lot of interpretation, schematization, and comparisons with Greco-Latin terminology. There were also, as Horten's critics were quick to point out, numerous mistranslations and misunderstandings. Horten was a deeply religious neo-Thomist with a natural inclination toward scholasticism bitterly resenting the positivistic antimetaphysical edges of contemporary German philosophy. Arabic-Islamic philosophy was for Horten an area where scholasticism still reigned supreme, a field in which metaphysical philosophy of Aristotelian dimensions was still possible. Horten deplored the "metaphysical blindness" of his orientalist colleagues and of the *zeitgeist* in general. His reconstruction of Islamic metaphysical systems was at the same time an apology for Christian theology as such and an antipositivist manifesto: "The Oriental takes from theology a deepening of religious experience and feeling and a heightening of his ethical motivation. For in theology all this is supported, motivated and vivified by a great system. Modern antipathies, which frequently only oppose the term "theology" and originate in an anti-metaphysical way of thinking have to be discarded."[22]

Horten is nowadays mainly remembered for his long and bitter polemical struggle with Louis Massignon. Horten had dealt also with the history of illuminationist theories (as-Suhrawardi, Molla Sadra Shirazi) and Islamic mysticism. And in the Sufis he thought he had discovered Indian influences, which brought him into sharp disagreement with Massignon, who insisted on understanding Islamic *tasawwuf* as an independent movement on its own terms. Horten's view of Islamic *tasawwuf* was generally rebuked.[23]

For Horten, Ibn Rushd was the "apologist of the Qur'an,"[24] an "apologist of Islam, whose sole endeavor was to reconcile Islam with the knowledge of his time"[25] and his position toward Ibn Rushd seems in this respect very close to Muhammad 'Abduh's position. On the whole, however, Horten's judgment of Ibn Rushd is surprisingly severe. According to Horten, Ibn Rushd was seriously overrated in Europe. The reason for this was what Horten called a medieval "optical delusion," by which expression Horten meant that in modern Europe Latin Averroism was identified with the teachings of Ibn Rushd. Horten says in his most popular book, *Die Philosophie des Islam*, "Averroës was one of the most reactionary and dependent spirits of the Islamic Orient. For him, philosophy was identical with

the philological establishment of what Aristotle had taught," and "Averroës'
attempt to nail down the human spirit on Aristotelian formulas had to fail
and can only be viewed as a symptom of decay of philosophy."[26]

Horten's great merit is that he put the nineteenth-century Arab re-
formists like Muhammad 'Abduh (1849–1905), the rector of the Azhar
Ibrahim b. Muhammad al-Bajuri (1783–1860), or Sayyid Abu l-Huda[27]
(died 1909), the famous Imam and confident of Abdülhamit II, firmly in the
line of Islamic philosophy. His essentialist vocabulary ("The Oriental . . .")
cannot be disclaimed, nor should we overlook that his book *Die Philosophie des Islams,* which was part of a series entitled *Geschichte der Philosophie in Einzeldarstellungen,* treated Islamic philosophy under the heading
"Das Weltbild der Primitiven und die Philosophie des Morgenlandes"
("The worldview of the primitive and the philosophy of the East"). Horten
was not responsible for this context. And it should in any case not make us
overlook that in his insistence on a surviving philosophical tradition in
Arabic and Islamic culture beyond Ibn Rushd's death, he may be closer to
historical truth than Renan was.

Ernst Bloch

The well-known German philosopher Ernst Bloch (1885–1977) developed, on the basis of Aristotelian and Hegelian concepts combined with
ideas of Judeo-Christian utopianism and principles of dialectical materialism and unorthodox socialism, a "philosophy of hope."[28] He was interested
in the phenomenon of religion and tried to trace postreligious elements of
enlightenment in established religious systems. In this vein, he wrote a
book, *Atheism in Christianity.*[29] And in his short article "Avicenna and the
Aristotelian Left," later to be published as a separate booklet, he tried to do
for Islam what he had tried to do for Christianity.[30] This article was an attempt to find a "subversive" materialist-atheist reading of the philosophies
of Avicenna and Averroës. As far as I can see, Bloch is the only contemporary Western philosopher who seriously tried to integrate, in the
persons of Avicenna and Averroës, medieval Arabic and Islamic philosophy into his own philosophy. A professor of philosophy in Leipzig, in
1955 Bloch received the National Prize of the German Democratic Republic. In 1957 he was prematurely and for ideological reasons forced to
retire. In 1961 he fled to the Federal Republic of Germany to become professor at Tübingen University and one of the best-known political refugees

in Germany. Bloch in Leipzig and Hermann Ley (born 1911), professor of philosophy in (East) Berlin, a specialist of medieval intellectual history, were the main channels through which the Syrian scholar Tayyib Tizini (born 1938) and others received the impulse of a Marxist reinterpretation of the history of Islamic philosophy and later of a program of cultural revolution.[31] This "subversive" reading of Averroës and Avicenna had its antecedents in attempts of Soviet historians to locate elements of materialist ideology in Islamic philosophy.

Bloch, who, of course, knew and had read Renan, developed a vision of Islamic philosophy which rested on the following premises: (1) Orthodox Islam was the main enemy of an Islamic "antifeudalist" philosophy and of the natural sciences; (2) Ibn Tufayl, Ibn Sina, and Ibn Rushd separated the secular from the religious and distinguished between religion and philosophy; (3) Ibn Rushd and Ibn Sina were pantheists, and pantheism was an important step in liberating man from religion; (4) Ibn Rushd's "naturalistic" concept of matter leads to the abolition of the Aristotelian dualism of (divine) form and (natural) matter. This indicates that basically Ibn Sina and Ibn Rushd can be seen as potential materialists and atheists.[32]

Bloch proves his case exclusively with quotations from Horten's German translations of Ibn Rushd and Ibn Sina, but violently attacks Horten's interpretation of both:

> It should not be disclaimed that the ex-Catholic theologian Max Horten, an Arabist not quite up to his enlightened topic, who translates, then comments on Avicenna and Averroes, denigrates these two "enlighteners," even denies their quality of enlightenment. Their naturalism is, according to Horten, not more than a "primitive misunderstanding" of scholasticism, facilitated by unsatisfactory Latin translations. According to Horten, Averroes changes surprisingly from an Anti-Orthodox to an "apologist of the Qur'an." This fits in badly with Averroes' "pantheist" tendency, which Horten cannot but concede. Regrettable is only that the Islamic orthodoxy in Averroes' time, which persecuted both Avicenna and Averroes and burnt their books, did not believe in their fidelity to the Qur'an, but defined this fidelity where it appeared as lip service. This clergy, unfortunately, registered the naturalism of the two philosophers more faithfully than a reactionary Arabist of today, post festum. And as far as the distinctly subversive effect of Averroism in the Christian Middle Ages is concerned, it seems that this "primitive misunderstanding" cannot be blamed on scholasticism whose least fault was primitivity.

Therefore, Avicenna and Averroes remain standing against the mufti-world of Islam. To assimilate them retroactively to this mufti-world is not a philology of reading-variants but a legend.[33]

Bloch, then, on the basis of his interpretation of Ibn Sina and Ibn Rushd, constructs a philosophical entity which he calls the "Aristotelian left." The term is coined following the established terms "Hegelian left" and "Hegelian right," two strands of post-Hegelian thought distinguish by historians of Hegelian philosophy after Hegel's death in 1831. The Hegelian right (F. H. W. Hinrichs, H. B. Oppenheim, J. E. Erdmann) opted for monarchy in Germany and tried to harmonize Hegel's religious philosophy with Christian orthodoxy. The Hegelian left (B. Bauer, L. Feuerbach) followed a liberal-democratic or even socialist course and developed a radical critique of established religion in the direction of pantheism or atheism. Bloch, in a bold analogy, constructs an "Aristotelian right" which in the Middle Ages led from Aristotle to Albertus Magnus and Thomas Aquinas and an "Aristotelian left" which led via Ibn Sina and Ibn Rushd to the Latin Averroists (Siger of Brabant) and via the universities of Paris and the Padova School to Giordano Bruno. According to Bloch, there is no absolutely neat separation between them; Christian scholasticism was not completely "right" and Avicenna and Ibn Rushd were not completely "left." But on the whole, Ibn Sina and Ibn Rushd belong to the Aristotelian left.

For Bloch, there are three main points in the teachings of this Aristotelian left: (1) The body-sould problem. Here, Averroës, in contradistinction to Avicenna, teaches the existence of an individual, human soul—but this soul ceases to exist with death; (2) The concept of "active reason" (*intellectus agens, 'aql fa "al*). This is a collective, nonindividual human capacity, a concept which in its essential points goes back to the teachings of Aristotle. In Bloch's terminology, it was against this doctrine of the Aristotelian left, namely the Latin Averroists, that the Aristotelian right, Albertus Magnus and Thomas Aquinas, wrote each a treatise *De unitate intellectus contra Averroistas* ("Of the unity of reason against the Averroists"); (3) The relationship between form and matter. This relationship implies the uncreatedness and therefore eternity of matter (*natura naturans*). The idea of a unique, divine causality does not have a place here.[34]

Bloch then reconstructs in the figure of Salomon Ibn Gabirol a pendant to the Aristotelian left, namely a "Neoplatonic left,"[35] which, he thought, lived on in various European pantheist "sects" (David of Dinant) and most brilliantly in Giordano Bruno. He goes on to say: "Philosophy became in the Orient as dangerous as natural sciences in Italy after the Galilei case."[36]

The link between Ibn Rushd's rationalism and enlightened thought with the concepts of atheism, agnosticism, and dialectical materialism was highly explosive. It was, to my mind, historically speaking for Ibn Rushd unsound and it was extremely counterproductive for the fate of the discussion of enlightenment in many parts of the Arab world. It had, of course, a Renanian tradition.

Hermann Ley

A leading authority on medieval European philosophy in the German Democratic Republic, Hermann Ley[37] (born 1911) was very influential for Syrian scholars like Tayyib Tizini and Nayif Balluz,[38] who studied in the GDR, as far as their reception of Ibn Rushd is concerned. An anti-orthodox reading of Ibn Rushd's philosophy was already foreshadowed by Friedrich Engel's statement that the life-centered free thought ("der lebenslustige Freisinn") of the Arabs was superior to that of the Roman peoples, that this prepared the coming of materialism and, therefore, of Marxism.[39] The most important Soviet experts in the field were probably S. N. Grigorian and his *From the History of the Philosophy of Central Asia and Iran in the 7th to 12th Centuries* and A. V. Saghadeev, *Ibn Rushd*.[40] This characterization of Ibn Rushd's teachings as a materialist transformation of Aristotle was to become standard Marxist-Leninist understanding and gained access to works like the *Great Soviet Encyclopedia.*

So it was against the leading Marxist ideology and therefore somewhat surprising when Dieter Bellmann, Arabist at the University of Leipzig, with a stroke of the pen and depending on Marx Horten, dismissed Bloch and Ley's whole theory by stating, "It can be accepted as a fact that al-Farabi . . . and Ibn Sina . . . as well as al-Gazali . . . and Ibn Rushd . . . used their natural scientific and philosophical 'knowledge' to substantiate and defend Islam and not to refute it."[41]

Bassam Tibi

Born in Damascus in 1944, Bassam Tibi teaches political science at Göttingen University and is a well known and prolific writer on the modern Middle East. Influenced by Theodor Adorno and Max Horkheimer (the so-

called Frankfurt school) and a student of Iring Fetscher, Tibi's view of Ibn
Rushd's philosophy comes very close to the one advocated by Roger Ga-
raudy in the latter's Marxist phase and to the just-mentioned views of
Ernst Bloch:

> The young Arab bourgeoisie had only its name in common with the Eu-
> ropean bourgeoisie of the period of enlightenment. It led a clerico-feu-
> dalist existence; its spirit owed more to Islamic orthodoxy than to Avi-
> cenna, Averroes, and Ibn Khaldun. These thinkers were even a great
> danger to the Arab bourgeoisie. Avicenna's and Averroes's naturalism and
> Ibn Khaldun's materialist philosophy of history are not so far from sci-
> entific socialism. In the last analysis, Marxism cannot limit itself to its
> Western sources.[42]

This resembled the view of Roger Garaudy. While still a leading Marxist
he wrote, "An Islamically educated Arab had had his utopian socialism in
the Qarmati movement, he based his rationalist and dialectical tradition on
Averroes, he sees the predecessor of historical materialism in Ibn Khaldun."[43]

Conclusions

1. The history of the reception of Ibn Rushd in nineteenth- and twentieth-century Europe inside and outside the orientalist tradition shows that
the question of what Ibn Rushd "really stood for" is unanswerable. The debates about what Ibn Rushd could mean today were remarkably independent of the research done in viewing and appraising the corpus of Ibn
Rushd's writings. Ibn Rushd was selectively interpreted almost indepen-
dently of the increase of reliable editions of Ibn Rushdian texts. Ibn Rushd's
name was claimed for the most contradictory currents. He was less remembered than discovered, less reconstructed than invented. In this respect, European and non-European interpretations were remarkably similar.

2. Ibn Rushd was seen as a precursor of the European Enlightenment—and I think this is a view which fitted and still fits into our time.
This is not a question which can be put in terms of: Did Ibn Rushd really
and objectively hold enlightened views? History is always the history of
people who write history. There is a legitimate element of reconstruction
in all historical views. Coming from a German tradition, I am perhaps par-

doned to quote Immanuel Kant, one of the fathers of German philosophy and of European enlightenment. "Enlightenment means:" Kant said, "Have the courage to use your judgment." And when asked, "Are we living in an enlightened age today?" he would answer, "No. But we are living in an age of enlightenment."[44]

Any judgment is, of course, always partially determined by history, and by social and cultural reality. Partially determined but not wholly determined. We can learn from Ibn Rushd and Immanuel Kant that there is no such thing as a definite stage of enlightenment, a stage forever completely and triumphantly achieved. Enlightenment is always a process bound to history. Ibn Rushd knew the Qur'an, and he knew it very well. He knew Islamic law, and he knew it very well. He knew Aristotle, and knew him very well. As a judge and a man of politics, he also knew the political, social, and cultural issues of his time very well. If enlightenment in the Kantian and in the Ibn Rushdian sense means basically to have the courage to use one's rational judgment, this judgment always pertains to a certain time and a certain space. I am not sure that the answers—some of them? all of them?—which Ibn Rushd found are appropriate now. I tend to think that the important points were not so much the answers as the questions that Ibn Rushd asked. And I am sure that Ibn Rushd's major importance lies in the fact that he combined a complete mastery of his own cultural background—he was the foremost Maliki scholar of his time—with a deep understanding of what was at this time contemporary scholarship. In Ibn Rushd's time, this cosmopolitan scholarship was embodied in Aristotelian philosophy. Let us try to do what he did, that is, know our own cultural background well, be aware of the social, political, and cultural issues and problems of our time, and have the courage to use all reserves of international academic scholarship and finally our own judgment to solve them. Then, even if somebody burns our books, our ideas will live.

Notes

1. Anke von Kügelgen, *Averroes und die arabische Modern. Ansätze zu einer Neubegründung des Rationalismus im Islam* (Leiden, 1994).

2. Thomas van Erpe, *Grammatica Arabica quinque libris methodice explicata* (Leiden, 1613).

3. Felix Klein-Franke, *Die klassische Antike in der Tradition des Islam, Erträge der Forschung,* vol. 136 (Darmstadt, 1980), p. 54

4. M. J. Müller, *Philosophie und Theologie von Averroes* (Munich, 1859). Cf. Max Horten, *Geschichte der Philosophie* (Munich, 1924), p. 329, n. 97.

5. Johann Fück, *Die arabischen Studien in Europa bis in den Anfang des 20 Jahrhunderts* (Leipzig, 1955), p. 173.

6. Ernest Renan, *Averroès et l'averroisme—Essai historique,* 3d ed. (Paris, 1866). Also in *Oeuvres Complètes* (Paris, 1949).

7. Ernest Renan, "L'islamisme et la science," in *Discours et Conférences* (Paris, 1887), pp. 402–409. Compare also "Der Islam und die Wissenschaft," lecture held in the Sorbonne on March 29, 1883, here quoted following Klein-Franke, *Die Klassische Antike,* p. 122. See also Elie Kedourie, *Afghani and 'Abduh. An Essay on Religious Unbelief and Political Activism in Modern Islam* (London, 1966), p. 41 and n. 131. This lecture was then commented upon by Jamalaldin al-Afghani in *Journal des Débats* of May 18, 1883.

8. Kedourie, *Afghani,* p. 42. Compare also Lord Cromer's verdict on Muhammad 'Abduh in J. J. G. Jansen: "I suspect that my friend Abdu . . . was in reality an Agnostic" in *Acta Orientalia Neerlandica,* Proceedings of the Congress of the Dutch Oriental Society, Leiden, May 8–9, 1970, P. W. Pestman, ed. (Leiden, 1971), pp. 71–74.

9. *Enzyklopädie des Islam,* 1st ed., s.v. al-Afghani, reprinted in H. A. R. Gibb and J. H. Kramers, eds., *Shorter Encyclopedia of Islam,* p. 85.

10. Kedourie, *Afghani,* p. 45.

11. Ibid., pp. 45f. and ns. 138–41.

12. Mustafa 'Abdalragiz, *Tamhid li-tarikh al-falsafa al-islamiyya* (Cairo, 1944).

13. A. Hourani, *Arabic Thought in the Liberal Age, 1798–1939* (Cambridge: Cambridge University Press, 1983), p. 163.

14. Renan, *Averroès et l'averroisme,* p. 1f.

15. Ibid., p. iiif.

16. Von Kügelgen, *Averroes und die arabische Moderne,* p. 414. Further examples include H. H. Schaeder, "Der Eintritt der Araber in die Weltgeschichte," in id., *Der Mensch in Orient und Okzident, Grundzüge einer eurasiatischen Geschichte* (Munich, 1960), p. 214. A different article by Schaeder, "Der Orient und das griechische Erbe," ibid., pp. 107ff., had been made known in the Arab world by a translation into Arabic done by 'Abdarrahman Badawi. Compare "Al-naz a al-insaniyya fi l-fikr al-'arabi," in *Al-Insaniyya wa-l-wujudiyya fi l-fikr al-'arabi, Dirasat islamiyya* 4 (Cairo, 1947), pp. 3–64; and id., *Ruh al-hadara al-'arabiyya, Dirasat islamiyya* 10 (Beirut, 1949), pp. 13f. Compare Jörg Kraemer, *Das Problem der islamischen Kulturgeschichte* (Tübingen, 1959), pp. 6, 26f., and the examples given by von Kügelgen, op. cit., p. 9, n. 48.

17. T. J. de Boer, *Geschichte der Philosophie im Islam* (Stuttgart, 1901), p. 167.

18. Compare, for example, Reinhard Schulze, "Das islamische achtzehnte Jahrhundert. Versuch einer historiographischen Kritik," in *Die Welt des Islams* 30 (1990): 140–59.

19. Otto Spies, "Max Horten 1874–1945" in *Bonner Gelehrte, Beiträge zur Geschichte der Wissenschaften in Bonn, Sprachwissenschaften (150 Jahre Rheinische Friedrich-Wilhelms-Universität, Bonn 1818–1968,* Bonn, 1970), pp. 327–29. Horten received a doctorate of theology in Jerusalem at the School of the Dominicans, a doctorate of philosophy in Beirut at the Universite St. Joseph with Louis Cheikho, and a doctorate of philosophy in Bonn in 1904, with a dissertation on al-Farabi. His 1906 *Habilitation* in Bonn was called "Semitic Philology and Islamkunde." From 1929 to 1935 he was a librarian in Breslau. Horten issued polemics against Louis Massignon on the genesis of Islamic mysticism. The best-known summary of his views is *Die Philosophie des Islams in Ihren Beziehungen zu den philosophischen Weltanschauungen des westlichen Orients* (*Geschichte der Philosophie in Einzeldarstellungen,* Abt. I: *Das Weltbild der Primitiven und die Philosophie des Morgenlandes,* Bd. 4) (Munich, 1924). Horten was a neo-scholasticist.

20. Max Horten, *Die Hauptlehren des Averroes nach seiner Schrift: Die Widerlegung des Gazali* (Bonn, 1913).

21. Max Horten, *Die Metaphysik des Averroes* (Bonn, 1912).

22. Horten, *Geschichte der Philosophie,* p. 192.

23. Compare H. H. Schaeder's critique in *OLZ* 30 (1927): 834–48.

24. Horten, *Hauptlehren* IV, AvK 15.

25. Horten, *Die Philosophie des Islams,* p. 86.

26. Ibid., p. 63.

27. For Abu l'Huda compare Werner Ende, "Sayyid Abu l'Huda, ein Vertrauter Abülhamid's II. Notwendigkeit und Probleme einer kritischen Biographie" in *Zeitschrift der Deutschen Morgenländischen Gesellschaft,* supp. III.2 (XIX. Deutscher Orientalistentag, September 28 to October 4, 1975, in Freiburg im Breisgau, Wiesbaden, 1977), pp. 1143ff.

28. Ernst Bloch, *Philosophie der Hoffnung* (Tübingen, 1965).

29. Ernst Bloch, *Atheismus im Christentum. Zur Religion des Exodus und des Reichs,* 1968.

30. Ernst Bloch, *Avicenna und die Aristotelische Linke* (Berlin, 1952; 2nd ed., Berlin, 1963).

31. Von Kügelgen, *Averroes und die arabische Moderne,* pp. 237ff.

32. Ibid., pp. 239f.

33. Bloch, *Avicenna,* pp. 29f.

34. Ibid., p. 33.

35. Ibid., p. 56.

36. Ibid., p. 62.

37. Among Hermann Ley's works are *Avicenna* (Berlin, 1923); *Studien zur*

Geschichte des Materialismus im Mittelalter (Berlin: Batunsky, 1970); of this, there is also a Russian translation (Batunsky); "Avicennas militanter Humanismus" in *Avicenna*, vol. 1, pp. 17–37; "Ibn Sina (Avicenna, 980–1037): Gründe für 1000 Jahre Rückerinnerung" in *Deutsche Zeitschrift f. Philosophie* (Berlin, 1980), pp. 1309–23; reprinted in *Islamic Studies in the German Democratic Republic*, special issue 10 (Berlin, 1982).

38. Von Kügelgen, *Averroes und die arabische Moderne*, pp. 237ff.

39. Friedrich Engels, *Dialektik der Natur* (Batunsky).

40. S. N. Grigorian, *Iz istorii filosofi Crednei Azii i Irana VII–XII* (Moscow, 1960), and A. V. Saghadeev, *Ibn Rushd* (Moscow, 1974).

41. Dieter Bellmann, "Bourgeois Arab Theories on the Cultural Function of Islam in Society," in *Islamic Studies in the German Democratic Republic* 10 (1982): 162.

42. Bassam Tibi, *Die arabische Linke* (Frankfurt am Main, 1969), pp. 9f.

43. As quoted in Tibi, *Die arabische Linke,* p. 10; Roger Garaudy, *Marxismus im 20. Jahrhundert* (Hamburg, 1969), p. 31.

44. Compare Immanuel Kant, "Beantwortung der Frage: Was ist Aufklärung?" *Werke* IV, p. 174, quoted by Peter Gay, *The Enlightenment: An Interpretation* (New York, 1966), p. 20; Joel Kraemer, *Humanism in the Renaissance of Islam. The Cultural Revival During the Buyid Age* (Leiden, New York, Cologne, 1992), pp. 147f.

15

Secularization in Turkey

Ioanna Kuçuradi
Professor of Philosophy,
Hacettepe University (Turkey)

To speak about secularization in Turkey is to show what Atatürk's revolution tried to achieve, *by means* of certain changes decided on in the 1920s and 1930s, by the Parliament of the newly established Republic of Turkey.

Let me first tell you what I understand from "revolution," that is, remind you of Albert Camus's conceptualization of revolution, which I find a very successful one. According to Camus "revolution" denotes "an injection of new ideas into historical reality,"[1] an "injection" of ideas which changes the "natural" course of history.

Now, if we look at Atatürk's revolution in the light of such a concept of revolution, it is possible to see (1) that it is a *cultural revolution* carried out politically; (2) that the main ideas and principles that Atatürk wanted to "inject" into the historical reality of Turkey show a specificity, which, I am afraid, even many people in Turkey are still not sufficiently aware of, that is, they are *ideas and principles deduced from the knowledge of the value of certain human potentialities;* and (3) the way those ideas and principles were "injected" appears to be different from the way followed in other, in fact very few, similar attempts. The changes made in Atatürk's

time in education and in matters related to education, constitute the core of
this revolution.

In connection with the first point: if by "culture" in this context we understand the world view and the conceptions of man and of what is considered valuable—including the norms—that prevail for a longer or shorter
time in a given group and determine all the expressions of life in that group,[2]
it is not difficult to see that on the one hand, the radical changes of social
institutions made in Atatürk's time are based on a *totally* different world
view and conception of what is valuable from those prevailing until his time;
and on the other hand, that the purpose of these social and legal changes was
to introduce those totally different views and conceptions in Turkey. "If we
saved ourselves within five or six years, this happened because we changed
our mentality"[3] he says in a speech he delivered in Kastamonu in 1925. And
in his opening address to the Parliament on November 1, 1937, he speaks
of "the great Turkish nation, which has accomplished a revolution not only
in its institutions but in its thinking as well."

Compared with the very few revolutions in the above-mentioned sense,
made until that time, compared, for example, with the French Revolution,
Atatürk's revolution shows the following striking specificity: the French
Revolution was an attempt to make the changes of world view, conceptions
of man and of what is valuable, that resulted from the Enlightenment in Europe, that is, to make certain changes that *had already occurred* in the intellectual world of Europe but had no impact on the social order, or determine this order. It was an attempt to change and reshape the prevailing
social relations according to *these historically new* ideas and conceptions
resulting from the Enlightenment. In other words: it was an attempt to
"modernize" or "secularize" the society in the etymological sense of the
term "secular" (*saecularis*), which means—among other things—"belonging to the age," that is, an attempt to *adjust* the social order to the new
ideas developed *there, in the same space,* where that order prevailed. This
was a secularization of the society, a reshaping of social relations, once established according to norms of the Christian religion, now according to lay
principles, yet *principles resulting from the Enlightenment.*

This historical background of secularization in Europe—provided that
no attention is paid to the specificity of the principles on which it is
based—is perhaps the reason why secularization or *laïcité* is now very
often defined as "separation of the state from the church or from religion."
This is nevertheless only a "negative" definition, in the technical sense of

the term, a definition which states nothing about the *specificity* of the ideas and principles on which secularization or "modernization" was based and which at present causes many difficulties in understanding the importance of secularization.

Atatürk's revolution is also an attempt to modernize the Turkish society, no doubt. Still, what distinguishes this attempt is, among other things, that its aim was to introduce to the reality of Turkey ideas and conceptions which were developed *not* in Turkey, but elsewhere. Atatürk and his collaborators tried to make first these ideas, which were the product of another intellectual world but which were proved to be more appropriate for the development of certain human potentialities, determine the order of social relations, *so that* this kind of idea and conception can develop and further develop also in Turkey. Thus considered, Atatürk's revolution appears to be a cultural revolution, carried out politically, through the modernization of the legal system and of the social institutions. It is a cultural revolution decided and opted for, as a whole, by the Parliament of the newly established Republic of Turkey under the leadership of Atatürk—a revolution aiming at introducing the ideas and conceptions of Enlightenment in Turkey.

The laws related to education, which were enforced by the Parliament in the 1920s, can show us what Atatürk aimed at and how he set these aims. These laws and the relevant debates in the Parliament are testimony to a most penetrating insight of Atatürk, an awareness of his, which we do not see at present in Turkey nor in the present world as a whole. This is the awareness of the necessity to avoid making valid *simultaneously* incompatible or contradictory principles and norms *on the same issue* and in general.

Avoiding this presupposes an evaluation of ideas and principles, as well as an evaluation of norms in the light of philosophical value knowledge. If no differentiation between ideas, principles, and norms is made from the viewpoint of their value—that is, if an idea, a principle, or any norm in general, is accepted without scrutinizing and answering the question whether in a given real situation it contributes to or hinders the creation of possibilities necessary for the actualization of certain human potentialities—or if all ideas and norms are considered to be *equal in value,* as certain fashionable views claim at present, then people can very easily establish incompatible norms that exclude each other in practice, something that leads to a chaos in which it is impossible to find a clue.

The enforcement of the *Tevhid-i Tedrisat Kanunu* (the Law for the Unification of Education) in Turkey in 1924 and the way that Atatürk followed in this respect, constitute an example of Atatürk's insight that I just mentioned. In a speech that he delivered in Bursa in 1922, that is, before the establishment of the republic, Atatürk says, "Nations which want to preserve logically unjustifiable traditions and beliefs can scarcely develop, if they can develop at all."

The main "places" where such traditions and beliefs were transmitted were the traditional schools and *Medresses,* in which the great majority of the children were trained. In addition to these schools a few modern schools and colleges were established in a few cities, starting in Selim III's time (at the end of the eighteenth century) and continuing in Mahmut II's time (in the middle of the nineteenth century). These incompatible educational institutions run parallel to each other.

Atatürk saw the problem. In a speech he delivered in Izmir in 1923 he mentioned, for the first time publicly, the necessity of the unification of education: "We have a problem," he says, "which, though obvious, everybody avoids to touch. What will become of the *Medresses*? . . . The educational institutions in our country must be unified. All children, young boys and girls, must be educated in the same way." The expression "in the same way" means obviously here "only in the modern schools."

Immediately after this speech Atatürk started paving the way for such a unification: in a speech he made in the Parliament on March 1, 1923, Atatürk speaks of the necessity of unifying the Ministry of Religious Law and Pious Foundations with the Ministry of Education. A hundred years of experience had shown that it is impossible to bring together the old institutions and the new ones and to synthesize medieval and modern mentalities.

Atatürk waited for the collaboration of these ministries for a whole year. But since this collaboration did not take place, Atatürk put the matter in the Parliament, on March 1, 1924, as follows: "We see that the public opinion favors an immediate application of the principle of unification of education. The danger of a postponement and the advantages of a rapid action must lead to a quick decision." The next day the Law for the Unification of Education was submitted to the Parliament by the Deputy of Samsun Vasef Bey, who justified his proposal by the harm that the parallel functioning of the incompatible educational systems had caused.

On March 3, 1924, the Parliament voted for the abolishment of the Ministry of Religious Law and Pious Foundations as well as for the Law for the Unification of Education. With the latter law all schools and *Medresses,* which were administered by the above-mentioned ministry or by private foundations, together with all other schools under the Ministry of Health and the army, were attached to the Ministry of Education.

Laws like those for "mixed education" (according to which boys and girls should be trained in the same schools), for the change of script and alphabet and the reorganization of Istanbul University in 1933, were further steps in carrying out the educational revolution in Turkey—a revolution aiming at Enlightenment in the Kantian sense: at "man's leaving his self-caused immaturity," which is "the incapacity to use one's intelligence without the guidance of another" and which is "self-caused if it is not caused by lack of intelligence, but by lack of determination and courage to use one's own intelligence without being guided by another."[4]

Thus, Atatürk's revolution appears to be an attempt to *secularize thinking* in Turkey, that is, to change the prevailing world view, conception of man, and the prevailing relevant norms *through* the secularization of social institutions and law.

The main ideas and conceptions that Atatürk tried to "inject" into the historical reality of Turkey are those of the Enlightenment, rather than the "positivistic world view," as is often assumed. And the basic principles on which he tried to base the new republic are the kind of principles we call today human rights.

This is what Atatürk tried to do. We have nevertheless to be well aware of the fact that *any* kind of ideas and norms—old or new ones—can be "injected" into a historical reality in the same way.

What we observe at present almost all over the world, also in some circles in Turkey, is a *desecularization of thinking*, for the moment, which is not only supported in many countries by religious fundamentalisms, but is also promoted by the demand to respect equally all cultures.

As long as we are unable to see the epistemological and axiological differences of world views, conceptions of man and of norms, that is, so long as we do not evaluate them philosophically before we attempt to promote any of them, the enemies of Enlightenment—be they well-minded or not, ignorant or very conscious of what they try to do—will gain more and more ground.

Thus, at the turn of the millennium we stand, as humanity, before a crucial choice: either to put enlightenment as one of the main objectives of education, which amounts to giving due place to the teaching of philosophy as a *cognitive field* of human endeavor, or, amid "the winds of freedom," to let the natural course of events lead where it runs: to a new Middle Ages.

Notes

1. *L'homme révolté* (Editions de la Pléiade, 1965), p. 516.
2. "Culture" in the plural sense, as I call it. For further distinctions, please see my "Cultures and World Culture," *Philosophy and Culture IV* (Montréal, 1988), pp. 457–60.
3. For all quotations from Atatürk's speeches, see "Atatürk," in *Islam Ansiklopedisi.*
4. "Was ist Aufklärung?" *Kants Werke* (Berlin: Akademieausgabe, 1968), p. 35.

16

Enlightenment in the Islamic World: Muslims—Victims of Mneumonic Success

Ghazala Irfan
Assistant Professor of Philosophy,
University of the Punjab (Pakistan)

As a student of philosophy I should define my terms before I embark upon my topic Enlightenment in the Islamic world. The question is: since the Islamic world is not a monolith and is as diverse as Saudi Arabia and Indonesia is there a unitary term of reference? Perhaps not. Also since the Muslims have been on the globe since 622 C.E. can I refer to them all as living in the here and the now and talk of them in general or as a stereotype? Definitely not. And so if my terms of reference are too broad and too extended do I have a reference at all? If my purview was historical, i.e., if I was discussing socio-politico-cultural issues I would have to demarcate spatial areas and temporal zones. However, I am taking the liberty of confining myself to a neuro-cognitive analysis of the mindset that has characterized the Muslim Weltanschauung.

Let me also acknowledge in advance the basic assumption I bring to my research:

Knowledge is like a kaleidoscope to which different civilizations have contributed. No one is better than the other in absolute terms; no one can be judged vis-à-vis the other or in terms of the other. Knowledge is a human enterprise. It is no one's legacy. Each one of us can partake of it ontogenetically or phylogenetically to the extent that we are able, so that there is no perfect model for others to emulate. However, despite the diversity we bring to this collective enterprise we can continue to analyze and evaluate and improve both within and without our unique contributions. It is in this spirit that I subtitle my paper "Muslims—Victims of Mneumonic Success."

"The magical number seven plus or minus two."[1] is the norm in the human information storage system called memory. The Muslims can boast of exceptional success in both number and verbal memory. The authenticity of the Qur'an is based on mneumonic virtuosity of storing and retrieving. Rhythm and rhyme facilitate the recall. Speaking out loud promotes the effect. Accuracy is guaranteed by the reliability of memory retained over years. God's word would have been distorted and adulterated but for skilled memory and recitation. Mneumonic devices therefore have a special place in Islamic theology. Preservation, perpetuation, and propagation of the message was dependent on one cognitive process—memory, which increased dramatically with drilling practices. It became all the more fundamental since imagery was a taboo and icons a blasphemy.

The paradox is that the acquisition of memory skills do not promote either the transfer of knowledge to other domains or the application and use of knowledge in other areas. For knowledge to be akin to power it must be both efficient, which it was, and effective, which it failed to become. It should increase comprehension and problem solving strategies. I should also dwell on the higher order of cognition, i.e., intelligence, concept formation, and logical activity. These are at the tail end of the information-processing chain. On the other hand, memory, together with perception, tends to occur earlier in the information-processing sequence. These components are not isolated from each other so that there is an integrated system. Only memory is inherently less complex than thinking, which involves the mental attributes of judging, abstracting, reasoning, imagining, problem solving, and creativity.

Let us not undermine the merits of memory. Much research has revolved around a "search for the elusive engram" or the trace and locus of neural changes that represent memory in the brain. It is taken to be both localized and distributed—"localized in the sense that peculiar brain systems represent specific aspects of each event and it is distributed in the sense that many neural systems participate in representing a whole event."[2] However, Larry Squire also suggests that memory may be more localized and be stored in the same neural systems that participate in perception. If this hypothesis is confirmed, it may force us to conclude that the Muslims used only a limited part of their brain—memory being cramped within a calcified vessel weighing only one-and-a-half kilograms.

The PET or PETT (positron emission transaxial tomography) scans seem to reinforce this hypothesis by being able to localize brain functions in different brain regions. In different experiments cerebral blood has been measured to show that episodic or personal memory experience and semantic or general-knowledge memory systems are supported by different regions of the brain. Tulving's research indicates, for example, that "the anterior regions of the cortex seem to be more involved in episodic memory than the posterior regions."[3]

In the 1950s research indicated two plainly visible parts of the brain. These were known as the right and left hemispheres of the cerebral cortex. Identical in appearance the two differ in function. The left hemisphere was associated with special functions such as language, conceptualization, analysis, and classification. The right hemisphere was associated with more mundane tasks such as getting dressed or knowing one's way around a city, recognition of faces and shapes, spatial processing, and integration of information over time as in art and music. Subsequent research endowed the right hemisphere with linguistic processing, especially written language. These findings tend to support the argument for localizations of functions as well. The question is did the Muslims neglect to use the left-hemisphere? And if evolution of hemisphere specialization be associated with flexibility of thought and "generativity" (ability to combine elements using rules to create new associations), then did the Muslims confine themselves unnecessarily?

In modern research neurologists support the view that some gross brain functions are related to specific areas, especially speech. The fascination of searching for the locus of the mind has an ancient tradition as well. Egyptian hieroglyphics suggest that knowledge is localized in the heart. Aristotle held the same notion although Plato maintained that the brain was the locus of the mind. What is of prime interest is how knowledge is represented in the mind, i.e., the question of acquisition, storage, transformation, and use of knowledge. The main theme to be traced is the line of demarcation between the structure or the makeup of knowledge and the process or the operations and functions of knowledge. Structure tends to be static while process is active. This dichotomy is disputable for processes, which, although constantly in flux, act in conjunction with the structure. Psychologists, however, continued to emphasize one or the other. Historically, Ebbinghaus presented the first scientific account of memory experiments (*On Memory,* 1885) by working on nonsense syllables. Structural properties were explored by William James in 1890 who introduced primary and secondary memory. Later hypothetical structures of short-term and long-term memory, pre-perceptual stores such as iconic (sensory) or echoic (auditory) memory became part of the experimental literature. Human memory was explained as "boxes in the head."

Without going into the details of historical interests, but not unmindful of the fact that the study of memory continues to be both interesting and enigmatic, let us move from structure to processes to connections. Neurocognitive studies now indicate that knowledge transcends a structural network based solely on memory. Connectionism or PDP asserts that knowledge is within the connections between pairs of units. Conventionally it was thought that knowledge is collected and stored in memory. What would be the implications of this drastic revision? To begin with the difference between knowledge and information may be necessary. Information may be derived from senses and may be stored in memory, but information is not the same as knowledge. Knowledge includes the organization of information in memory. Philosophers distinguish between declarative knowledge and procedural knowledge; declarative knowledge is explicit and factual while procedural knowledge is implicit and is demonstrated through performance. One example of this is knowing that a bicycle has two wheels and handlebars is declarative but riding it is procedural. One does not necessarily lead to the other. Another example may be cited from swimming where declarative knowledge of floating, body movements, and breathing in water does not ensure being actually able to swim. Epistemologists refer to this distinction as "knowing what" and "knowing that" the former being based, as in episodic recall, specifically on memory whereas knowing that or knowing how refers to skill learning. Procedural knowledge also incorporates the performance of various cognitive activities, for it has a marked problem-solving organization. It also presumes that human cognition is always purposeful, directed to achieving goals, and to removing obstacles to those goals. The prime example of procedural knowledge is the knowledge of the grammar of our first language. This knowledge is not something we can articulate but can display it in using the language.

Now if the knowledge available to the Muslim is memory-based and memory-bound, i.e., primarily declarative and information storing, rather than using it in novel permutations, it automatically remains stagnant and incapable of growth. Also, any trace of procedural knowledge would atrophy from disuse. The phenomena of functional fixedness and *Einstellung* effect reinforce this hypothesis. Functional fixedness refers to the failure to solve a problem due to inability to experiment with objects or environment in novel ways; *Einstellung* or set effect is a mechanization of thought which prompts a problem solver to become biased due to availability of previous knowledge. It thereby inhibits rather than facilitates. Conversion of declarative factual knowledge of a domain into procedural representation is therefore an imperative that Muslims are advised to pursue. In all earnestness let it be pointed out that chess players—supposedly the whiz kids regarding cognitive activity—are not particularly more intelligent in domains other than chess. This narrowness of expertise is an all-pervasive pattern so much so that memory-span skills cannot be transferred from digits to letters. No wonder Hafiz-e-Qurans could never be considered sages. The exception to prove the rule was Avicenna who had memorized the Qur'an by age ten.

The case of the person who scored the highest scores obtained on tasks involving memorization in an experiment conducted by Hunt and Love in 1972 is a case in point. Despite the high score of 136 in IQ tests (Wechsler Adult Intelligence scale) he confessed that he had difficulty putting lead in a pencil.

What is of concern to educators, since most of us here are academics, is that transfer in knowledge is very narrow in scope so that people learn a variety of narrow responses to very specific stimuli only.

Similarly, from studies of experts all available evidence indicates that there are very definite bounds on how far skills will transfer, for expertise in one domain does not guarantee success in another area. Positive transfer occurs only to the extent that the two domains involve the same knowledge, i.e., use of the same facts, productions, and patterns. The only positive side to this specificity in the transfer of skills is that there is hardly any negative transfer in which learning one skill makes a person worse at learning another skill. The clearly documented kind of negative transfer, however, is the set effect. Thus with Muslims memory training, drilling, and development did not ensure optimal performance in other cognitive domains. Despite that, in the education system in Pakistan today, for instance, rote learning is the modus operandi so that memory devices continue to remain rampant. Let us peruse common college-study-skills courses designed to improve memory for text material to analyze whether mneumonic devices in themselves really are successful. The central feature of these modern-day techniques, strangely enough, is their question-generation and question-answering characteristics. It may sound paradoxical but may be the moot issue—that which contributes most, even to good memory, is question making. Two of the more publicly accessible techniques are the SQ3R or later PQ4R methods of Robinson (1961 & 1972). Let us examine the latter. The PQ4R method derives its name from the six phases it advocates. These are:

1. Preview
2. Question
3. Read
4. Reflect
5. Recite
6. Review

The important component of the PQ4R technique is reviewing the text with questions in mind.

Perhaps the Muslims' passion for certainty, since they are the repositories of infallible knowledge and truth, bar them from pandering to their inherent curiosity. Maybe a shift from certainty to probability may enlighten them. The deductive logic model of Aristotle, which inspired and influenced the Muslims, only reinforced the inclination toward certainty, for in a deductively valid argument the conclusion must be certain, provided both the premises are true. In contrast, in the inductive logic model the conclusion can only be probable even if the premises are true. Thus in the deductive model:

If all residents of Pakistan like mangoes and x is a resident of Pakistan, then x likes mangoes is true.

In the inductive model:

If x likes mangoes and is a resident of Pakistan and
y likes mangoes and is a resident of Pakistan,
then if z is a resident of Pakistan, the assumption that he likes mangoes is only probable.

Of course, deduction and induction are complementary to each other. Rather we can distinguish between them only in theory and not in fact. However, the focus on one rather than the other has important consequences.

Now therefore if logical systems and reasoning consist of rules of inference that permit true conclusions to be derived from true premises but which conclusions are either certain or probable, the question here would be why not choose to look where the light is and so why settle for probability when certainty is guaranteed. The irony is that the choice seems so very logical in itself. The problem with certainty is that further questioning seems irrelevant and further inquiry seems redundant. Thus conjectured knowledge or hypotheses formation, evaluation, and judgment, activities that promote enlightenment, were far from the Muslim purview. Also the nature of God in Islam, as in all monotheistic religions, being all-comprehensive and all-pervasive, and being not just omnipotent (all-powerful) but omniscient (all-knowledgeable), left a small world for the Muslim to explore. If all that we can know is either limited or wrong, why not abandon the process of knowing to one who is able and capable of knowing. Since this God is not reluctant to impart and transfer his knowledge, why compromise on quality? Why not inherit the knowledge that is infallible? This may be the reason that knowledge in the Islamic mold is content-based rather than process-based, the emphasis being on "what" as previously mentioned rather than the "how" to acquire or the even more subversive "why."

The other more redeeming feature of this complete infallible knowledge is that it is not time-barred but eternal. Consequently the process of having to combat obsolescence or the self-renewing and self-revising activity remained foreign to the Islamic mindset. Even *ijtihad* was confined within certain parameters. There was no concept of free inquiry per se. The entire gamut of knowledge was in fact defined in terms of faith, faith being the more basic and the most fundamental of all terms.

Let us now divert our attention to what is referred to as higher-order cognition, i.e., thinking or what occurs temporally toward the end of the sequence of information processing. By bringing out the salient features of thinking one may, by contrast, be able to identify the essence of the human genius. Solso[4] defines it as a "process by which a new mental representation is formed through the transformation of information by complex interaction of the mental attributes of judging, abstracting, reasoning, imagining, and problem solving." What distinguishes thinking from memory is that in thinking information is transformed rather than retained as in memory. Also thinking is directed toward and leads to problem solving, being vital and dynamic, whereas memory remains static in comparison, although solutions to problems are influenced by memory factors. Moreover, thinking may result in the formation of a new mental representation which may continue to expand and evolve. Memory may become an impediment to this expansion for the tendency to perceive things in terms of their familiar uses is not easily overcome. Reference has already been made to functional fixedness which may lead to nonproductive solutions. The name given to the cognitive activity that results in novel or original ways of viewing a problem is creativity. We have a few conceptual frameworks with which to understand creativity. Four sequential stages were described by Wallas in 1926.These were:

1. Preparation or the formulation of the problem and making initial attempts to solve it.
2. Incubation or the dormant period when the problem is allowed to lie fallow.
3. This is followed by the third stage of illumination where an insight to the problem is achieved.
4. After the euphoria of discovery the final stage is that of verification when the solution is put to the rigors of testing and retesting and confirming.

A current theory based on a multivariate approach is espoused by Sternberg and Lubart. They contend that creativity is rare for it must include six attributes working simultaneously. The factors of creativity that they enumerate are:

Process of Intelligence
Intellectual style
Knowledge
Personality
Motivation
Environmental context

Is creativity genetic or is it a function of our culture and education? Is it possible to train for creativity, i.e., can creativity be enhanced? These questions are not only of pedagogic interest but significant in the analysis of the Islamic perspective on Enlightenment—it is imperative that there be a paradigm shift from memory to creativity. Diversity and flexibility as solutions seem all too simplistic, but let us turn to intelligence—the epitome of human functioning—to provide us with one. Let us also refer to the two types of thinking hypothesized by J. P. Guildford in 1969. He distinguishes between convergent thinking where recall of factual information is emphasized as compared to divergent thinking which requires generation of a variety of responses. There are no correct answers in the latter as compared to the former where one needs to zero in on memory and come up with exact answers. It is necessary to clarify that Guildford did not see only the number or quantity of responses to be significant; it was the creativity of the responses that mattered or rather the number of creative responses. Now creativity thrives only in the right atmosphere—one that is not inhibiting but free; one that is not constrained but unhindered. These constraints may not necessarily be internal or cognitively determined but external and social determined. Unfortunately, suffocation in Islamic societies is all too real a phenomena where free inquiry is suppressed and philosophy ostracized.

In Western industrial societies separation of the state from the church allows for a parallel paradigm within broad Christian parameters. This is not just a socio-historical phenomenon but also ascribed to Christ who had clearly distinguished between that which is Caesar's and that which is God's. This means that there are two distinct realms, the secular and the religious, which need not be in conflict but which also must not be confused. Islam right from the start acquired an ethos uniting the spiritual and the temporal in one community. Secularism was therefore never tolerated within the precincts of Islam, Turkey being the modern exception. The fact that Islam claims to be a way of life rather than a religion, i.e., a "Deen," means that it spreads its tentacles to every facet of life. It does not confine itself to the relationship between God and man but also includes very specific rules of conduct between man and man, i.e., it incorporates individual and social behavior within the state. This is rigidly defined and suffocatingly imposed. Does this promote creativity or intelligence? To find an answer let us seek an analysis of human abilities that characterize intelligence. In compiling a list most theorists consider adaptation to one's environment the hallmark of human intelligence. The question now is: Do the Muslims live in the highly technologically advanced cyberworld of the twenty-first century? Or do they take a defensive stance and take refuge in the safe cocoon of stereotypical responses of an era long gone, suspending all analyses. These responses may have become inappropriate, counter-productive, or even self-defeating.

Let us return to other facets of the phenomenon that is intelligence so that we can continue to assess the Muslim mindset. Charles Spearman hypothesized in 1904 that intelligence consists of "g" or general factors and "s" or specific factors. He maintained that it was possible to exhibit unusually high ability in one or more specific factors while exhibiting poor ability in other factors. Mention has already been made of specificity and the lack of transfer to other domains. Guildford extended the concept of factor analysis conceptualizing mental abilities within a three-dimensional framework. In this complex mosaic of intellectual components the first dimension incorporated the operations required in a task such as convergent and divergent thinking and memory. On the second dimension were products of those mental operations such as relations, system transformation, and implications. On the third dimension were the specific contents of a problem—figural, symbolic, semantic, or behavioral. A less complex and more elegant model was proposed by Cattell in 1965. Intelligence for him comprised two major subfactors which he named crystallized abilities and fluid abilities. The former were associated with accumulation of facts while the latter with the ability to understand abstract and sometimes novel relationships as exhibited in inductive reasoning. All these models denounce crystallization for it leads to invert ideas—ideas that are fossils of a time in the remote past and not fashioned in the information-processing model of the present. This model of vitality and dynamism was not alien to the early Muslims who were both revolutionaries and evolutionaries, who were willing to imbibe Greek philosophy and knowledge. This cross-fertilization of ideas was disseminated to the West. Ibn Rushd (Averroës) earned the title "commentator" by translating Aristotle. The group of rationalists called Mu'tazilites even discussed meta issues and debated over the fundamental problem of reason and faith and reason and revelation. Ibn Rushd even interpreted the sacred text allegorically.

No nostalgia for the past is being advocated just the aversion to change in the present is being questioned, for change is not always for the worse although it seems disconcerting. A critique—the essence of enlightenment of the social and intellectual bases—is being recommended: This critique is not for the sake of criticism but to be able to discern what is relevant and worthy. Progress—a characteristic of enlightenment—is being contemplated. Not just the toleration that Locke espoused but tolerance as a fundamental doctrine is being vindicated. A commitment to self-critical reform is being expressed. The defensive attitude of accepting only because it is ours is being questioned, for knowledge is not a legacy of any one nation or community.

If we put the Muslim societies under the lens of reason we would find them seriously wanting—free thought is stifled and superstitions abound. In Pakistan in the 1970s Fazal-n-Rehmah, an enlightened scholar, had to flee the country because he gave a symbolic interpretation to "Miraj" (the Prophet's ascension). Much censorship still exists. Intellectual freedom is feared. Reforms, social or academic, will not be forthcoming unless the scholars of the Muslim community anchor their hopes in enlightened attitudes and values. In the cognitive domain this entails exorcising the ghost of mneumonics so that the brain is not bounded and the mind is not bonded any more. It also entails making the paradigm shift from specificity to what could be subsumed under the term *synesthesia*.

Lest this rigorous self-analysis seem too harsh and be misconstrued to understand that some sort of genetic determinism bars them from cultivating alternatives, let us consider some pedagogical explorations so that initial steps to move to synesthesia are envisaged. Let us reiterate that philosophers do not claim definitive answers or solutions; in fact they decry them. Einstein's relativity theory in science has forced all knowledge to forego absolute standards. Within Newtonian theory time was assumed to be the basic quality and velocity was defined in terms of it (velocity = distance/time). With the Einsteinian shift time and velocity are defined in terms of each other for neither concept is considered more basic. Whether philosophico-psychological hypotheses or imagination or science fiction is the forerunner of science, or whether scientific advancements prompt new permutations of philosophical theory, it is acknowledged that one fertilizes the other. Thus they intersect and interconnect. Such a model should convince the Muslims that diversity of norms and standards is the key to being relevant in the cyber age. Whether we are in accord or in discord, whether we like it or not, a "United States of the World" or a "Global Village" (McLuhan)[5] is the reality we have to reckon with. Small islands of particular and specific types may not be able to thrive in such an environment. Our quest for synethesia is an option worth exploring.

The origin of the term is borrowed from a condition in which information from one sensory modality is coded in another modality. This could mean that an image can conjure up a sound. Sensations of vision are experienced in audition, e.g., Shelley's "A soft yet glowing light, like lulled music." Conversely, "the sound of colors" is not just a poetic metaphor but that yellow and white are bright, red and green intermediate, and black and brown dark. High pitches of sound are thus associated with bright colors and low pitches with dark colors. Walt Disney is credited with synesthetic ability and his creative endeavors are to a large extent based on his cross-modal ability. This research discounts also the much trumpeted conflict between sight and sound. Analyses theorizing the "inability of oral and intuitive oriental cultures to meet with rational visual cultures" (McLuhan) become suspect. If the two were entwined and intertwined no clear line of demarcation would exist. Such synoptic and synesthetic activity would mold and meld into a common heritage of knowledge for all.

Notes

1. G. A. Miller, "The Magical Number Seven, Plus or Minus Two: Some Limits on Our Capacity for Processing Information," *Psychological Review* 63 (1956).

2. Larry Squire, *Memory and the Brain* (Oxford: Oxford University Press, 1987).

3. Endel Tulving, *Elements of Episodic Memory* (Oxford: Oxford University Press, 1983).

4. Robert L. Solso, *Cognitive Psychology,* 3rd ed. (Boston: Allyn & Bacon, a division of Simon and Schuster, Inc., 1991), p. 405; see also John R. Anderson, *Cognitive Psychology and Its Implications,* 3rd ed. (New York: W. H. Freeman & Co., 1990).

5. Marshall McLuhan, *Understanding Media: The Extensions of Man* (London: McGraw Hill, 1965).

17

Fundamentalism in India

Ramjee Singh
Director, Gandhian Institute of Studies (India)

Fundamentalism is considered merely a reaction against the liberalizing tendencies of modern thought. It has been a reaction against something new. The term "fundamentalism" is used to designate what is more generally called a conservative type of thought as opposed to liberal or modernist tendencies and as a name of a specific conservative movement with its own organizations and agencies devoted to the propagation of a definite doctrinal program.[1] Needless to say that, in the past it has been used in the context of Christian thought. However, today it is being used in a wide sense including religious fundamentalism of all types—Islamic, Zionist, Hindu, Buddhist, and so on. It is thought to be an extreme position characterized by the belief that the Bible or the Quran or the Vedas are verbally accurate renderings of the word of God, and their writers inspired to the smallest detail of revealed truth.[2] Thus it stands for strict adherence to traditional, orthodox tenets of belief.[3]

Hopkins says that, "India always has been a land of religions."[4] At least four religions—Buddhism, Jainism, Sikhism, and different strands of Vedic-Brahmanic religion—are of indigenous origin. However, "the national form of Indian religion is Hinduism."[5] But other world religions like Christianity,

189

Islam, and Zoroastrianism also have deep roots in India. At the same time there is an underlying unity in the religious life of India.[6] Indian culture is a continuous process of synthesis. It has assimilated not only the religious beliefs and practices of the Aryans and the pre-Aryans (like the Negrits, Mongoloids, the Dravidians, and so on) but also of many other races like the Sakas, the Sethians, the Hunas, the Gurjars, and the Pratiharas. The cultural history of the Muslims also is an integral part of Indian culture. Similarly the pre-Islamic Indian culture is as much the heritage of the Muslims of India as of the Hindus. India's relations with the Arab world did not start with the dawn of Islam; trade between the West Coast and the Arabian Peninsula was a part of its ancient history. Arab traders and the religious men after the advent of Islam (570 C.E.) came to South India even before Muslims came as invaders, starting with the conquest of Sind by Muhamad-bin-Kasim (711–713 C.E.).[7] In the eighth century Arab settlements in the south multiplied due to an increase in the commercial activity. The Zamorin rulers of Calicut patronized the Arab merchants and they were permitted to construct mosques and religious institutions and follow Islamic personal law. Quazis were endowed with full powers to decide disputes. Similarly, the original Christians are scattered in the southern peninsula of India. These Martoma Christians, and a later group of Christians, fleeing from persecution in the Middle East, arrived in India for refuge in 350 C.E. . Thus, the "Syrian Christians" are the original Christians of India. They were never persecuted by the Hindus, Buddhists, Jainas, or Muslims but the zealous Christian missionaries from the Occident persecuted them and burned their literature because of their so-called deviations from European beliefs and practices.[8] St. Thomas and his disciples came to India with the gospel of Jesus[9] and founded the Christian church in Southern India in the seventh century. Jesuit missions were well received in the court of Emperor Akbar (1556–1605), but his tolerance for all religions was disliked by the Jesuits, who had already set up an Inquisition court at Goa. A mixture of motives of trade and missionary zeal led many missions of the Roman Catholics, Protestants, American Methodists, and Baptists, up to Mother Teresa from Albania to work with honor and distinction in India. Even after partition of India, precisely on religious lines. India today has the second-largest Muslim population in the world (150 million) and India's Constitution has declared India a secular state, where all citizens enjoy equal rights, irrespective of caste, color, creed, religion, or sex.[10] There is complete freedom for every citizen to practice any religion he or she chooses,[11] and no discrimination is made on this account.

This separation of religion and state has been a characteristic feature of the Indian political system. The Hindu rulers allowed Muslims and Christians to practice their faith with freedom according to *Alamgiri,* which are authoritative works of Mogul emperors. The children of Israel received hospitality in India several centuries before the beginning of the Christian era. The Zoroastrians, the first group of Pilgrim fathers in history, fleeing from Iran before Muhammadan persecutions, were hospitably received by a Hindu Prince and given land to build their temple. Neither the Jews nor the Zoroastrians have been persecuted in India. Muslim mystics, saints, and Sufis have always been looked on with veneration by the Hindus. Medieval Indian society was influenced by the rise of the Sufi among the Muslims and the Bhakti movements among the Hindus. Among the Muslim saints, Sufis, and poets, there are the names of Mohaddis, Amir Khusro, Niza-muddin Auliya, Sharafuddin Yaha Manyari, Sh. Amars, Miyan Mimi, Sah Mohibullah, Sh. Burhan Shaffari Bulle Sah, Rahim, Raskhan, and others. Among the Hindu mystic saints we have Raidas, Meera, Sankaradeva-Madhavadeva, Ramdas, Tulsi, Sura, Thyagaraj, and others who also have advocated universal humanism. Kabir and Nanak are symbols of human unity. A Muslim laid the foundation of the Sanctum-Sancturium of the Sikhs at Amritsar. Devotional cult is basically against all fundamentalism. Even during the modern Indian Renaissance, the voice of liberalism is always heard. Ramakrishna-Vivekanand advocated "universal religion," so Tagore stood for the "religion of man," Bhagawandas pleaded for the "essential unity of all religions," and Gandhi lived and died for upholding "equal respect for all religions."

This legacy of liberalism has been wisely inherited by the great Moguls and other Muslim monarchs. Unlike the Muslim rulers in Arabia and Africa, Muslim rule in India was almost secular because propagation of Islamic religion was not their objective. Muslim rulers even offered gifts to Hindu temples and royal assistance to classical Hindu schools. From Emperor Babar (*Babarnama*) to Auranzeb (*Adbe Alamgiri, Rukat Alamgiri*) and Tippu Sultan, they had prohibited cow slaughter to respect the sentiments of their Hindu subjects. They did not play the role of "defenders of faith" or "custodians of faith" but acted as the chief of the law-and-order machinery. This is one of the reasons for four hundred years of uninterrupted Muslim rule in India but also provided for a Hindu devotional reform movement to grow without state interference. Not to speak of liberal Muslim rulers like Akbar, Darashikoh, Bahadur Shah, Tippu, and the like, Muslim political establishments in India with a few exceptions, like Sultan Sikandar of Kashmir, Firoz Tuglaque, Sikander Lodi, and some others, rejected the repugnant intolerance and antihumanistic fundamentalism of some Muslim theologians and interpreters. This even led to repeated tensions between the Muslim political rulers and some of the fundamentalist Muslim theologians in India. Ziauddin Barni's *Tarikh-I-Firozshahi* (pp. 42–72) and *Fatwa-I-Jahandari* show ample evidence that Muslim rulers denied the mandate of some of their theologians for state interference in the religious practices of the Hindus or even for persecuting them.

We can conclude that exclusiveness of thought or behavior is alien to Indian culture. What it aims for is not the monopoly of a particular religion or culture but that particular groups follow particular cultures or philosophers with a spirit of coexistence and harmony. Indian history does not point to any massacres, forcible mass migrations, religious bans, forced conversions. Buddhism and Jainism challenged the Vedic orthodoxy and its authority, but this was done by the pen, not the sword. This led to a cross-fertilization of ideas and cultures. The cultural diversity of India can be explained only on the basis of its sociocultural dynamics of tolerance of doctrinal differences and cultural forms. What is not accepted is that any philosophy or religion should think of lording it over the others. Change from one philosophy or religion is not indeed prohibited; what is specifically forbidden is nonintellectual methods of persecutions or declaring any particular religion as the state religion and treating other coreligionists as second-rate citizens. Hinduism, by its character and constitution, has never been an exclusive religion. In it there is room for worship of all prophets of the world. It is also not an evangelical or missionary religion. It has no taste for religious conversion. It tells everyone to worship God according to his own faith or *dharma* and so it lives at peace with all religions. In short, it is not a religion of the prison.

There is thus an underlying liberalism and tolerance for other views in the Indian psyche and its racial unconscious that is aware of plural truth claims or faith in alternative standpoints. A nonabsolutistic cultural frame has become the characteristic Indian way of thought and action. The Hindu doctrine of spiritual level of competence of a person (*adhikars*) advocates that the truth should be formulated in accordance with the level of understanding and competence of different persons who all differ from each other. This also serves to promote nonfundamentalism. Then there is also a faith that we can worship the essential formless divine being in any form of one's own choice (*ista-devata*). This means that no one form can claim to be intrinsically more desirable than another, so that the desire to convert others or bring about uniformity in belief and worship is uncalled for. This brings so much catholicism in thought and behavior that even the belief in God is not adhered to. There are a good number of skeptics, agnostics, heretics, atheists, and the like in the Hindu fold who enjoy freedom of thought. The Buddhists and the Jainas not only denied the very existence of God but also challenged the authority of the Vedas and the Vedic priest and yet Lord Mahavira and Lord Buddha were regarded and revered as incarnations of God by the Hindus. The most ancient Indian scripture, called the Vedas (knowledge), is eclectic enough to declare: "The one Reality, the learned speak of in many ways."[12] Next to the Vedas, the most hallowed and philosophic treatises, called the Upanisads (secret knowledge), follow the same line. "Cows are of many different colors but the Milk of all is of one color, white: so the proclaimers who proclaim the Truth, use many varying forms yet the Truth enclosed in all is one or as streaming rivers pass in the sea, abandoning all separate name and form and merges into the State Beyond."[13] Next to the Vedas and the Upanisads, the most venerated and popular work, called the Gita (*Song Celestial*), tries to elucidate the same catholic spirit: "All men approach Me, so do I accept them; men on all sides follow My path."[14] "All human beings, though they seem to walk on divergent paths are marching to One God."[15] "Even as the several senses apprehend the different qualities of the same thing, so many lines of searching sciences show aspects, numerous of the One Lord." "Whatever form any devotee with faith wishes to worship, I make that faith of his steady." Echoing the Vedic spirit, the Jain heritage is even more eclectic, when Samantabhadra, while paying his obeisance, expresses the same spirit: "In you, O Lord arise all viewpoints, even as rivers rise out of the ocean and just as the ocean cannot be seen in those rivers so long as they remain separate, even so you cannot be seen in the separate viewpoints." The Jain philosophy of nonabsolutism (*anekantavada*) and conditionality of judgment (*syadavada*) are classic instruments of the foundational basis of catholicity. According to this theory, we are not the sole possessors of truth and the rest are in the clutches of devils. Even in the monistic system of Vedants, three different levels of reality corresponding to three levels of perspectives provide abundant scope for catholicity of thought and judgment. Its doctrine of nonviolence is the very antithesis of fundamentalism and aggressiveness. The famous scholar-poet Pushpadanta supports this spirit beautifully: "Whatever paths the ordinary mortals, according to their varying tastes and aptitudes adopt for seeking the Lord, by each and every one of those paths is He attainable, as the sea is to the waters of all the rivers running toward it." Like the Jaina doctrine of nonabsolutism, the Buddhist doctrine of *vibhajyavada* and the doctrine of the Middle Path (*madhyama pratipada*) are ample proofs of methodological and ideological nonfundamentalism. The Great Emperor Ashoka's Edict says: "Whoever honors his own sect and disparages another man's does his own sect the greatest possible harm."

Hence, what has been happening in India on the religious front, like the rise of fundamentalism, is only an aberration and mostly politically motivated. The Indian Freedom Movement, from 1857 to 1947, has a tradition of religious harmony. The last of the Moguls, Bahadur Shah Jafar, had become the hero of both Hindus and Muslims against British imperialism. During Gandhi's leadership, the Hindus zealously fought together with their Muslim brethren the battle of Khilafat. Due to the British policy of divide and rule, the country was divided on communal lines and its bitterness continues. This naturally created division in the minds of men. The rise of fundamentalism is the result of hopes belied, frustrations, and mistrust. However, even now, after the division of the country on religious lines, the Indian state is an ideal of secularism. It has the second-largest Muslim population in the world living with equal rights. At least two eminent Muslims have occupied the supreme position of the president of India. It has inducted Muslims, Christians, and Sikhs into other high positions of the country without discrimination. Besides, India developed intimate relations with Afghanistan, Iraq, Iran, Indonesia, and other Islamic countries. It fought most valiantly for the right of self-determination of the Palestinian people. It has maintained most cordial relations with Egypt and the Arab world.

Because of the very fact that India has a synthetic culture, it cannot become fundamentalist. This synthesis and growth of mixed culture is a proof against insolence, pride of a particular race or religion. There has been constant give and take between the Aryans and the Dravidians, between the Vedic Brahmanas and the Sramanas, between Hindus, Muslims, and Christians. What to speak of philosophy and religion, there has been sharing together in the fields of language and literature, art, and music, folklore and festivals. Notwithstanding political rivalries confined mostly to the corridors of power, people in India do not like extremism or fundamentalism.

However, there is no denying the fact that even as aberrations, both Islamic and Hindu fundamentalisms have raised their ugly heads in India's recent past. Muslim fundamentalism is a worldwide phenomenon whether it is in Libya or Iran, Afghanistan or Pakistan, Bosnia or the Sudan. The fact is that most of the Muslim countries have adopted a theocratic state structure and set up an organization of Islamic countries on the global plane and that there has been growing intolerance toward freedom of expression and writing in some parts of the Islamic world. All these have their impact on the minds of Indians. The majority of the Hindus feel disillusioned with Muslim leadership, as, primarily under their influence, India was divided. Not only this, almost all political parties in India try to make some appeasement and use the Muslims as their vote banks. This has created a reaction in the Hindu mind and they have become more conscious of their own religious identity. But nonfundamentalism has been an article of faith with the people of India. Forcible conversion, destruction of places of worship, have no approval. India is a multiethnic country with a distinctly pluralistic heritage. The current belligerent posture of Hindutva is a passing phase. That is why the Ram-wave has not only been halted in Indian politics but has received a setback after the Ayodhya tragedy. Fundamentalism among Muslims also has received a severe jolt and saner sections of the Muslims have asked the Babri Masjid agitation to stop. India has two kinds of identity: cultural and political. Political identity is firmly rooted in a secular and federal constitution with all-India political parties and unified administration. The question of the political identity of India is thus too important to be brushed aside. It is one of the largest democracies with the finest judiciary at the apex of the world. It has shown remarkable unity against secessionism and any external threat. However, its spiritual and cultural identity distinguishes itself from the West and this is a common heritage. So far as its sociocultural identity is concerned, it is based on the fellowship of diversity in unity, which has the quality of creativeness and universalism. The cultural tradition and identity has always been synthetic and adaptive with values of tolerance, accommodation, and coexistence.[16] Milton Singer, M. N. Srinivas, and Yogendra Singh maintain that Indian society has been adopting and assimilating itself. Narayan has shown that "tolerance and respect for others' views and feeling" has been "the hallmark of Indians over the centuries." This signifies the pluralist character of Indian cultural identity. Srinivas is perhaps realistic when he says that those who deplore various forms of subnationalism such as ethnicity, communalism, linguistic consciousness, and regionalism are unaware that they are all parts of the package of nationalism itself when it hits a developing country and the danger of such nationalism is an everpresent one. Hence the uniformitarian model is unsuitable for multiethnic societies like India. To obliterate every religion other than one's own is a sort of Bolshevism in religion.[17] The Indian solution seeks the unity of religion not in a common creed but in a common *quest*. It believes in a unity of spirit and not of organization, a unity which secures ample liberty not only for every individual, but for every type of organized life that has proved itself effective. Deeper experience of reality is no monopoly of any particular prophet or church. The world would be a much poorer place if one creed absorbed the rest. God has bestowed upon India a rich harmony and not a colorless uniformity. Ramakrishna, who had tried successively Hindu, Muslim, and Christian symbols as means of *sadhana,* compared "different religions to the *ghats* (shores) around the same tank." Hence, Vivekananda says, "There never was *my* religion or *yours,* my national religion or your national religion; there never existed many religions, there is only the one—expressing itself in its various ways.[18] The famous Rock Edict of Emperor Ashoka clearly warns to "avoid the extolling of one's own religion to the decrying of the religion of the other or speaking lightly of it without occasion or relevance.[19] India has been a laboratory of synthesis of facts and creeds. There has been synthesis of Vishnu and Siva cults, Aryan and non-Aryan cultures. After Ashoka's efforts to establish a universal religion, Emperor Akbar and Saint Kabir tried to bring Hinduism and Islam together. So Vivekananda also pleaded for synthesis of Islam and Vedanta. Brahmas tried to bring together Hinduism and Christianity, Ram Krishna, Vivekananda, Tagore, Iqbal, Gandhi, Radhakrishnan, and Nehru and all leading lights of modern India, provided religion a cosmic dimension, all-embracing and all-inclusive, as the world or the same God. The third president of the Republic of India, Dr. Zakir Hussain, has said, "Providence has destined India to be the laboratory in which the greatest experiment of cultural synthesis will be undertaken and successfully completed."[20] In the Indian mind, there is no rivalry among religions for supremacy or for superiority. Indeed, a good Hindu, as Gandhi used to say, would admonish the Muslim to be a better Muslim, a Christian to be a better Christian, and so on.[21] Emperor Ashoka valued neither gifts nor honors so highly as that there should be a promotion of the essential elements of (high) religion in all religions; there should be no exaltation of one's religion and finding fault with others.[22] Indian secularism is the logical outcome of this philosophy of religious tolerance, which is its natural character and its philosophical faith in alternative standpoints and *homo hurarchius*. Indian culture hates proselytization and persecution because it knows that it will be unspiritual and counterproductive. Besides, the Hindu socioreligious arrangements are so structured that spread of its dogmas by force is impossible. The Hindu king was no caliph and there was no Hindu sword to propagate religion by wars or by sanguinary persecution to force consciences.[23] *Orthopraxis* is more central to man's life than *orthodoxy*. Therefore, Ashoka pleaded only for *dharma* or, as Gandhi said, "ethical religion." Vivekananda says, "It is not the man who believes a certain something, but the man who does the will of the Father in heaven, who is right. On this basis—being right and doing right—the whole world can unite."[24] The Indian approach to relativization of religions is not reduced to mere pragmatic and intellectual levels, because true religion is of intuitive order. "Religion is not the acceptance of academic abstractions or the celebrations of the ceremonies, but a kind of experience."[25] Here there is a tolerance not at the lower intellectual, but at a higher intuitive and different levels. The popular model of the interrelationship of different religions can be understood as many rivers leading to the sea"[26] or "colors of a spectrum of light,"[27] or as pluralism of languages referring to the same reality.[28]

Conclusion

Both ideologically as well as historically, Indian culture has been secular in character except for a very few minor aberrations. Perhaps, this was its genius and also its destiny. However, Indian secularism is not necessarily either antireligious or antitheistic. Since ancient times up to the present period, there has been a dissociation of religion and politics in India. In the ancient Hindu period, even during the long regime of Muslim and Moghul kings, this cult of secularism continued with only a few exceptions. This is one of the reasons which has allowed the Hindu Bhakti movement to grow uninterruptedly. However, there is no denying the fact that the most grievous wounds to Indian secularism were inflicted by playing the imperialistic game of "divide and rule" and dividing the country on Hindu-Muslim communal lines in 1947. If there would have been a religious state in India at that time, it could have been only a Hindu state with more than 90 percent Hindu population, but it is interesting to observe that the idea of India being anything but a secular state was never seriously raised in the Indian Constituent Assembly, not even by the Hindu Mahasabha, a Hindu organization. The founding fathers of the Indian Constitution guaranteed equal fundamental rights to all citizens, including full religious freedom. This has been recently upheld both by the people at the mini-general election, ousting substantially such forces trying to mix up politics with religion, as well as in the recent full-bench verdict of the apex court of the country that secularism is the "basic structure" of the Indian Constitution and any government which violates this principle is bound to be dismissed. In fact, such a faith in nonfundamentalism is both its heritage as well as its sociological compulsion. There are some grounds:

(1) Firstly, we know that in the field of speculative knowledge or knowledge of final truth, it is difficult to say that a particular theory is false or true. Hence any absolutistic stance is wrong. Therefore the Indian genius has devised several ideological weapons to fight fanaticism, like the philosophy of nonabsolutism (*anekanta*), relativity of judgment (*syadvada*), levels of knowledge and reality, all-inclusive universalism, and so on. While philosophical systems represent varying stages in an ascending order, they are coordinated by a "synthetic process" so that a sublime picture of synthesis might emerge.

(2) Secondly, the Indian mind believes in the principle of the dignity of man and respect for individuals. Liberty of individual conscience is granted to the maximum. That is why there is a rich store of philosophical systems and religious schools flourishing side by side. There is no tradition of persecution or inquisitions for practicing any faith like skepticism, agnosticism, atheism, materialism, and so on. There is, thus,"ideological autonomy" or "*swaraj* in ideas." This tradition of "individual freedom" has been continuing up to now. This is the strongest pillar of Indian secularism and catholicism.

(3) Indians are constrained to believe that in the sphere of ethics, "*there are truths but not one truth.*" "To one who has such a desire, any doctrine that the pattern of the ideal life should be the same for all is intolerable."[29] There is not even one idea about God or reality. There is not one single path of self-realization or salvation. There are paths of knowledge, action, devotion, and so on, all equally good. This is not cheap compromise at the cost of truth but a way of life to foster diversity in the pursuit of ideal ends.

(4) It is true that the majority of people are Hindus in India; hence all other religious societies are influenced by its usages and action and vice-versa. Hinduism is not a proselytizing religion. However, as a reaction to

Christianity, the Arya Samaj launched its *Shuddi* (reconversion) movement to reclaim for the Hindu fold people who had been converted to Islam or Christianity. However, this has not been able to become a popular and regular feature, as we find in Christianity or Islam. Recently in South India, when the entire village of Meenakshipuram was converted to Islam, there was strong resentment in Hindu society and a bill called "Freedom of Religion" was moved in the Indian Parliament by a private member so as to curb religious conversion either through "fraud, force or temptation." But a great hue and cry was raised by evangelical religionists, mainly Christians, and the bill was withdrawn with the consent of the Hindus, who constituted the majority.

(5) The democratic structure of the Indian state and the inclusion of articles 14, 15, 16 (right to equality, no discrimination), 25 and 26 (freedom of conscience and right freely to profess, practice, and propagate religion, and freedom to manage religious affairs including religious institutions), and 29 and 30, providing for the protection of minorities, are the safest guarantees against fundamentalism. No political party can afford to go against the minorities because they have the balancing vote. The Indian judiciary is perhaps the most impartial as well as the most strong. The Election Commission is also extremely impartial and nonpartisan. Over and above, there is absolute freedom of press in India. All these provide an insurance against fundamentalism in India.

India's religious heritage is unmatched in the world. Practically all living religions of the world have found refuge in the land. India gave hospitality to Judaism, Zoroastrianism, Christianity, and Islam. The geography of India points to her natural isolation, but her history reveals a record of uninterrupted contacts with the outside world. She has been engaged not only in rewriting but also in reconstructing her own past history. Religion is not an "ism," not a bundle of creeds, beliefs, rites, and rituals, but it is the inner nature of man and our whole life. It is that which holds together or upholds the integrity of the individual, of society, of the cosmos. It is useless to give a particular label like Hindu, Muslim, or Christian to this reality. It is "eternal" (*sanatan*), and "universal," it is "ethical" and "spiritual."

Notes

1. *Encyclopedia Britannica* (1964 ed.), vol. 9, p. 1009.
2. *New Webster English Dictionary,* p. 384.

3. Syed Ali, "India's Cultural Traditions: Hindu-Muslim Synthesis," *Tolerance in Indian Culture,* R. Balsubramanian, ed. (Delhi: I.C.P.R., 1992), p. 71.

4. E. B. Hopkins, *The Religions of India,* 2d ed. (New Delhi: Munshiram Mancharlal, 1970), p. 1.

5. Max Weber, *The Religions of India* (Illinois: The Free Press, 1958), p. 4.

6. K. Morgan, *The Religion of the Hindus* (Delhi: Motilal Banarsidass, 1987), p. 6.

7. Ali, "India's Cultural Traditions," pp. 72–73.

8. H. T. Mazumdar, *India's Religious Heritage,* vol. 1 (Delhi: Allied Publishers, 1986), p. 148.

9. "And he said unto them. Go ye into all the world, and preach the gospel to the whole creation," Mark 16:15.

10. Constitution of India, preamble: India shall be a "Sovereign, Socialist, *Secular* Democratic Republic" which will "secure to all its citizens" (emphasis added).

11. Article 14, Justice, Liberty, Equality and Fraternity. Equality before the law; Article 15 prohibits discrimination on grounds of religion, race, caste, sex, or place of birth; Articles 25 and 26 mandate freedom of conscience, the right freely to profess, practice, and propagate religion, and freedom to manage religious affairs, including religious institutions; and Articles 29 and 30 provide for the protection of minorities.

12. Rgveda, I. 164, 46.

13. Quoted by Bhagavan Das from the Upanisads in *Essential Unity of All Religions,* 6th ed. (Bombay: Bhartiya Vidya Bhavan, 1960), p. 75.

14. Bhagavad Gita, IV. 11.

15. Ibid., III. 33.

16. Milton Singer, "The Modernization of Religious Beliefs" in Myron Weiner, ed., *Modernization: The Dynamics of Growth* (New York: Basic Books, 1968); M. N. Srinivas, *On Living in a Revolution and Other Essays* (London: Oxford University Press, 1992); and Yogendra Singh, *Modernization of Indian Tradition: A Systematic Study of Social Change* (Delhi: Thomson, 1973).

17. R. K. Radhakrishnan, *The Hindu View of Life* (London, 1927), p. 42.

18. *The Gospel of Ramakrishna* (New York, 1907), p. 151.

19. Swami Vivekananda, *The Complete Works,* vol. 4, p. 180

20. *Edicts of Emperor Ashoka,* S. Murthy and A. N. K. Ayangar, trans. (Madras: Adyar, 1951), *Rock Edict* XIII, pp. 33–37.

21. Quoted by Mazumdar in *India's Religious Heritage,* p. ix.

22. *Edicts of Emperor Ashoka,* p. xiv.

23. Bacon spoke of "Mohamet's sword."

24. Swami Vivekananda, *Complete Works,* vol. 5, p. 273.

25. Radhakrishnan, *The Hindu View of Life,* p. 13.

26. Swami Vivekananda, *Complete Works,* vol. 1, p. 390.

27. K. M. Pannikar, *The Inter-religious Dialogue* (New York, 1978), pp. 21–22.

28. Ibid., pp. xxiv–xxv.

29. P. F. Strawson, *Freedom and Resentment and Other Essays, Social Morality and Individual Idea* (Methuen, 1974), pp. 28–29.

18

The Islamic Perspective on Enlightenment: Principles and Implementation

S. M. A. Shahrestani
Chairman, International Colleges
of Islamic Science (UK)

This paper will begin with a clarification of the definitions of the principle words and phrases used in the paper, such as enlightenment, *salafiyya,* and fundamentalism. The paper then moves on to an evaluation of the Islamic perspective regarding enlightenment in order to determine whether Islam supports or rejects this principle. To achieve this the paper is split into two main parts, the first dealing with the Islamic principles and the second dealing with the actual implementation.

The great period of European Enlightenment is usually recognized as being the eighteenth century, and central to this movement was the belief in the need to benefit from more knowledge in order to free oneself from ignorance, misunderstanding, or false beliefs. Furthermore, proponents believed that it would be reason and science rather than religion which would achieve an advancement in human progress. Hence the goals of rational man were considered to be knowledge, freedom, and happiness.[1]

By its very nature enlightenment is in direct opposition to those who believe in a strict adherence to ancient or fundamental doctrines, and who believe that no concessions should be made to modern developments whatsoever (such people are said to be *salafiyya*). It is only natural that these two opposing views should be engaged in a continuous struggle, with such accusations as being either backward or innovators and fabricators.

The question which presents itself at this stage is whether one belief is right and one is wrong. The philosophers at the forefront of the European enlightenment movement, such as Voltaire, Rousseau, and Montesquieu, concentrated their efforts upon a confrontation with the established church's beliefs as well as the feudal system. This determined struggle against the church was a result of the philosophers' knowledge of Christianity, but it manifested itself as a struggle against all religions.[2] It was this attitude which caused them to deviate in their judgments about religion and caused even greater tragedies, and which time has shown to be proof that we should never eliminate religion from society altogether.

Let us now turn to a definition of fundamentalism. Fundamentalism means to maintain the literal interpretation of the traditional beliefs of an ideology. Every ideology will have certain fundamentals which must be adhered to in order for the ideology to be upheld and practiced. For example, Islam has certain fundamentals which every Muslim must adhere to in order for them to be considered Muslim. If a person does not believe in these then he steps outside the boundaries of Islam. Clearly this understanding of fundamentalism is very different from that given to it today, which always imbues it with highly negative and false connotations. It is these clear differences in the meaning of fundamentalism in theory and in practice that leads us to investigate the meaning more thoroughly.

In Islam, as with any ideology, there are, as we have mentioned, certain fundamentals which must be accepted and followed wherever and in whatever time the Muslim lives. These fundamentals will never change, and are accepted by all Muslims. In issues which are not considered to be part of these fundamentals, differences of opinion are considered acceptable as long as the opinion is based on a strong foundation.

In the light of all this, this paper wishes to look at two of the groups among the Muslims who are considered to be fundamentalists in the true sense of the word. The first group is known as the Imamiah fundamentalists. They are followers of the Shi'a Ahlul Bay't school of faith. This group is composed of those Muslims who consider rational reasoning to be their fourth source of Sharia, and they consider it necessary to use the mind's faculty of reason in order to reach an acceptable conclusion. As such they hold that they ensure Islam's progress and development throughout all times.

The other group is known as the *salafiyya* fundamentalists. They believe that they must look only to the teachings of their ancestors, and reject the process of reasoning as an acceptable source of the laws. As such they are seen to be in favor of avoiding anything which will change the existing rules and laws. The point we want to make here is that there are many types of fundamentalists, not all of which should be viewed in a negative light and seen to be against enlightenment.

In order to show this more clearly, we are going to firstly concentrate on investigating the true Islamic vision of this issue, as based upon its basic principles and authoritative sources. The question we are attempting to answer is thus whether Islam supports enlightenment or not. We will then attempt to see whether this view is actually implemented by Muslims in practice.

The Islamic View of Enlightenment

It is accepted that the basic sources of the Islamic teachings are the Qur'an and Sunna, and thus it is only correct that we begin our investigation with a verse from the Qur'an: "Therefore give good news to My servants, those who listen to the word, then follow the best of it; those are they whom Allah has guided and those are they who are the men of understanding."[3] It is from this verse that we can distinguish a great challenge, as well as three general points. The challenge is the permission which one can take to be granted from this verse for Muslims to listen to and discuss all contradicting arguments and to then select the best one. If we were to investigate any other religion or ideology we would not find such freedom present in them. This is because they all consider their ideas to be correct and the only way to reach salvation, and they will accept no investigation into other ideas. The three points which can be taken to have arisen from this verse are as follows:

1. God makes it clear that he will limit his guidance to those who explore the truth through reason. As such it is clear that God recommends people to think and develop themselves.

2. The ability to think and reason is a gift which God has confined to human beings above all other creatures; therefore it is clear that man should use this ability. The following hadith confirms this and shows that reason is a source of knowledge: "The men of reason are those who are the possessors of understanding minds, about whom God has said, 'But none mindeth save the possessors of understanding minds.' "[4]

3. As the Qur'an is the word of God and thus can never be wrong, God
is not afraid to allow people to carry out their own research and scientific
experiments into different areas, as God is confident that the true researcher
will always come back to the Qur'an at the end of the day. As a result Islam
allows complete freedom and openness in the search for the truth. This is
in complete contradiction to other beliefs, which do not allow their adherents any such freedom, as they fear that if they allowed this they would lose
their followers.

Having considered this challenge and the three above points, it is possible for one to argue that this verse provides an excellent example of
Islam's view of the use of reason. Such freedom in evaluating all the different views and choosing the best one is in reality the true meaning of enlightenment, both in theory and in practice. As Ibn Rushd said in his book
Fasl al-maqal, "On this basis, according to rational conditions, we should
look to the works of our predecessors."[5] In other words we should took to
the work of our past scholars, but if we find something which is not acceptable or appropriate, then we should politely reject it.

Furthermore, the Qur'an, which is the basis of Islam and its first source
of law, gives man both the guidance and the tools by which he can understand the universe and thus improve his condition. In other words, the
Qur'an itself provides the necessary mechanism by which enlightenment
can be achieved, as it allows man to understand and enhance his methods
of learning and development as times change and new discoveries are
made. Thus the goals of rational man, which can be defined as knowledge,
freedom, and happiness, can all be obtained from the Qur'an.

It is vital for a book which needs to cover all the necessary issues
which relate to the living code of human beings to contain guidance on
both those issues which are static and those which are changeable. To
clarify what we mean let us expand a little more. Some matters such as
man's relation to his bodily needs, to his environment, to nature, to other
creatures, and to the universe, are all things which will never change, and
are considered to be established matters for which the rules and laws will
never need to change. On the other hand, there are other matters where
changes will take place, such as in areas of technology and science, as well
as in intellectual, social, and political developments as time goes by, and
which the Qur'an must also provide rules and laws for. Thus one may argue
that the Qur'an, which says, "Nor a grain in the darkness of the earth, nor

anything green nor dry but [it is all] in a clear book"[6] should include all of the following:

First, it should be so comprehensive that all those aspects of human beings which do not change at any time, nor become affected by changes in man's progress, are included. We can call such aspects of life as the fixed or established codes of life. In reality it seems to be very problematic for humans to recognize these unchanging aspects of life, but if we overlook any of these then there will be some problem in the individual's personality or in the society. At the same time, the Qur'an should include verses which provide knowledge and rules to provide for the development and progress of human beings in all their shapes and forms. Furthermore, such verses should be revealed in a way which is understandable for both the uneducated and the knowledgeable, not just at the time of their revelation but hundreds of years afterwards as well. They should thus be relevant to both those who they were revealed to as well as those who have passed through scientific revolutions and live in a world very different from that of their ancestors. Is the Qur'an such a book?

The answer is, quite simply, yes, as the almighty God says in the Qur'an: "He it is Who has revealed the Book to you; some of its verses are decisive, they are the basis of the Book, and others are allegorical; then as for those in whose hearts there is perversity, they follow the part of it which is allegorical, seeking to mislead, and seeking to give it [their own] interpretation, but none knows its interpretation except Allah and those who are firmly rooted in knowledge."[7] Therefore, the decisive verses in the Qur'an are those which cover the unchangeable aspects of human life (as we called them earlier, the fixed ones). They are plain and can be understood by whoever has a command of the Arabic language. Whereas the nondecisive (allegorical) verses are those which cover the progressive elements of human life and the mind. Their wordings can be taken to have different definitions, or the structure of the script can be such that it causes the reader to produce different understandings, which are not necessarily what God intended. Since this can create uncertainty as to what God intended by these verses, it is not acceptable to act upon them until one has consulted the knowledgeable people, who are authorized to interpret them. The reason behind this preventive measure is to stop those who have mischief, self-interest, or bad intentions from fulfilling their desires through their own interpretation of such verses.

Second, the authorized interpreters of the Qur'an are those qualified people who have spent many years studying the Qur'an and its related sciences, and it is to these people that we are allowed to refer to (as indicated by the above verse). If this limit is not laid down, any person will be able to interpret the verses however they like, most likely in their benefit and interest. Such people are using their minds alone to interpret the verses; they have no regard for the word of God, and this is by all accounts unacceptable. This is the same conclusion reached by Ibn Rushd in *Fasl al-maqal,* in which he states that it is expected that scholars will reach different interpretations of the Qur'an, depending upon how qualified they are. As a result these differences mean that the interpretations are not binding, nor carved in stone.

Third, Muslims who belong to the first group that we mentioned, the Imamiah fundamentalists, believe that God has already introduced such firmly rooted and knowledgeable people, by virtue of the hadith, "I am leaving two weighty [precious] things: the Book of God and my progeny."[8] He then named all of those who have the right to interpret the Qur'an one by one, thus excluding all others.

It is upon this matter that I contend the arguments of Ibn Rushd and other scholars, since they consider the righteous interpreters as those who God described as "those who believe in Him."[9] We should point out that here Ibn Rushd contradicts himself in relation to the nonbinding nature of these scholars' interpretations. Furthermore, many scholars rely on the saying of Ibn Abbas, which says, "I am one of the firm rooted . . ."[10] yet this itself is in contradiction to the verse, "But none knows its interpretation except Allah."

Fourth, if the Qur'an is going to be active and useful up until the day of judgment, then it needs an interpreter for all the time that it exists. In the absence of such interpreters, Islam has allowed scholars to diligently deduct the Islamic laws according to the rational principles and needs of the time, although at the same time being within the framework of established Islamic principles and the variable progressive needs of every time. This is what is meant in the hadith: "Thus God will dispatch a reformer in order to revive their religion on the birth of every century."

Thus one can conclude that there is not a better system to give rational, modern, and enlightened system for all those established aspects of human life, while at the same time covering all the variational changes in life throughout the different centuries, and regardless of culture or civilization. Meanwhile, the same system safeguards the basis of Islam by negating the significance of the interpreters where they give different ideas. This provides an obstacle for those who have mischief in their hearts or a lack of knowledge, and might thus dilute the principles of Islam, thus keeping it clean from any intellectual disease. This system is present in the Qur'an, which is the first source of Islamic jurisprudence.

It can be argued that there are many verses in the Qur'an that not only encourage but actually insist upon the use of reason and rationality in order to achieve enlightenment and liberalization. The importance given to the mind in the Qur'an cannot be ignored or overlooked. The evidence for this can be seen to be present in the Sunnah of the Prophet and his progeny, through the books of hadith and sirah, many of which have devoted an entire chapter to the use of reason. Furthermore these are so numerous that even if some of the narrators can be questioned as to their genuineness, we cannot disregard all of them, and if some are not clear, we cannot ignore all the others which are very clear in their meanings.

To clarify this, what follows are some examples of such verses and hadiths:

Almighty God said: "Do you not consider the kingdom of the heavens and the earth and whatever things Allah has created."[11] "And [as for] these examples, We set them forth for men, and none understand them but the learned."[12] "And they think on the creation of the heavens and the earth: Our Lord! Thou hast not created this in vain!"[13] "Surely the vilest of animals, in Allah's sight are the deaf, the dumb, who do not understand."[14] And "Most surely in the creation of the heavens and the earth and the alternation of the night and day, and the ships that run in the sea with that which profits men, and water that Allah sends down from the cloud, then gives life with it to the earth after its death and spreads in it all kinds of animals, and the changing of the winds and the clouds made subservient between the heaven and the earth, there are signs for a people who understand."[15]

As for traditions: "Reason is that by which God is worshiped and a place in Paradise earned."[16] "Don't boast of a person performing too many prayers and observing too many fasts until and unless you determine what degree of reason he possesses."[17] "The initiation, the development, and the power of any task productive of any advantage cannot be undertaken without reason which has been designed by God as a light and ornament for His creation. It is through reason that man recognizes his creator. . . . It is through reason that they can discriminate between good and bad. It is through reason that they understand that darkness [the evils] lies in ignorance and the light [every good] lies in knowledge. All these facts are known to men through reason"[18] and "God has deputed the Prophets as His messengers to make the people wise and mindful of God. The more they accept and believe in these messengers the greater is their God consciousness. The wisest among men is he who knows about Godliness most. And he who is the most perfect in his reasoning enjoys the highest status among men, in this life and the life hereafter."[19]

Thus one can argue that it is impossible given such evidence to ignore the importance of rationalism in Islam. It can be seen how Islam encourages us to study the universe and all its contents in order to utilize its resources and in correcting our methods of understanding in order to have a better life and to improve ourselves continuously. The significance of this evidence is the role it plays in the acceptance of either analogy (*qiyas*) by some Muslims, or pure logic by others, as the fourth source of Sharia, which can be used only when there is no clear law from any of the other sources. In my opinion analogy can be used only if the cause of any law is given by God. In the absence of any such clear cause, we cannot use this method, as this would involve induction, which does not lead to certainty. Deduction through logic is therefore, one can argue, the correct method of finding the Sharia, in the absence of others, and thus it is clearly apparent how enlightenment is illuminated in the Sharia.

The Qur'an, some argue, is also made of parts which call for obedience and belief in what God has sent, without reasoning or having any empirical evidence. On this basis the following verses may be said to contradict what we have so far said about the nature of the Qur'an and Islam. For example, Allah says in the Qur'an:

"This Book, there is no doubt in it, it is a guide to those who guard [against evil]. Those who believe in the unseen and keep up prayer."[20] "Those to whom We have given the Book read it as it ought to be read. These believe in it; and whoever disbelieves in it, these it is that are the losers."[21] "Nor is Allah going to make you acquainted with the unseen, but Allah chooses of His apostles whom he pleases; therefore, believe in Allah and His apostles; and if you believe and guard [against evil], then you shall have a great reward."[22] And "[As for] those who fear their Lord in secret, they shall surely have forgiveness and a great reward."[23]

The above verses are in fact also based upon rational reasoning. The argument here is that there is certain knowledge that should be conveyed to others in the form of commands which should not be questioned, for three reasons: (1) No human can have access to all knowledge; (2) In relation to those matters which God has not sent revelation upon, it is fruitless for us to try and understand or explain them, as we will never be able to reach such a level through our own minds; (3) An individual will be unlikely to find the answer to his questions regarding why he should or should not do an action; thus in the meantime he needs to be able to seek the knowledge of those who are qualified in Islamic matters in order to know and understand one's duties.

From the day each individual reaches puberty, he must know what he is obliged to do, as well as what he is not obliged to do. Thus God has set some definitive guidelines for him, which enables him to carry out his duties straight away. However, even though this allows every person to know what he should do to safeguard himself in this world and the next, they are encouraged to search and analyze their beliefs in order to be further satisfied as to the reasons behind their duties. In regard to this Ibn Rushd says, "Not all humans can perform the task of reasoning due to the differences in their abilities. Not only that, some cannot even follow analogical discussions. Since it takes time and is difficult to learn the reasoning process, and since the Sharia comes with the aim of teaching all people, it is necessary that the Sharia covers all methods of teaching and all levels of understanding."[24]

This is thus the enlightenment program as defined by Islam, which is continually correcting and developing the society throughout all times and places. It thus ensures happiness and justice with all those established aspects of human life. However, excessive liberalization also presents a danger for society, since while it may improve one aspect of human life, it destroys others. One should therefore work within a given framework in order to safeguard the prosperity of human life and to protect from deviation or failure.

Islam, we argue, thus encourages Muslims to study all ideas and beliefs, whether they are in favor of or against Islam. In fact we argue that it is compulsory for all scholars of Islam to study other schools of philosophy, analyzing them and then either accepting or rejecting them depending upon how far they are compatible with Islam. This is in complete contradiction to the view held by Western scholars of Muslim scholars, who they see as reactionary fanatics or short sighted. In reality I wonder how much do the philosophers of Enlightenment really know about Muslim scholars? How much did Voltaire, Rousseau, or Montesquieu know about the Islamic view of enlightenment, or on the methods of deduction in Sharia? Did they even know about the different Islamic philosophical views on the various aspects of life? How many of them read the works of Sheikh Al-Toosi[25] or Allamah al-Hulli[26] or the other eminent scholars of jurisprudence before them? For example, how many Western scholars know that the Jewish philosopher Baruch Spinoza's work is in fact a reflection of the works of Ibn Rushd? This is itself pointed out by Abu Rayyan in his book *History of Islamic Philosophical Thought,* when he says, "There is no doubt that the work of the Jewish philosopher Baruch Spinoza, in reconciliating philosophy with religion and in the interpretation of the religious scripts in order to conciliate them with rationalism especially in his paper [on theology and politics], is in fact a reflection of the works of Ibn Rushd in this field."

It is thus clear that one may argue that despite the fact that only a small amount of Ibn Rushd's work has been translated, it has still had a significant effect on a number of Western scholars in relation to enlightenment. It should also be borne in mind that Islamic scholars have naturally had far more of his works at their disposal. It is reasonable then to say that Western scholars could learn a great deal more about Islam and enlightenment if they were to pay more than just perfunctory attention to these Islamic works.

Muslims and Enlightenment

There is clearly an important question here which needs to be answered. Furthermore, if this is the view of Islam toward enlightenment, why are some other Muslims, such as the *salafiyya* fundamentalists, who we mentioned earlier, in such open and confrontational opposition to any such progress or change, to the extent that leads them to open and often violent rebellion against the governments of their countries?

The answer, one can say, rests with what seems to be a general flaw in human nature. This is evidenced by the fact that if you analyze any community or people, regardless of their beliefs or systems, however sacred their ideals, there is always a major segment of that community that does not wish to fully implement the beliefs of the society, or who actually openly rebels against them. For example, many Jews do not implement the Torah, many Christians do not implement the Bible, Marxists do not follow the teachings of Karl Marx, Communists do not implement the teachings of Lenin. This can also be applied to nations and governments. For example, many governments refuse to follow or obey either the United

Nations or Security Council resolutions. This is all unfortunately the direct result of weaknesses in human nature.

One such weakness is that many humans tend to listen to their emotions rather than their minds, especially in regards to their own benefit. The result is that they tend to follow whoever can provoke their emotions and manipulate their feelings in the cleverest way. On the other hand, whoever tries to inform the people of what is right, through rational and intelligent means, is often dismissed. Thus those who refuse to use methods of propaganda, and instead simply want to tell the truth in a dignified way, will always be unsuccessful with the people. Unfortunately, this weakness is the same for all human beings, whether they are secular, Hindu, or Muslim. The result is that while it is easy to win the support of the people by extravagant promises and declarations, the reality of implementation once power is won is frightening and difficult, and in the end results in misery and suffering.

As for the Muslims, according to Ibn Rushd they can be divided into three groups: "People's natures are different; there are people who concede to rational reasoning; those who concede to dialectical arguments, as if they are logical ones; and those who concede to speech as if they are logical proof."[27] The first group are those who adhere to the sciences of Islam, and who have deep wisdom and piety. They are those who insist upon the necessity of investigating what God has allowed and what He has forbidden. They diligently deduct the laws from the recognized sources and insist upon their implementation. This group of Muslims is made up of those who are themselves able to practice deduction due to their knowledge and understanding, as well as those who, due to their lesser knowledge, simply follow these scholars. As Imam Askari[28] says in his hadith about these Muslims, "Thus whoever from amongst the scholars is protecting himself [from evil], is custodian of his belief, resists his desires, and submits to the orders of his Lord, then it is necessary for the public to follow him."[29] This is also specified by Ibn Rushd in his writings on this issue. These Muslims are those who understand the importance of using reason and rationality. They adhere to reason within its correct context and thus they are said to be adherents of the Enlightenment school of thought.

The second group of Muslims are those about whom Ibn Rushd said, "There are those who concede to dialectical arguments as if they were logical ones, since they do not have the capacity to do otherwise."[30] This group prefers not to accept reason as a source of knowledge, as they argue the mind is too misleading to accept it as such. Instead they prefer to use intuition, as perfected through deep contemplation and periods of retreat. Many take this belief so far as to simply submit to God's laws without necessarily understanding why. Some of these Muslims choose to practice Sufism, which they see as the only way to safeguard both this world and the next.

We must point out that we disagree with Ibn Rushd's belief that they follow this path due to lack of capacity to reason. While it is true that some of this group follows this path due to a lack of ability to use their reason, there are still many among this group who enjoy a very high level of intellect, such as Abu Hamed al-Ghazali and Ibn Sina, who both prefer the use of intuition over reason. For example, al-Ghazali says, "Sufis prefer knowledge which comes from intuition,"[31] while Ibn Sina in his book *Ta'liqat* (Commentaries), says, "Human beings are not able to know the whole truth of things, and we do not know of things except their propers and accidents."[32] This matter is further discussed in our chapter on the sources of knowledge, in the "Theory and Knowledge" course at the International College of Islamic Science. Here we prove that reason is a quality bestowed upon man that allows him to distinguish between right and wrong, but that it needs to refer to consciousness and to what we have learned from divine sources.[33] In short this group of Muslims rejects any kind of philosophical study, wisdom or enlightenment. They take shelter under the following verse: "O you who believe! Take care of your souls; he who errs cannot hurt you when you are on the right way; to Allah is your return, of all [of you], so He will inform you of what you did."[34]

The third group of Muslims are those who, one can say, have gone astray and who have misled others. Many of them are unlearned in matters of Islam, but there are also some who are considered to be highly educated members of the Ulema. These are those who have been overcome by their own desires of wealth, power, or fame, and who have gone on to claim that the only way to reform is by the means of a strict adherence to the rigidity of the initial Islamic principles. As a result they often attack other scholars' doctrines or *fatwas* and accuse them of blasphemy by means of innovation (*bida*). From this position they have often gone on to exploit the ignorant and the faithful but naive elements of Muslim society. As we mentioned earlier, the majority of people are like herds who follow any shepherd; they rely on their emotions rather than their wisdom, and all too often follow their desires without thinking of the consequences. We believe that it is the leaders and followers of this group who are today calling for *salafiyya* fundamentalism. This group can thus be viewed as the opposers of enlightenment and of the intellectual rational schools of thought.

What has been discussed so far is a brief insight into the Islamic perspective on Enlightenment in principle and practice. in order to give a living example of what we have discussed, a number of short examples will be given in relation to the achievements of some of the contemporary Muslim scholars of the enlightenment school.

The first example is Jamaluddin Al-Afghani,[35] who saw political reform as a necessary prerequisite for other reforms in the cultural, religious, and economic fields. He builds his opinion on the belief that the Muslim *ummah* cannot question its rulers, while the system that is implemented upon them is totalitarian. It is important, he argues, that the political system be reformed in order to allow people to have their house of representatives, where they can call their rulers to account. He goes on to say that the use of reason should be unleashed, and the door of *ijtihad* opened, in order to benefit from modern scientific and technological advancements. He rejected the old way of memorizing the Islamic texts by the Ulema. He argued that "human beings are one of the biggest mysteries of nature, and he can only achieve what once seemed impossible through science and reason, thus making what may once have seemed to be a fantasy, a reality."[36] In addition Afghani opened up the modern civilizations in order to take what was positive from them, thus setting up a new way of thinking.

Following in his footsteps was Afghani's student Sheikh Muhammad Abdu,[37] who participated in a journal called *Al-'arwa al-wuthqa* as a platform from which to advocate the use of reason in order to understand the religion. He said, "It is important to free our thinking from simply following, and to use reason, one of the strongest powers invested in humans."[38] Among his achievements are his reformation of many social and religious institutions, such as the judiciary, Muslim land trusts, and methods of teaching in Al-Azhar. He also formulated a project to reform education in Egypt, as well as teaching in Dar al-'Ulum, which was established in the nineteenth century, thus making it into a university which combined both religious and modern education.

Following along this line was Sheik Abdul Hamed bin Badis,[39] who was a prominent Islamic reformer in Algeria and who challenged the French policy that was aiming to both exploit the wealth of the country while destroying its Islamic identity. His method of confronting French domination was through the preparation of a generation of students who would be capable of standing up to the French. In order to achieve this he established many schools to teach both Arabic and the Qur'an, as well as the different subjects related to Islam. In addition he established with a group of friends the "Algerian Islamic Muslim Group" and published many different papers in order to get his message through to the people.

In Lebanon there was Sayid Abdul Hussain Sharaf-edin,[40] who was trying to challenge secular education in the country, which was being spread by the French. He established Al-Jaaferiyya school to combine the traditional and modern method of teaching to create a well-educated generation. His activities were not confined only to education, but went further to reform society, and by doing so, helped the people. He also established a Charity and Piety association and the Imam Sadiq club, which was intended to be a meeting place for the youth. His activities were not simply confined to Lebanon; he also went to Egypt in an attempt to bring unity in *fiqh* between Shi'a and Sunni Muslims. He eventually discussed this matter with the mufti of Al-Azhar, Saleem al-Bissri.

In Iraq there was Sayid Hebattudin Shahrestani,[41] who played an important role in the reform movement and was one of the leading figures in the 1920s revolution. He was a reformer of the modern Islamic education and he was the first education minister when the Iraqi government was established. He initiated the first cultural program for the Iraqi schools and institutes, where a combination of modern and traditional education was taught. He was the first to establish a university for higher education, which bore the name "Ahlul al-Bay't University." He taught the science of atoms, and he was the first to prove the connection between empirical science and the Qur'an and Sunna, indicating where Islam talked about all modern achievements in science. In this field he wrote books such as *Al-Hai'a wal-Islam*,[42] *Al-mu'jiza al-khalida*,[43] and *Al-dala'el wal-masa'el*.[44] He also produced a journal titled *Majallat al-ilm,* which was a leading journal in its time. As for social and political reforms he played an important role in the Palestinian cause, where he cooperated with Sheik Amjad Zahawi. Shahrestani always stated that human happiness would be achieved "when the colors on the map of the world are eliminated." Thus his aim was always to work for the benefit of people in general.

Also in Iraq there was Sheik Muhammad Hussain Kashif al-Ghifa,[45] who was prominent in the Islamic reform movement, where he cooperated in 1931 when there was a conference regarding the salvation of Palestine, and where he closely cooperated with the mufti of Palestine, Amin al-

Husseni. In one of his books, *Al-muthul al-ulia fel Islam la fi bhamdoun,*[46] he gave an intellectual program to protect morality in society.

Finally, in recent decades Shahid Al-Sadr[47] in Iraq was one of the most outstanding Islamic reformers, who called for reforms in various matters, such as politics, society, and economics. He materialized his thoughts onto paper, and these books have become valuable sources of knowledge. For example, *Falsa fatuna* represented a moderate view between the extremes, while his book *Iqtistaduna* presented an Islamic economic method that is completely compatible with the ongoing changes in society. In addition he wrote *Al-bank al-la rabawe fe al-Islam,* where he presented an international monetary system. Lastly he wrote *Al-usus al-montiqiyya lil istikra,* where he proved that the method used by the empiricists was never certain unless it complied with God's laws.

As we have seen, there have been many enlightened Muslims who have called for reform in their societies, where they have often faced the aggression of their leaders on one side and narrow-minded people on the other. Many were killed, exiled, or imprisoned for attempting to bring about such reforms.

Conclusion

It has been shown that Islam as represented by the Qur'an and Sunna calls for the use of reason in order to distinguish between right and wrong, although such use of reason stops on matters of worship. The Qur'an has two types of verses, one type of which is fixed, the other being changeable, thus being capable of suiting each place and time. This is why the Qur'an is the permanent miracle. This quality of the Qur'an made it clear that people would not be allowed to make changes which were based upon their personal interests. As we have attempted to show, Islam is not a utopian ideology that cannot be implemented in practice; as we have shown, there are many Ulema who have called for reform throughout history.

What we are witnessing today by the *salafiyya usulia* who are actively resisting reform are just individual movements which unfortunately have objectives which contradict those of Islam. They are in reality the same as many international movements under which countless lives have been lost under the pretext of reform.

In the end I would like to call the participants of this conference to realize that the only way we will overcome the present conflicts is through dialogue, which itself will not occur until we are willing to discuss such matters with openness and clear intentions. This type of conference is perhaps more capable of achieving such dialogue, as it, more than any other organization, is in a position to bring people with different points of view together, and enable them to achieve the necessary discussion.

Notes

1. *Encyclopedia Britannica,* p. 504.
2. M. Rosental and B. Yudin, eds., *Al-mawsu'a al-falsafieh,* Samir Karam, trans. (Beirut: Dar Al-Taliah), p. 145.
3. Qur'an, Zumar (39): 17–18.
4. Al-Kulaini, *Usul al-kafi, The Book of Reason,* vol. 1(Iran: WOFIS, 1978), p. 31.
5. Ibn Rushd, *Fasl al-maqal,* p. 31.
6. Qur'an, Anaam (6): 59.
7. Qur'an, A'lay Imran (3): 6.
8. Al-Tirmidhi, *Bab manaqib ahl bayt al-nabi,* 199/13.
9. Ibn Rushd, *Fasl al-maqal,* p. 40.
10. Muhammed Husain Tabatabi, *Tafsir al-mizan,* vol. 3, p. 44.
11. Qur'an, Al-Araf (7): 185.
12. Qur'an, Al-Ankabut (29): 43.
13. Qur'an A'lay Imran (3): 191.
14. Qur'an, Al-Anfal (8): 22.
15. Qur'an, Al-Baqarah (2): 164.
16. Al-Kulaini, *Usul al-kafi,* vol. 1, part 1 , p. 26.
17. Ibid., p. 63.
18. Ibid. p. 67.
19. Ibid., p. 41.
20. Qur'an, Al-Baqarah (2): 2.
21. Ibid., (2):121.
22. Qur'an, A'lay Imran (3): 178.
23. Qur'an, Al-Mulk (67): 12.
24. Ibn Rushd, *Fasl al-maqal,* p. 54.
25. Al-Shaykh Al-Toosi (Shaykh al-Ta'ifa), founder of the Najf seminary, died in 1067 C.E.
26. Al-Allama al-Hulli, founder of the Hillah Seminary, died 1325 C.E.
27. Ibn Rushd, *Fasl al-maqal,* p. 33.
28. Imam Hasan al-Askari (846–874 C.E.), the eleventh infallible Imam of Imamiah Shi'a.
29. Tabari, *Al-ihtijaj,* vol. 2, p. 263.
30. Ibn Rushd, *Fasl al-maqal,* p. 33.
31. Mulla Sadra, *Sharh usul al-kafi,* p.447.

32. Mulla Sadra, *Al-afsar, al-safr al-awwal* (first book), p. 391.

33. M. A. Shahrestani, lecture on "Research Methods," a fourth-year course at the International College of Islamic Science.

34. Qur'an, Maidah (5): 105.

35. Jamaluddin Al-Afghani (1838–1897), a Muslim philosopher and thinker.

36. Muhammad Amara, *Jamaluddin al-afghani,* p. 270.

37. Muhammad Abdu (1849–1905), a prominent scholar and jurist and the mufti of Egypt in 1899.

38. Muhammad Amara, *Al-Islam wa al-mar'a fi ra'i Muhammad Abdu,* p. 140.

39. Sheikh Abdul Hamid bin Badis (1887–1940), a prominent Algerian scholar and reformer.

40. Sayid Abdul Hussain Sharaf-edin (1870–1957), a prominent Muslim (Imami) scholar and jurist in Lebanon.

41. Sayid Hebattudin Shahrestani (1878–1963), a prominent Muslim (Imami) scholar, jurist, and philosopher.

42. The book *Al-hai'a wal-Islam* (Islam and Cosmology) proves that Islam agrees with the new astronomical theories; it was translated into many different languages.

43. The book *Al-mu'jiza al-khalida* (The Eternal Miracle) proves the miracles of the Qur'an and shows how its laws adapt to contemporary developments.

44. A series of publications in which answers were given to contemporary religious questions.

45. Sheik Muhammad Hussain Kashif al-Ghifa, a prominent Muslim (Imami) scholar, jurist, and thinker of Najaf.

46. A book written in response to "Middle East Friends Association" in order to open the dialogue between Muslims and Christians.

47. Shahid Seyed Muhammad Baqir Al-Sadr (1933–1980), a prominent Muslim (Imami) scholar, jurist, and philosopher, martyred by the regime of Saddam Hussein.

19

The Third World and Enlightenment

Mahmoud Osman
Ambassador to Indonesia, Egyptian Foreign Ministry

The relation between the Third World and the concept of "enlightenment" is intrinsically organic. The prevailing impression, across the borders of the Third World countries, is that there is all but a total absence of a well-defined notion about enlightenment. The term has various usages within the otherwise monolithic Third World countries. Whereas common, uncontroversial, and well-established definitions for such terms as "development," "economic growth," and "modernization" are discerned in the Third World, rarely do we come across an equally clear and undisputed meaning of the term "enlightenment" in this part of the world.

As this paper will endeavor to clarify, the Third World is—in a broader sense—divided into two ubiquitous blocks: the Islamic world and the Hinduist-Buddhist societies in Asia. As for the basically Christian Third World countries in Africa south of the Sahara and in Latin America, in my point of view they do not essentially represent a vital segment with immediate correlation to the issue of enlightenment we are dealing with.

If I am to start by focusing on the Third World societies belonging to the first monolithic part, namely the Islamic world, it appears that the concept of enlightenment is particularly vibrating and pivotal. Furthermore, it is increasingly preoccupying the minds of political and intellectual circles alike. Indeed, enlightenment is currently a component inevitably permeating the day-to-day lexicon in this part of the world. Hence, the thematic subject of this seminar derives its utmost relevance and significance.

Without running the risk of being deluged with controversial definitions of the term, "enlightenment" will be discussed throughout this paper essentially as to indicate the preparedness of Third World countries—psychologically, ideologically, and politically—to relate to the values and concepts adopted by a group of nations on which the Third World is commonly relying as a source of economic aid and technological know-how. The problem is further complicated whenever norms and orientations of life observed within this group of nations are also coveted by Third World countries.

The dynamics of the situation lead predictably to a cultural schizophrenia which makes injecting more potent doses of enlightenment into the fabric of Third World societies all the more necessary.

Ironically, the affiliation by several Third World countries to remarkably progressive ancient cultures ran contrary, at certain moments, to the aspirations of these very societies for an acceleration of modernization. The Islamic world, in particular, was invariably preoccupied over more than seven centuries (between the eighth and the fifteenth centuries) by tedious labor concentrating on interpretations, summarizing, and rewriting of Islamic heritage. Such invaluable use of energies was at the expense of employing powers of creation and innovation. A prototype manifestation of the adage that, "Memory functions at its best whenever mind ceases to work," was created.

Over many centuries most, if not all, intellectual undertakings in the Islamic Third World countries were primarily devoted to "divine issues." In no part of the Third World societies were the rights of God rather than the rights of people so vigorously defended as in these societies, regardless of the fact that it is obviously human rights rather than God's that ought to be defended since God is omnipresent.

The overenthusiasm by Muslim theologians to "interpret," "clarify," and "narrate" has allowed the scrupulous and literal application of religious texts to occupy a predominant level in the intellectual milieu irrespective of contemporary considerations. Therefore, the Muslim world was left with no option but to coexist, during the later decades of the nineteenth century and throughout most of the twentieth century, in total bewilderment as to how to tune the predominantly religious climate to the exigencies of their daily life on one hand, and the attempts to bring their political, educational, and institutional apparatuses in line with their European parallels, on the other.

The struggle between the two schools of thought in several Muslim societies, Egypt being no exception, has worn out the intellectual stamina and distracted the educated classes for many decades. By the end of the day, there was no outright triumph from this Byzantine, seemingly fruitless debate. While developed societies were strenuously and consistently devising methods conducive to widen their very scopes, upgrade their socioeconomic conditions, and incessantly break new ground in technological fields, the developing societies were (and still are) immersed into an ever-protracted debate revolving around the ultimate theme: Is Islam solely religion or state as well?

The inquiry started shortly after the death of Prophet Muhammad. Apparently, it is currently ongoing. While the developed societies have coined the newly introduced term of "sustainable development," the developing societies seemed to consecrate instead a sustainable debate with no categorical result in sight.

The problem has acquired a rather serious turning point during the last decade, primarily due to political upheavals affecting the ideological texture of both developing and developed societies. I will confine my remarks in this context to the following two components.

First, during the Cold War, the Third World was preoccupied either by struggling against Communism on one hand, or against imperialism on the other. The termination of the Cold War has confronted the Third World with a dilemma culminating in opting for a rather convenient alternative, namely, fundamentalism. Thus, parts of the Third World were put on a collision course with the concept of enlightenment.

Second, concomitant with the termination of the Cold War, certain models have emerged in the Third World typifying a feasibility, relatively speaking, of establishing a full-fledged state on bases derived from Islamic tenets and precepts. Conspicuous among those are the Iranian, the Sudanese, and the Algerian models. I do not intend to dwell on the political and ideological nuances which make these models distinctively different. I merely wish to point out that as the twentieth century is drawing to a close, certain models within the Third World attempted to vindicate, from their own perspective, that Islam has dual functions permitting the establishment of both state and religion combined.

The Arab-Israeli conflict has also produced a dimension equally feeding on fundamentalism. I am alluding to the movements of Hamas and Hezbollah. Needless to say that the sporadic successes achieved now and then by these two movements are expected to engender, though indirectly, an already active fundamentalist tide within the Islamic world. The atmosphere portrayed above is anything but amenable to ushering in the perception of enlightenment into Third World societies. Worse still are the unfolding currents targeting writers, artists, and journalists known to uphold secular and progressive perspectives. The situation indeed calls for devising a strategy congruent with the magnitude of the fundamentalist tide. I, hereby, propose that the following approach could be considered:

First, the debate arguing that Islam is a twofold religion and state—started ever since the eighth century and in apparent continuum ad infinitum with no decisive conclusion—has to be brought to an end. The perpetuation of this debate has proven to be an exercise in futility. It is, furthermore, an intellectual war of attrition that continues to drain the creative powers of many spheres in Third World countries.

Second, the different values and concepts of enlightenment, successfully adopted by the developed countries, may be considered and introduced through fostering education, scientific thinking, and freedom of expression along with other major components of human rights.

By so suggesting, we would be actually offering a gesture of reverence and approbation to Prophet Muhammad's aphorism, "You [leaders of the Islamic nation] are the best judges as to how affairs of your societies can be best conducted and governed."

The persistence of such insoluble inquiry over fourteen centuries is a testimony to certain inadequacies immanent in our psyche. It equally reveals a deep-seated sense of apathy on the part of Muslim clergy who customarily tend to invoke from the literature only the convenient while obscuring all that is to the contrary.

A major scourge obstructing any possibility for a normal flow of enlightenment—as far as the Islamic countries are concerned—appears to be that the postulates are invariably dealt with as debatable issues, and the unequivocally clear to the mind is discussed at length as ambiguous or enigmatic. These traditions are a drain on the otherwise potentially creative minds in Third World countries.

Moreover, at other instances, certain actors within the Third World seem to believe that enlightenment and liberalism lead—by definition—to concepts of nationalism and liberation. Since several Third World countries happen to belong to a rich heritage derived from creative ancient civilizations, a distinct sense of identity occasionally leads these actors to develop a feeling of self-reliance that suggests to them that it would, in fact, be redundant to borrow from the West. Why should we emulate developed societies—so the argument goes—if we have our own roots and sources in every field?

Predictably, the cultural and technological gap separating developed and developing countries continues to widen. To illustrate, I recall that when the United States of America launched its first manned space vehicle to land on the moon, Muslim theologians in a certain Third World country, while denouncing the step, showed some compassion when they expressed relief that the moon was full at that moment. Had it been a crescent, they exclaimed, the spacecraft and its astronauts would have crashed—back to Earth—into pieces.

The gap was not formed during contemporary eras. In fact, it goes back to the twelfth century or earlier, when an eminent thinker—al-Ghazali— criticized sciences copied from foreign cultures. As is well known, al-Ghazali exhorted the nation to embrace the "Ash'ari" tradition, that is, resigning everything to God's will.

The Third World countries currently suffering from political Islam are in dire need of invoking values of enlightenment as a viable panacea, if only the plague is to be contained. Politicizing Islam was put into focus particularly in the Middle East, ever since the 1950s. Employing Islam as a political weapon was not only resorted to by indigenous peoples of the region. The West itself contributed in its own way to the practice. The United States of America was first to conceive the establishment of an "Islamic Pact" to protect the region—though not cogently—from the Communist threat. The same pretext, more or less, was used to justify liberating Muslim Afghanistan from the Soviet invasion. It is ironic, however, that American academic, political, and diplomatic activities are today closely monitoring the intriguing phenomena of political Islam.

What about enlightenment in non-Muslim Third World countries? It is interesting to note that these countries do not consider enlightenment as an exigency for advancement and progress as it is in our region, since nations belonging to equally high religions and dogmas—particularly Hinduism and Buddhism—have some self-fulfillment in this regard.

Hinduism is essentially an extrovert religion of spectacle. It is popular in its practices and is also considered a religion of the learned. It cannot be understood if the Vedanta and Samkhya have not been fully comprehended. Furthermore, Hinduism does not know the contradiction between the religious and secular environments; consequently, a Hindu, even if he belongs to a group, considers himself alone to be responsible for his salvation. Interestingly enough, there is no Hindu term corresponding to what we call "religion"; there are, rather, "approaches" to the spiritual life.

As for Buddhism, suffice it to recall that the simple definition of the Buddha is "the Enlightened One," in both epistemological and metaphysical respects. The meaning of *buddhi* is "supreme enlightenment." Therefore, Buddhism is primarily conceived as experiential in nature and purpose. It concerns the life, here and now, of each sentient being and thus interrelatedly of all existence. Buddhism, lastly, covers more than thirty Asian states.

Back to the Middle East, it has been noted that enlightenment has been experimented with in the region intermittently. There has never been a consistent, uninterrupted application of the concept in this part of the Third World. Even when it was applied, it was done in a timid and apologetic manner. Symbols of enlightenment in our cultural life have never been able to dislodge themselves from the inhibition posed by the religious current. These symbols, likewise, were obliged at certain moments to flatter the religious current to secure their survival.

The type of enlightenment we need in our region is the one which is uninhibited, unbridled, and consistent with values enshrined in the definition given by Kant: "Enlightenment is the migration of man from the subconscience, which is the inability of man to use his mind without getting assistance from others." In our region, however, and in view of the magnitude of the problem, perhaps we should waive the condition referred to by Kant regarding dependence on others.

20

Islam and Enlightenment

Yehia Howeidy

Abstract

Culture in general has an imaginative aspect easily found in folk knowledge, in historical traditions, and in anthropology. Religion itself is the embodiment of this kind of culture. It has indeed a divine or a revealed nature, besides its psychological basis; nevertheless, its imaginative aspect is undeniable and uncontested. This imaginative aspect functions socially and leaves its imprints on some of our habits, not merely habits of conduct, but also trends in thought, which can be described from this angle as spiritual. It goes without saying that it is our duty to respect and revere those habits but not to the point that we worship them in a way that they become as partners of God himself.

Our holy book, the Qur'an, wages a well-known campaign against what is commonly called ascribing partners unto God, considered as the utmost action of blaspheming. God is one. This means that we ought not worship anything or anyone except the Almighty. Now, those partners with God are not merely the stones or statues found around the Kaaba during the life of our prophet, but they include those mental habits deeply rooted in our traditions since the *Al-jahiliah,* and which have affected our lives until now.

The campaign of Islam against polytheism is especially targeted against those mental habits or those idols. The famous motto of monotheism must be understood in this framework. In some respects, Islam's stand against the idolatrous aspects of religion might be considered as a kind of secularization or as a profaning of idolatry's so-called sacredness with its exaggerated importance, for the sake of preserving the sacred honor and dignity of humanity. This very same campaign is no doubt an act of enlightenment, which removes those mental habits that create taboos, cause strains in our social life, spread fears, and thus become true impediments to the free will of mankind. Getting rid of them and purifying our lives from their exaggerated influence, or at least dismantling them by removing their false sacred cover, while respecting them at the same time, enable men and women to promote their actions more freely and with more creativity, in accordance with their full dignity. In the meantime, such actions are liable to intensify the creed of monotheism, which is considered to be the essential call of Islam and is accepted by the three revealed religions. Furthermore, these acts of enlightenment provide a basis to unify the three religions or at least to pave the way for a fecund and a rich dialogue of religions based on the dignity of humanity.

21

Religious Truth and Philosophical Truth according to Ibn Rushd

A. El Ghannouchi

Abstract

Islamic thought has remained during all its history strongly marked and haunted by the theological spirit. It is characterized by a negative dialectical cadence, which has brought it back to its point of departure, if not further back. This happens each time it risks a step ahead. In the end, it is the reactionary spirit of orthodox theology which prevails.

It is thus that *ash'arism* answers to *mu'tazilite* rationalism, which brings down *jahmist* fatalism. Two freethinkers, Rhazes and Ibn Rawandi, answered this by attacking all religions and prophets. Al-Farabi and Avicenna, although their thinking was different from these philosophers, subscribed to a double syncretism (Aristotelian/Neoplatonic and philosophical/theological) to hide their heterodoxies. This irritated al-Ghazali and justified his attacks against philosophers. He strongly advocated a strict religious integrality. The dawn of secular thought, revindicating the distinction between religion and philosophy, represented by Ibn Tufayl and Averroës, was the answer to that. But Ibn Taymiyya, the most reactionary theologian, condemned Averroës and all who followed his example of practicing the pagan sciences of the Ancients. Since then the Islamic world has been drowned in obscurantism.

PART TWO

FIVE DIALOGUES ON AVERROËS AND HIS INFLUENCE: REMEMBERING GEORGE HOURANI

22

Free Inquiry and Islamic Philosophy:
The Significance of George Hourani

Paul Kurtz
Professor Emeritus of Philosophy,
State University of New York at Buffalo (USA)

I

My task in this paper is to make some comments about George Hourani, first, because many of you knew him personally and admired his work; second, because this conference is sponsored in part by a fund that he and his wife bequeathed to the State University of New York at Buffalo to support Islamic studies; and third, most significantly, because George Hourani contributed importantly—though in his quiet and reserved way—to the effort to reevaluate the foundations of Islamic thought by focusing on the rationalistic strains within it.

George Hourani was born in Manchester, England in 1913 of Lebanese parentage. He took a degree at Oxford in 1936 and his Ph.D. from Princeton in 1939. He taught at Government Arab College in Palestine from 1939–1948, which was under the British mandate. He and his wife Celeste Habib (of Egyptian extraction) came to the United States in 1950. Hourani taught at the University of Michigan from 1950 to 1967, where he became professor of Islamic history and philosophy and helped to build the Department of Near Eastern Studies. In 1967, I am pleased to say that as

233

chairman of the Council on International Studies, I was instrumental in bringing him to SUNY at Buffalo, where he became professor of philosophy. He was elected chairman of the Philosophy Department from 1976 to 1980 and helped to smooth frazzled nerves after the revolutionary battles of the preceding years in this department. Hourani became president of the American Oriental Society in 1978–79 and associate editor of their journal.

Most importantly, in a series of books and papers, he sought to uncover the rationalistic sources in early Islamic thought. This is especially seen by his publication of Ibn Rushd's work *On the Harmony of Religion and Philosophy* (1961), *Islamic Rationalism: The Ethics of Abd al-Jabbar* (1971), *Essays on the Islamic Philosophy and Science* (1975), and *Reason and Tradition in Islamic Ethics* (1985). George Hourani became a Distinguished Professor at this University. Incidentally, he was at first denied this honor by his colleagues because they said that he was not a "philosopher." I fought hard for him, and the department, which was then under the strong influence of analytic philosophy, agreed to name him as Distinguished Professor, though of "Islamic Thought and Civilization." (I mention this because thankfully today we are beyond such a narrow definition of philosophy. Many thought that Marvin Farber's work on phenomenology was not doing main-line philosophy. Indeed the kind of philosophical inquiries that we engage in here at the Center for Inquiry—humanistic and pragmatic and drawing on the Dewey tradition—is not considered to be "genuine philosophy," whatever is meant by that.) It was a great honor to have known and worked with George Hourani, a man of great integrity and moral character. George and Celeste Hourani left a substantial portion of their estate to the Department of Philosophy, the income of which enables conferences such as this to proceed.

I wish to concentrate on the central interests of George Hourani's work. It is directly related to our celebration of the eight hundredth anniversary of Averroës's death. As everyone here knows, the Muslim philosophical tradition did much to preserve the ancient classical Greek texts—especially those of Aristotle and Plato. There was a kind of philosophical renaissance from the ninth to twelfth centuries among Islamic scholars, who translated the Greek texts into Arabic. Among the great figures were al-Farabi (873–950), Ibn-Sina (Avicenna) (980–1037), and Ibn Rushd (Averroës) (1126–1198). Had it not been for these philosophers, especially Averroës, the works of Aristotle in particular might have been lost to the West. At the first Cairo conference on the relationship between Averroës and the subsequent European Enlightenment this was pointed out. Averroës was widely read in Latin and Hebrew translation, and this brought Aristotle to the West and liberated philosophy in a sense from its dogmatic theological grip.

An important work by George Hourani in our own day was his own translation and commentary on Ibn Rushd's work on *On the Harmony between Religion and Philosophy*, the English edition of which was published in 1961.

In his introduction to the work, Hourani states that this classic, written about 1179–80, "sets out to show that the Scriptural Law (*shar'*) of Islam does not altogether prohibit the study of philosophy by Muslims, but on the contrary, makes it a duty for a certain class of people, those with the capacity who are 'demonstrative' in scientific reasoning. Apparent conflicts between the teaching of Scripture and philosophy can be reconciled by allegorical interpretations of Scripture, though such interpretations must not be taught to the common people" (p. 1).

Hourani goes on to observe that as soon as Greek philosophy was introduced into Islamic circles, a tension between it and orthodoxy arose. At the very foundations of Islam stood the Qur'an, which prescribed definitive beliefs and actions for believers to follow. Legal opinion about right and wrong could be decided chiefly by reference to the Qur'an and the Tradition. Any doubt about this was to be resolved by the consensus of the learned. Any independent reasoning by lawyers, he says, was to be used only in interpretation of the Scripture, and not by attempting to define right or wrong on independent grounds. Granted that some implicit philosophical issues arose, and some concessions were made to the principles of rationality, but there was little or no reference to Greek philosophy to resolve such a dispute. Such was the opinion that prevailed among the Asharites in the tenth century. Thus Greek philosophy (*falsafa*) seemed unnecessary. When it was introduced in the mid-ninth century it appeared to many to be dangerous; for it appeared to have the pretension of science and it claimed to give us demonstrative knowledge about the world. No person who studied this literature could fail to be impressed by it. Writings about the empirical sciences did not worry the orthodox. When such philosophers spoke about the universe or the destiny of man, however, the question was raised as to whether they agreed with the Qur'an and the Tradition.

Hourani maintains that a stunning blow to rational philosophy was delivered by al-Ghazali (1058–1111). In his treatise *Tahafut al-falasifa* (*The Incoherence of the Philosophers*), he attacked the philosophers' claim that the world was eternal (contrary to Islamic principle of divine creation), the implausibility of physical bodily resurrection, and other so-called heretical views. Hourani states that it was Ibn Rushd's task to reply to al-Ghazali and to harmonize the two different systems of thought. The objection to philosophy was that it propounded doctrines about God and the world that deviated from the Scripture: it could not thus be an inquiry that the Scripture condones. Ibn Rushd denied these charges. He said that since religion is true, the Muslim community knows definitively that demonstrative studies do not lead to conclusions that conflict with Scripture. "For truth does not oppose truth, but accords with it and bears witness to it" (Hourani, p. 22). Since he accepts both as true, he denies that there is any inherent contradiction between them. The method of reconciliation that he proposed was to use metaphorical and allegorical interpretations of the Scripture. However, he goes on to state that since philosophers can achieve the truth directly, Scripture is unnecessary at the highest level of inquiry. This was a matter in which Islamic philosophers, including Ibn Rushd, had to be discreet. Philosophers may be aware of the obscurity and apparent contradictions of the Qur'an, but they need to proceed to unravel the inner meanings. According to Hourani, Ibn Rushd had to deal with the fact that we have objective knowledge of the world, which is not derived from Scripture, but from science and philosophy.

Thus he is concerned with defending the right of qualified philosophers to pursue their inquiries, including scriptural texts. He is accordingly defending freedom of inquiry, at least in this qualified sense. Ibn Rushd is surely not a democrat, and he is not defending the unlimited right of free inquiry for any and all thinkers. Indeed, he wishes to restrict education to a limited elite.

II

Why then should we make such a big fuss about this today? Perhaps because free inquiry has been under such heavy attack in our own day, from political and ecclesiastical sources. An enduring feature of modern culture is the vital role that freedom of thought and conscience have played. Free inquiry is surely essential to the development of modern philosophy; that is, the right to engage in untrammeled free, creative, and critical thought, without fear or recrimination. This is best exemplified perhaps by Descartes, who began to doubt all his previous beliefs and attempted to re-establish them on a firm foundation—clear and distinct ideas and deductive inferences from them. In this process of self-examination, Descartes came to question his previously held beliefs, based on authority, faith, feeling, or his senses. Free inquiry became pivotal in the development of the new science of the fifteenth and sixteenth centuries: all previously held theories of the universe had to be tested by reason and experiment. Even Aristotle's authority and the views by the Church had to be questioned. No discipline could be investigated without the free play of the intellect, and without fear of punishment. Freedom of thought and conscience was crucial to the democratic revolutions of the seventeenth and eighteenth centuries—the government was held to be limited in its power; it should allow for individual dissent and tolerate alternative points of view.

The continuing battle against authoritarian regimes, which sought to limit freedom of thought and to censor or prohibit free expression has been ongoing. In the name of a Higher Truth, Absolute Morality, or Piety, despots have always sought to curtail free inquiry.

In the twentieth century the great battle was against totalitarian ideologies—whether fascist or communist. These sought to use the power of the state to enforce ideological conformity to stamp out dissenting viewpoints.

The confrontation of the free mind with theological dogmatism is an ongoing saga in human history. The Roman Catholic theologians sought to censor Bruno and Galileo. Orthodox Jews excommunicated Spinoza. Protestant fundamentalists insisted upon the teaching of creationism along with evolution in the schools. Thomas Jefferson opposed any "tyranny over the mind of man," whether religious or political. Increasingly the separation of church and state and the development of a plurality of denominations has led to a modicum of toleration and modus vivendi—though orthodox religionists attempt to bridge the wall in the light of its dogmas.

Today there is an ongoing struggle between freethinkers and Muslim fundamentalists, who consider blasphemy and atheism the greatest sins, and do not tolerate any questioning of the articles of faith. The fate of Salman Rushdie, who earned a *fatwa* from the mullahs of Iran and Taslima Nasreen, who was condemned by the fundamentalists of Bangladesh, exemplify this conflict. For the fundamentalist, "blasphemers" and atheists do not have the right to life, but are to be killed. Of the seventeen great sins, apparently unbelief is the greatest, more despicable than murder or theft.

It is well known that Averroës himself suffered repression in his own day. Although he was able to do his work because of the patronage of his caliph, Abu Ya'qub Yusuf, who was interested in philosophy and indeed urged him to provide commentaries on Aristotle, nearing the end of his life his books were prohibited and burned, and he was insulted by a mob. Hourani quotes from his biographer Ansan: "The worst thing that happened to me in my affliction was when I and my son Abdullah entered a mosque in Córdoba at the time of the evening prayer, and some of the lowest of the common people made a commotion against us and ejected us from it" (p. 39).

Fortunately, a year later, just before his death at 72, he was restored to favor and the ban was lifted. Regrettably, however, after the death of Ibn Rushd, his works went into eclipse and the hostility of al-Ghazali to philosophy prevailed. Hourani deplored that fact. As a result, Averroës's writings remained largely unknown to Islamic scholars until the middle of the nineteenth century, though as I pointed out, Averroës's translation and commentaries of Aristotle had a great influence in Europe, and some historians have traced the Enlightenment in part to the influence of the Averroists. Many of us today look back to Averroës and point to his role in order to persuade Muslims to soften their attitude toward free inquiry.

III

Professor Alfred Ivry objects to the reinterpretation of historical figures in the postscript to his paper in this volume (pp. 122–24). Ivry states that "many speakers at the (Cairo) conference . . . presented Averroës as a figure of contemporary significance, emphasizing his dedication to scientific pursuits, philosophy, and democratic values."

Ivry agrees that Averroës for the most part was a champion of science and of a naturalistic and nominalistic philosophy. His political philosophy was antiauthoritarian and perhaps to some degree democratic. However, Ivry correctly points out that Averroës was not truly democratic in spirit and was sympathetic to Plato. It is surely hard to find a devotee of democracy in the twelfth century. Ivry states: "Adopting Averroës for contemporary liberal political purposes is therefore problematic, and threatens to distort his life and work." No doubt, says Ivry, Averroës used allegory for philosophical, personal, and political purposes in order to enable philosophical inquiry to continue. But are we entitled to allegorize Averroës himself, to create a person with modern sensibilities? he asks. Postmodernists, who do not believe in objective history, perhaps can construct history to suit their purposes. Ivry suggests that we need to be cautious in how we read Averroës and we should not seek to use him for our political purposes. "Philosophers must be wary of lending themselves to such methods."

It seems to me that his chastisement is well taken. Nevertheless, may I register some dissent to his dissent? Philosophers have always interpreted the past in the light of present needs. Socrates was considered a chief inspiration for Neoplatonism, but he had also been preempted by analytic philosophers in the last generation, who considered him to be an inspiration for philosophy—insofar as he sought definitions of basic terms and concepts. Aristotle had been used by the Averroists to topple dogmatic theology, but he was also preempted by Aquinas, and used in the twentieth century by naturalists as well.

Similarly, Marxist humanists in the post-World War II period sought to reinterpret Marx's message by looking back to his early *Economic and Philosophical Manuscripts*. On the basis of this they maintained that Marx was an authentic humanist who wished to liberate us from alienation and emphasized the philosophy of freedom. Many orthodox Marxists disagreed with this reading of Marx. Nonetheless the interpretation led in no small measure to the humanization of communism and the overthrow of its totalitarian character in Eastern Europe, at least among intellectuals, which only demonstrates that reinterpretations may have a vital role to play.

In the present context I think it eminently worthwhile to reexamine the history of Islamic thought in order to find tendencies that were rationalistic and permitted some freedom of inquiry. Some writers such as Renan in the nineteenth century went so far as to consider Averroës a freethinker. This interpretation perhaps goes too far. Many philosophers have looked backwards to find precursors for their present position, and this process is not without some justification. Surely there are other philosophers of Islam besides Averroës who agreed with a freethought and rationalist agenda—though no doubt in a modest way. And George Hourani among others has pointed this out. The great confrontation today between reason and tradition in ethics, between democracy and theocracy, human rights and authoritarian systems, have considerable significance in the present confrontation between Islam and Western democratic values. Many intellectuals desire some kind of cultural reformation of Islam, and they hope that with scientific, technological, economic, and political changes this will occur. One way of contributing to this is by pointing out the rich heritage of the Islamic tradition, which did permit some freedom of intellectual interpretation and perhaps approaches in a very modest way the Protestant Reformation and its demand for freedom of individual conscience. In any case, those who believe that Islam is in need of a renaissance, or reformation, or enlightenment, wish to return to its intellectual precursors—and this is not without some justification.

Another aspect of this problem concerns the role of rationalistic ethics in Islamic thought. Hourani has pointed to the fact that Abdu al-Jabbar had attempted some philosophical inquiries. In his book *Reason and Tradition in Islamic Ethics* (1985), Hourani points out that the standards of character and conduct in society are derived from several sources. One is tradition—in the Muslim world the Qur'an and the Tradition provide the conventional framework. There is a real difference in the Muslim tradition between philosophers, who wish to use reason, and the Asharite tradition, which prefers religious dogma.

The main virtues taught by the Qur'an were: "piety, i.e., humble obedience and fear of God," and, adds Hourani, "justice, the avoidance of wrongdoing, benevolence, gratitude to God, chastity, the performance of ritual duties and legal obligation." Ethical commandments insofar as they are derived from God express a form of ethical voluntarism and subjectivism (as emphasized in the Asharite tradition and al-Ghazali).

The philosophical tradition takes a different approach. The great question, says Hourani, is whether a Muslim is ever authorized to decide issues that go beyond scriptures and tradition. For example, how does the Muslim solve moral dilemmas or deal with new problems never foreseen within the Qur'an? And here Hourani recommends the use of reason to resolve moral issues. He has argued that there is an objective basis for moral choice and that ethics in one sense is autonomous and independent of theological premises. This no doubt is a radical thesis for the traditional fundamentalist approach. Yet it is possible that those within the Islamic tradition have been and can be persuaded to adopt a more liberal approach. In 1984 Hourani wrote:

> In spite of the resurgence of fundamentalism in several Muslim countries,
> I believe fundamentalism is bound to fail in competition with the many
> good things offered by modern life and a more relaxed society: freedom
> above all—for women to choose their husbands and their dress, to be able
> to drive cars and go out without veils, for minorities not to suffer dis-

crimination or persecution, for boys and girls to attend the same schools and colleges, for everyone to listen to the music they like, to be able to criticize the government and religious leaders without fear of reprisal, unlawful detention, or torture, freedom to lend and borrow money with interest without having to resort to legal fictions (Hiyal), etc.

There are still strong forces of liberalism in many Muslim countries; Egypt, Turkey, Jordan, Tunisia, Kuwait, probably in Malaysia. But they lack a firm theoretical grounding in Islamic thought. . . . Fundamentalism and even Sunnite conservatism are attempts to cling to the safety of the past, which can have only temporary success. If I had a choice of what intellectual paths Muslims should follow—a choice which I do not have looking at Islam from outside—I would start over again at the points where the early jurists and the Mutazilites left off, and work to develop a system of Islamic law which would openly make use of judgments of equity and public interest, and a system of ethical theology, which would encourage judgments of right and wrong by the human mind, without having to look at scripture at every step. The Mutazilites were correct in the doctrine that we can make objective value judgments, even if their particular theory of ethics had weaknesses, which would have to be revised by modern ethical philosophers and theologians. So I think this is the best way for Muslims to revive Islam, and I wish them success at this formidable task.

I submit that the reappraisal of Averroës by this seminar in a modest way makes contributions to this development so vitally necessary in the world today. I don't think that we need necessarily distort history in looking back to the Islamic renaissance of the ninth to twelfth centuries, but that we can reevaluate and reinterpret it and hopefully contribute to the modernization, secularization, and humanization of Islamic culture. This culture plays an increasingly important role in the world, and it needs to enter into dialogue with Western philosophies and to try to seek an accommodation. And above all it needs to come into the modern world. Islamic culture still remains premodern. It is important if it is to make progress that the further modernization of Islamic thought and values—and particularly freedom of thought—be encouraged.

23

The Philosopher and the Understanding of the Law

Jorge J. E. Gracia
Professor of Philosophy,
State University of New York at Buffalo (USA)

One of the tenets of the rationalist interpretation of Averroës is that, for him, the philosopher is the arbiter of the meaning of the law. Indeed, even those scholars who do not defend a strictly rationalist interpretation of his thought, frequently agree with this understanding of it.[1] I shall argue in what follows that not only did Averroës not hold that the philosopher is the arbiter of the meaning of the law, but that, even if he had, such a view would go contrary to some of the basic principles of his philosophy. The philosopher, I shall show, does not and cannot know the meaning of the law with the certainty which the philosophical method is supposed to yield. So, unless we are prepared to believe that Averroës contradicted himself in a rather obvious way—and I do not believe for a moment he did—we must accept that this tenet of the rationalist interpretation of Averroës is mistaken. This conclusion has important implications for the determination of the relation of Averroës to the Enlightenment, but I shall leave speculations on that score to others.

Let me begin by summarizing what I have explained elsewhere in more detail concerning Averroës's view of the interpretation of the law.[2] The law (*shar'*) refers to texts in which God has revealed Himself and His views to humanity. These texts are called *the law* because they contain God's commands for human conduct, but they can also be called *scriptures* insofar as they are texts to be studied.[3]

Averroës divides the law into two types of texts: Texts which have an apparent meaning only (*zahir*) and texts which also have a hidden meaning (*batin*).[4] The difference between these two types of texts is that the first do not use symbols whereas the second do.[5] Because the first do not use symbols, their interpretation poses no difficulties and they can be understood by everyone who is a competent user of the language in which the texts are rendered. "Everyone" includes three classes of knowers: the rhetorical class, the dialectical class, and the demonstrative class.[6] (I shall return to this in a moment.)

The interpretation of texts which have a hidden meaning poses difficulties, because the use these texts make of symbols requires that they be interpreted allegorically (*ta'wil*), that is, that the words they use be understood to mean something other than their ordinary meaning.[7] Now, in some of these texts, the meaning of the symbols are well known to everyone and, therefore, these texts pose no difficulties of interpretation to any of the three classes of people mentioned. These texts are allegorically understood, but their understanding is the same for everyone. But there are some texts in which this is not so, and this opens up the question concerning who is responsible for their correct interpretation. The view of Averroës I am disputing holds that, for him, it is the philosopher who can determine the correct interpretation of these texts.

I have three reasons to dispute this view. The first is that, for Averroës, there is only one way to establish that a particular interpretation of a text of the sort we are discussing is correct: unanimity (*ijma'*). But he holds that unanimity is not possible to achieve. Therefore, we can never be certain that a particular interpretation of a text, the meaning of whose symbols is not known to everyone, is the correct one.

Religions have devised many ways of determining when an interpretation of a sacred text is correct. For example, some religions make personal intuition the criterion of certainty: I am certain that a particular understanding of a text is correct if I have a personal intuition to that effect. Some other religions find the criterion of certainty in the opinion of an authoritative body or a person of authority: I know a particular interpretation of a text is correct if that is the interpretation sanctioned by a person or body of persons regarded as authoritative. And there are other possibilities, such as tradition and combinations of various criteria. However, Averroës does not consider any of these, and explicitly favors only unanimity, which, as already noted, he finds impossible to achieve.

> That unanimity on theoretical matters is never determined with certainty, as it can be on practical matters, may be shown to you by the fact that it is not possible for unanimity to be determined on any question at any period unless that period is strictly limited by us, and all the scholars existing in that period are known to us (i.e. known as individuals and in their total number), and the doctrine of each of them on the question has been handed down to us on unassailable authority, and, in addition to all this, unless we are sure that the scholars existing at the time were in agreement that there is not both an apparent and inner meaning in Scripture, that the knowledge of any question ought not to be kept secret from anyone, and that there is only one way for people to understand Scripture.[8]

Clearly, the conditions of unanimity are impossible to meet.[9] Moreover, Averroës makes explicit that this impossibility applies in particular to allegorical interpretations; there is no possibility of unanimity concerning these.[10]

The second reason to dispute the view that, for Averroës, the philosopher is the arbiter of the correct interpretation of texts which use symbols whose meaning is not evident to everyone is that Averroës explicitly opposes the view which holds that we can be certain which interpretations of these texts are correct. The reasons he gives for this position are practical. He believed that the contrary view leads to abuses of all kinds. First, because claiming a correct interpretation of hidden meanings involves making the interpretation public among those who are not capable of understanding them, and this leads to unbelief. Those who do not understand the interpretation lose their faith; and those who put forward the interpretation for them become unbelievers for contributing to the unbelief of others.[11] Second, because claiming to have such a correct understanding and presenting it to nonqualified people causes division and hatred:

> Thus the Mu'tazilites interpreted many verses and Traditions allegorically, and the Ash'arites did the same, although they used such interpretations less frequently. In consequence, they threw people into hatred, mutual detestations and wars, tore the Scriptures to shreds, and completely divided people.[12]

To claim a correct interpretation of these texts is wrong. Therefore, scholars should keep their interpretations to themselves and they should tell nonscholars that God is the only arbiter of the correct interpretation of the texts He has given us.

> With regard to an apparent text, when there is self-evident doubt whether it is apparent to everyone and whether knowledge of its interpretation is possible for them, they should be told that it is ambiguous and its meaning known by no one but God.[13]

These two reasons are important and I believe are sufficient to show that Averroës did not hold that there is anyone who can know with complete certainty when an interpretation of a text which uses symbols whose meanings are not evident to everyone is correct. And, if this is so, then he could not have held, without contradiction, that philosophers can be the arbiters of the correct interpretation of these texts. But there is an even more important reason in support of this position, although it is not as explicit as the ones discussed so far.

For Averroës there are three different methods through which one can reach assent, that is, there are three ways through which one can draw a conclusion (*qiyas*).[14] Moreover, because a conclusion for him is always a conclusion of deductive reasoning, these methods are deductive. Consider the following deductive argument:

All S is M
All M is P
Therefore, All S is P

According to Averroës, the three methods through which one can infer the conclusion of this argument are the following: the demonstrative (*burhan*), the dialectical (*jadali*), and the rhetorical (*khitabi*). The conditions of the demonstrative method are as follows: (1) The argument must be valid, that is, the conclusion must follow necessarily from the premises; (2) the premises of the argument must be true; (3) the premises must to be known to be true either because they are self-evident or because they are derived from other demonstrative arguments; and (4) the argument must not use symbols.[15] The following argument would qualify as demonstrative for Averroës:

1. All triangles are geometrical figures with three angles.
2. All geometrical figures with three angles have angles which to-gether measure 180 degrees.
3. Therefore, all triangles have angles which together measure 180 degrees.

This argument qualifies as demonstrative because it fulfills the four specified conditions. The argument is valid and its premises are true and known to be true, for premise 1 is self-evident and premise 2, although not self-evident, is the result of some other demonstrative argument. Moreover, none of the terms used in the argument has symbolic meaning. The meanings of the terms in the argument are the standard meanings in the language.

The second method of reaching conclusions is the dialectical.[16] The dialectical method shares with the demonstrative method conditions 1 and 2: The argument must be valid and its premises must be true.[17] But condition 3 is not the same: the way the truth of its premises is known is different from the way the truth of the premises of the demonstrative argument is known. For the premises of the dialectical argument are neither self-evident nor conclusions of demonstrative arguments. The premises of this kind of argument are known to be true on the basis of revelation. Finally, it is not clear whether condition 4 applies. Averroës does not state clearly whether the dialectical argument can use language symbolically, although I am in-clined to hold that it does not because the use of symbolic language is char-acteristic of rhetorical arguments. In any case, it is obvious that the defin-ing characteristic of dialectical reasoning is that the premises of this kind of reasoning are based on revelation, that is, belief. The following, then, qualifies as a dialectical argument:

1. Eating pork is forbidden by the law.
2. All that is forbidden by the law is bad for humans.
3. Therefore, eating pork is bad for humans.

Clearly, Averroës would regard the premises of this argument as true, for they are contained in the law or can be easily deductively derived from it. But he would say the argument of which they are premises is dialecti-cal because neither of the premises is self-evident nor the conclusion of a demonstrative argument. They are known to be true on the basis of faith and thus the certainty we can have of the truth of the conclusion of the argument too depends on revelation. Note, however, that the language used in this illustrative argument is, like the language used in demonstrative arguments, nonsymbolic.

The third method of reaching conclusions is the rhetorical.[18] Again, the rhetorical method shares with the demonstrative and the dialectical methods conditions 1 and 2: This argument is supposed to be valid and to have true premises. Moreover, like the dialectical argument, the premises of this kind of argument are based on belief rather than on self-evidence or demonstration. But, unlike the demonstrative and the dialectical, the rhetorical argument uses symbols. This is the defining characteristic of rhetorical reasoning. The following qualifies as a rhetorical argument:

1. God is the creator of man.
2. Man is a being with free will.
3. Therefore, God is the creator of a being with free will.

This is a valid argument with true premises and the premises are known to be true through revelation. The argument, then, would appear to be dialectical, because its premises are not known on the basis of self-evidence or demonstration. However, what is characteristic of this argument is not its dialectical character; its distinctive character is that it uses language symbolically. The term "creator" which it uses to describe the relation between man and God is used metaphorically, because God is not strictly speaking the creator of man. Indeed, strictly speaking, and in accordance with the Aristotelian framework Averroës adopts, God is not creator of anything. God is rather the Final Cause of the universe, the object of desire which makes change possible. His function is to explain change, not to explain the existence of the universe.

Now, according to Averroës, philosophers use demonstrative reasoning, theologians use dialectical reasoning, and preachers use rhetorical reasoning.[19] All three use arguments that are valid and have true premises, so the conclusions they reach are also true. Averroës firmly believed in the truth of the conclusions reached not just by philosophers, but also by theologians and preachers, provided they follow the rules prescribed by their disciplines.[20] There is no evidence Averroës ever held that theology and preaching lead to falsity. Still, it is quite clear he held philosophers know their conclusions demonstratively; theologians only believe their conclusions; and preachers are unclear as to their ultimate meaning, because the views they expound are cloaked in symbols.

Now, to know that an allegorical interpretation of a text that uses symbols is correct is to know something like this:

Text T means M.

Moreover, this must be a conclusion of an argument, for it involves assent and there are only the three methods of assent we have discussed: demonstrative, dialectical, and rhetorical. Now, the interpretation of Averroës I am disputing would have to hold that the conclusion of an allegorical interpretation such as the one I have provided, in which the text uses symbols, must be of the demonstrative sort, for the philosopher, qua philosopher, uses only the method of demonstration. Such an interpretation, then, must be based on a demonstration which proves that the particular symbols used in the text have the particular meanings claimed in the interpretation. For example, to conclude that the word "creator" used in a text from the Qur'an means "First Cause," requires a demonstrative argument. But is it possible to give such an argument for this fact? The answer is negative, and I do not believe that Averroës ever thought it was possible to provide such an argument. For the meaning of symbols, unlike the meaning of nonsymbolic language, is precisely what is at stake in the allegorical interpretation, and the philosopher has no claim to know with certainty what that meaning is. The reason is clear: There is no self-evident principle (or set of principles) or demonstrations from which the philosopher can derive the connection between a particular symbol and its allegorical meaning. There is, and there cannot be, no self-evident principle or demonstration for the fact that "creator" means "First Cause."

Note that the issue need not concern the connection between a particular sound (or sounds) and a meaning, or a particular mark (or marks) and a meaning. The issue is not the connection between some written marks on this page, say "creator" and the meaning "creator." The issue has to do rather with concepts. It concerns the fact that the concept of creator actually means "First Cause" rather than "creator." For Averroës surely accepted the Aristotelian view of the conventional character of language. Indeed, if he had held otherwise, he could not have consistently maintained that *any* demonstrative knowledge is possible.

In short, the philosopher cannot possibly have demonstrative knowledge of the meaning of symbolic language, because there are no self-evident principles or demonstrations from which such knowledge could be derived. Therefore, the knowledge the philosopher has of the meaning of texts which use symbols whose meanings are not generally evident cannot be certain.

But, then, we may ask: Is the philosopher's knowledge better than the knowledge theologians and preachers have of the meanings of those texts? I am inclined to speculate that the answer is affirmative, but the reason is not that the philosopher knows with certainty what these symbols mean. His knowledge is superior to the knowledge of the preacher because the philosopher does not use symbols in the allegorical interpretations he gives. So, his interpretation of symbolic texts advance, in principle, the process of knowledge over what the preacher offers. And the philosopher's knowledge is superior to that of both the theologian and the preacher insofar as the philosopher proceeds by using self-evident principles and conclusions of other demonstrations, and therefore has a better grasp of the interpretive possibilities of the texts in question, whereas theologians and preachers base their conclusions on revelation. Indeed, this may be the reason why it is the philosopher who bears the responsibility for allegorical interpretation. But the philosopher can have no demonstrative certainty about his conclusions concerning correct allegorical interpretations, and, indeed, it is altogether possible that he may be wrong and that the theologian and the preacher are right. For the philosopher can offer no demonstrative proofs of his allegorical interpretations of texts and only demonstrative proofs can yield the certainty which characterizes the philosophical method.

Notes

1. George F. Hourani, Introduction to Averroës, *On the Harmony of Religion and Philosophy* (London: Luzak & Co., 1967), p. 24. Averroës's treatise is also known as *The Decisive Treatise*.

2. Jorge J. E. Gracia, "Interpretation and the Law: Averroës's Contribution to the Hermeneutics of Sacred Texts," *History of Philosophy Quarterly*, forthcoming.

3. Hourani, Introduction to Averroës, *On the Harmony of Religion and Philosophy,* p. 19. For reasons of economy I shall not discuss the notions of text and interpretation here, but the reader will find further details in Gracia, *A Theory of Textuality: The Logic and Epistemology* (Albany, N.Y.: SUNY Press, 1995) and *Texts: Ontological Status, Identity, Author, Audience* (Albany, N.Y.: SUNY Press, 1996).

4. The first is often referred to as "literal" as well. See Hourani, Introduction to Averroës, *On the Harmony of Religion and Philosophy,* p. 24.

5. Averroës, *On the Harmony of Religion and Philosophy*, trans. George F. Hourani, p. 78.

6. Ibid., p. 59.

7. Ibid., p. 50.

8. Ibid., p. 52.

9. This applies both to theologians and to philosophers who are believers. Ibid., p. 57.

10. Ibid., pp. 53, 54, and 57.

11. Ibid., p. 66.

12. Ibid., p. 68.

13. Ibid., p. 66.

14. Ibid., p. 64.

15. Averroës is not very explicit on all these conditions, but his intention is to follow Aristotle. For Aristotle, see *Posterior Analytics* 71b20. I have not listed all the conditions Aristotle mentions, but only the pertinent ones for our argument.

16. Cf. Aristotle, ibid., 71a6 and *On Sophistical Refutations* 165b3.

17. Note that the syllogism (valid deductive argument) in question need not be perfect. Enthymemes qualify as well.

18. Cf. Aristotle, *Rhetoric* 1401a2.

19. Averroës, *On the Harmony of Religion and Philosophy*, pp. 49, 65.

20. Ibid., p. 50.

24

Averroës on the Harmony of Philosophy and Religion

Thérèse-Anne Druart
Professor of Philosophy,
The Catholic University of America (USA)

At the very beginning of the *Fasl al-maqal* or *The Decisive Treatise*, sometimes known as the *Harmony Between Religion and Philosophy*, Averroës gives us a definition of philosophy or *falsafa*.

> If the activity (*fi'l*) of "philosophy" is nothing more than study of existing beings and reflection on them as indications of the Artisan (*al-sani'*), i.e., inasmuch as they are products of art (*masnu'at*) (for beings only indicate the Artisan through our knowledge of the art in them, and the more perfect this knowledge is, the more perfect the knowledge of the Artisan becomes), and if the Law has encouraged and urged reflections on beings, then it is clear that what this name signifies is either obligatory or recommended by the Law.[1]

Putting aside the question of determining whether or not Averroës accepts this definition of philosophy or more precisely metaphysics, we are confronted with the complex issue of causation and its impact on the questions of God's knowledge and of the eternity of the world, two of the main bones of contention between Averroës, who presents himself as the cham-

253

pion of the philosophers, and al-Ghazali, the champion of religion so often referred to in this brief text.

Al-Ghazali himself was very aware of the importance of causation for the whole debate. In his *Munqidh* or intellectual biography, sometimes known as *Deliverance from Error*, while appraising physics or natural philosophy and related questions, he plainly states:

> The basic point regarding all of them is for you to know that nature is totally subject to God Most High: it does not act of itself but is used as an instrument by its Creator. The sun, moon, stars, and the elements are subject to god's command: none of them effects any act by and of itself. (*la fi'l lishayin minha bidhatihi 'an dhatihi*).[2]

This is expressed in more technical terms in the *Incoherence of the Philosophers* in the section concerning the natural sciences, first question:

> The connection between what is customarily believed to be a cause and what is believed to be an effect is not necessary, according to our opinion; but each of the two [namely, what is believed to be a cause and what is believed to be an effect] is independent of the other. The affirmation of one does not imply the affirmation of the other, nor does the denial of one imply the denial of the other; the existence of one does not necessitate the existence of the other, nor does the non-existence of one necessitate the non-existence of the other.[3]

This is followed by the famous analysis of the burning of a piece of cotton in which al-Ghazali argues that fire is not the acting cause for the burning of the piece of cotton.

It seems therefore interesting to examine how Averroës handles this issue in the appropriate section of the *Incoherence of the Incoherence,* particularly since Averroës is on very tricky grounds. After all, what exactly is the position of the philosophers on this issue? Avicenna in his *Metaphysics*, Treatise VI, chapters 1 and 2, had already taken serious distance from the position that the supposedly observed cause is the true agent or acting cause. As for al-Ghazali himself, Marmura and Richard Frank have shown that he is less than straightforward on this very issue since at least in the passage of the *Incoherence* of which I have quoted some lines he presents no less than two or three theories on causation.[4] The last of these is none other than a variation on an Avicennan theme, even grants the existence of natures, and yet can be accommodated to leave space for miracles, and in particular for Abraham's surviving and not being burnt after having been thrown into the fiery furnace.

How does Averroës handle these two first-rate pieces of philosophy, which both claim that the true acting cause is not the observed one? I am afraid the philosophical answer is: "not too well," even if Barry Kogan tried to make the most of it to defend him[5]. In his desire to avoid trouble among ordinary people who need to act morally or virtuously, Averroës takes it that the learned among the philosophers do not permit discussion of the principles of religion such as miracles, the existence of most of which appears to him incompatible with the views of the philosophers that there is a necessary connection between the observed cause and its effect. Since the denial and discussion of the principles of the Shari'a denies human existence Averroës states that "it is necessary to kill heretics (*zanadiqa*)[6]" and dodges serious philosophical problems. I intend, therefore, to look briefly at some aspects of Avicenna's position and that of al-Ghazali before evaluating Averroës' comments on this passage since it seems to me that Kogan did not pay enough attention to some of its aspects.

Avicenna : *Metaphysics*, VI, 1 and 2, or the True Acting Cause Is Not the Observed One

The title of chapter 2 is rather significant:

> The Solution of the Question Which Arises Concerning the Opinion of the True Philosophers [Who maintain] that Every Cause Exists Simultaneously with That Which is Caused by It, and the Verification of the Discourse Concerning the Acting Cause (*al-'illa al-fa'iliyya*).[7]

In this chapter Avicenna argues that some people are ignorant of what a cause truly is. "The builder, and the father, and the fire are not really causes for the subsistence of the things which they cause"[8] and they are not even causes of their existence. So what is a true cause? It is that which provides the form, that is the incorporeal substances. Such true efficient and essential causes which are finite in number must exist simultaneously with their effects whereas the causes which precede the things caused are causes either accidentally or as supporting and may be infinite in number. The builder, i.e., a craftsman or voluntary "agent" is not really the agent of the building, the father, i.e., a member of a natural species is not the real agent of the son and fire, a natural "agent," therefore, is not the real agent of burning but simply an accidental agent or a supporting cause which requires a matter to act. When matter is needed then matter has power over the effect coming into being since the procession or emanation requires the appropriate recipient. Avicenna uses the Neoplatonic principle that whatever is received is received at the mode of the receiver. So if the appropriate disposition is not present in matter, the form cannot be received and there is no effect. The accidental or supporting causes, therefore, provide the dispositions which allow the true agent to be effective. The famous "Giver of Forms"[9] requires matter to act. On the other hand, the ultimate or first true cause is able to act "after" absolute nonexistence and therefore without matter and this procession (*sudur*) is creation (*'ibda'*) and nothing has power on such effect, and, therefore, its cause.[10]

Fire, therefore, is not a true acting cause since it precedes the burning and its own form derives from the Giver of Forms, i.e., the tenth separate intelligence. Chapter one had clearly explained what the root of the problem was: many people—and this in fact includes Aristotle—had confused cause of motion and cause of existence. Avicenna spells it out in the following manner:

> The reason is that the metaphysicians do not intend by the agent the principle of movement only, as do the natural philosophers, but also the principle of existence and that which bestows [existence] (*mufidu*), such as the creator of the world (*al-bari lil-'alam*). But the natural acting cause does not bestow existence as distinguished from movement.[11]

Fire is not a true cause of existence but only an accidental cause or necessary disposition for burning to appear. Avicenna's position undermines the claims of ordinary people about the observed cause. Sensory experience may show that fire precedes or even accompanies the burning but such concomitance does not show a necessary connection between the fire and the existence of the burning. The real agent is beyond sensory impression but fire, which is simply an accidental or supporting cause, provides the dispositions which are a necessary condition for the efficacy of the true agent's act and, therefore, keeps at least some level of causal efficacy.

Al-Ghazali: *The Incoherence of the Philosophers, Concerning the Natural Sciences, First Question*

This section is preceded by al-Ghazali's review of the natural sciences and his affirmation that he only sees problems with four points, the first of which is naturally the assertion by the natural philosophers that "this connection observed between causes and effects is necessary."[12] Al-Ghazali thinks he must contest this view because it does not allow for miracles which interrupt the usual course of nature (*al-'ada*), such as Moses' changing a rod into a serpent. Philosophers simply interpret such "miracles" allegorically, except in certain limited cases. Al-Ghazali concludes this introduction with stating that one needs to deal with this question in order to assert miracles and to support "the doctrine on which the Muslims base their belief that God has power over everything"[13] as possible.

Al-Ghazali then presents two points against the philosophers and their affirmation that there is a necessary connection between what is customarily believed (*fi al-'ada*) to be a cause and what is believed to be an effect. In a first move he presents the view of some philosophers who claim that "the acting cause of burning is fire exclusively and that fire acts by nature."[14] In stark contrast al-Ghazali states that it is God who is the only acting cause of burning by creating blackness in the cotton, etc, whereas fire which is inanimate does not have any act whatsoever (*fi'l*). He then argues that observation proves only one thing, i.e., that the so-called effect occurs together with the so-called cause, since this does not prove that it occurs through the agency of the other[15]. He then comments that this is the very argument that the philosophers who talk of the "Artisan," i.e., God (and Averroës did so at the very beginning of *The Decisive Treatise*[16]), cannot refute. He then asserts that since the philosophers assert that the father is not the acting cause of his son or of his sight, they should also assert that the fire is not the acting cause of the burning. Indeed, this is what "true" philosophers[17]—he must be referring to Avicenna—hold. Hence what we observe and what are customarily taken for causes are only preparatory and preliminary for the subject's reception of the forms emanating from the Giver of Forms. Clearly, for him, the perceived "causes" contribute nothing to the action but simply allow the subject to receive those forms. Al-Ghazali seems to have reappropriated Avicenna's conclusion in such a way that the so-called observed causes are no longer even causes of motion—Avicenna had left them this role—and, therefore, have no causal role whatsoever.

Such a reformulation allows for God's freedom and full power to do whatever is possible, since these so-called causes have become preparatory and preliminary things which are simply instruments entirely caused by Him.

Moving to a second point al-Ghazali presents an opponent who claims that "the predisposition [in the affected subject] for receiving the forms occurs through causes that are observed and present."[18] This second view seems to restore at least some kind of act to what observers habitually dub "acting" causes. They provide a new kind of disposition which will ensure a new kind of reception. This explains why one and the same apparent agent, sunlight, for instance, whitens the fuller's garment but blackens his face. In that way the efficacy of the act of real agents depends on the existence and mode of existence of a disposition capable of receiving it. The disposition has some power over the act of the acting cause and, therefore, if Abraham is a true human being and the fire is a true fire, poor Abraham must necessarily burn when thrown into the fiery furnace.[19]

Al-Ghazali denies this necessity since he holds that principles of existence or God act by will.

> If it is affirmed that the acting cause [God] creates burning through His will, when cotton and fire are in contact, then it is possible, according to reason, that He may not create burning when contact [between cotton and fire] exists.[20]

The adversary will counterattack by claiming that such a view would completely undermine uniformity and regularities in nature, but al-Ghazali retorts that God can create knowledge of the nonexistence of some possible and, in so doing, substitutes to the necessity of natures the notion of custom ('ada) or customary behavior in both the course of things and in our knowledge of it which is based on past customary recurrences. Hence God can create effects without their usual concomitant and even create in a prophet the knowledge that He will do so.[21] Sensory experience can lead, therefore, to knowledge construed as habitual and for the most part, but does no longer show a necessary connection between what is erroneously construed as a cause and its supposed effect.

Averroës's Reply in the *Tahafut or The Incoherence of the Incoherence*

Averroës begins by stating that denying "the existence of acting causes which are *observed* in sensible things is sophistry . . . for he who denies this can no longer acknowledge that every act must have an agent."[22]

Why this should follow is not clear to me since in al-Ghazali's most antithetic formulation there is still one agent who is the agent for every "act," i.e., God. Then, even if fire is no longer considered the agent of burning, it does not follow that there is no other agent for the burning since al-Ghazali claims God is this agent.

Averroës then goes on to argue that if we deny the existence of acting causes which are observed in sensible things science will be impossible since necessary knowledge will be impossible. To substitute a "custom" or "habit" (*'ada*) for the necessary connection does not solve anything because the notion of "custom" or "habit" is vague and it is not clear whether it refers to the agent, i.e., God, or to existing things, or to our "habit" to form a judgment about such things. In its strict philosophical sense as defined by Aristotle the notion of "habit" cannot apply to God nor to existing things and, therefore, can only apply to an act of our soul determined by its nature, but al-Ghazali denies that there are natures[23]. Averroës here rightly points to the fuzziness of the notion of "habit" used by al-Ghazali but seems unable to conceive of it outside of the Aristotelian framework.

Averroës then moves to examine the first version of a reformulation of the Avicennan position which al-Ghazali seems to have deemed equivalent to or at least compatible with his own view that there is only one agent. Surprisingly Averroës assimilates it to a second version, that of an opponent who grants some causation to the supposedly observed cause in producing predispositions that determine whether and how forms are received and, therefore, limit the efficacy of the power of the true acting cause. Averroës blurs the differences between these two theories and simply claims that they are illusions and have not really been affirmed by anyone. He then asserts that since separate principles have knowledge they must act by choice even if out of two contraries only the better can proceed. Rejection of the miracle of Abraham surviving the fiery furnace should not be put at the door of the philosophers but rather at the door of heretical Muslims and since denying miracles denies human existence, heretics or free thinkers must be killed[24]. In fact Averroës spends little time dealing seriously with the philosophical points but rather focuses on the social dangers arising from the denial of miracles. Even Kogan who ingeniously tries to absolve Averroës of the philosophical sin of not taking seriously al-Ghazali's argument that observation cannot tell us anything about a necessary connection between the so-called cause and effect confesses that the defense is essentially political.[25]

Commenting then on al-Ghazali's claim that the principles and God act through the will and not necessarily, Averroës reiterates that such a view abolishes any observation of the existence of causes and effects and claims that

> no philosopher doubts that, for instance, the fire is the acting cause of the burning which occurs in the cotton through the fire—not, however, absolutely, but in relation to an external principle which is the condition of the existence of fire, not to speak of its burning.[26]

What exactly is meant by the external principle being a condition (*shart*) rather than a cause of the existence of the fire, not to speak of its burning, is not spelled out though Averroës claims that philosophers only disagree about whether such a principle is a separate principle or an intermediary. Vagueness is of the order and we can only regret that Averroës in his zeal to avoid discussing the very possibility of miracles and to convince others to do the same by threatening them with execution was led to dodge dealing carefully with a serious philosophical issue. He misses the opportunity to present a careful analysis of the relation between primary and secondary causes.

Obviously Averroës wants to distance himself from the position that the real agent is not the observed agent but rather a separate being or God. Thus, he seems here to make of God not an "Artisan" or even an acting cause but simply a condition of existence and of the act of a being. Yet, both Avicenna and al-Ghazali claim that such a position is the position of true philosophers. He, therefore, rejects a philosophical position not on philosophical grounds but rather on political grounds. One may well wonder if in doing so Averroës is not giving up his right to be called a true philosopher. Neither philosophy nor, I think, what he calls its "milk-sister," i.e., the Law or religion,[27] end up being well served at least in this particular discussion.

Notes

1. Translation taken from Averroës, *On the Harmony of Religion and Philosophy*, transl. and ed. by George F. Hourani (London: Luzac, 1961), p. 44; Arabic: Ibn Rushd (Averroës), *Kitab fasl al-maqal*, ed. by George F. Hourani (Leiden: E.J. Brill, 1959), pp. 5–6.

2. Translation taken from *Freedom and Fulfillment, An Annotated Translation of al-Ghazali's* al-Munqidh min al-dalal *and Other Relevant Works of al-Ghazali* by Richard Joseph McCarthy, S.J. (Boston: Twayne, 1980), p. 76; Arabic from Al-Ghazali, *Al-Munqid min adalal (Erreur et Délivrance)*, ed.and transl. by Farid Jabre, 2nd ed. (Beirut: Commission Libanaise pour la Traduction des Chefs-d'Oeuvre, 1969), p. 23.

3. Translation by Arthur Hyman taken from *The Incoherence of the Philosophers* section in *Philosophy in the Middle Ages*, ed. by Arthur Hyman and James J. Walsh, 2nd ed. (Indianapolis: Hackett, 1983), p. 283; Arabic: Algazel, *Tahafot al-Falasifat*, ed. by Maurice Bouyges, S.J. (Beirut: Imprimerie Catholique, 1927), p. 277.

4. Michael E. Marmura, "Al-Ghazali on Bodily Resurrection and Causality in the Tahafut and the Iqtisad," *Aligarh Journal of Islamic Thought* 2 (1989): 46–75; Richard M. Frank, *Creation and the Cosmic System: Al-Ghazâlî & Avicenna* (Abhandlungen der Heidelberger Akademie der Wissenschaften, Philosophisch-historische Klasse, Jahrgang 1992. 1. Abhandlung. Heidelberg: Carl Winter Universitätsverlag, 1992), particularly, ch. 3: "The Ordering of Causes and Events within the World," pp. 22–46, and Michael E. Marmura's review of that book, "Ghazalian Causes and Intermediaries," *Journal of the American Oriental Society* 115 (1995): 89–100. On al-Ghazali's conception of Causality, see also Ilai Alon, "Al-Ghazali on Causality," *Journal of the American Oriental Society* 100 (1980): 397–405; and B. Abrahamov, "Al-Ghazali's Theory of Causality," *Studia Islamica* 67 (1988): 75–98.

5. *Averroës and the Metaphysics of Causation* (Albany: State University of New York Press, 1985), particularly ch. 3, pp. 71–164.

6. Arabic ed. by Maurice Bouyges, S.J., Averroès, *Tahafot at-tahafot.*, 2nd ed. (Beirut: Dar el-Machreq, 1987), p. 527, l. 11.

7. Translation by Arthur Hyman, taken from *Philosophy in the Middle Ages*, op. cit., pp. 247–55, and in particular, p. 252; Arabic in Ibn Sina, *Al-Shifa' Al-Ilahiyyat (La Métaphysique)*, ed. by G.C. Anawati and S. Zayed, intro. by I. Madkour, 2 vol. (Cairo: Organization Générale des Imprimeries Gouvernementales, 1960), vol. 2, pp. 258–68, and p. 264, ll. 2–4, in particular. The Medieval Latin translation of this passage can be found in *Avicenna Latinus, Liber de philosophia prima seu scientia divina, V-X*, ed. with notes by S. Van Riet and with an intro. by G. Verbeke (Louvain: E. Peeters; Leiden: E.J. Brill, 1980), pp. 291–306, and. p. 300, ll. 92–94, in particular..

8. Hyman's transl., op. cit., p. 252; Arabic, op. cit., p. 264, ll.6-; Latin, p. 300, ll. 95–99.

9. By the "Giver of Forms" or "dator formarum" Avicenna means the Agent Intellect which in his system is the tenth separate Intelligence.

10. Hyman's transl., pp. 253–54; Arabic, p. 266, l. 9, p. 267, l. 9; Latin, p. 303, 63–p. 305, l. 94.

11. Hyman's translation, pp. 247–48; Arabic, p. 257, ll.13–15; Latin, p. 292, ll. 19–23.

12. Arabic, pp. 270, l.13–p. 271, l. 1. A translation of most of al-Ghazali's text can be found interspersed with Averroës' response in *Averroës' Tahafut al-tahafut (The Incoherence of the Incoherence)*, transl. with notes by Simon Van den Bergh, vol. I (London: Luzac, 1969), pp. 311–33.

13. Arabic, p. 276, l. 3, simply says "has power over everything" but more carefully p. 285, l. 4, states that God "has power over everything that is possible."

14. Hyman's transl., p. 284; Arabic, p. 278, ll. 10–11.

15. Hyman's translation, p. 284; Arabic, p. 279, ll. 3–5.

16. *Incoherence*, Arabic, p. 279, l. 12; *Decisive Treatise*, Arabic, p. 5, l. 12, see first quotation in this paper.

17. Arabic, p. 281, l. 1; Hyman's translation, p. 285. This may be an echo of Avicenna's reference to true philosophers in the title of *Metaphysics*, VI, 2.

18. Hyman's translation, p. 285; Arabic, p. 281, ll.11–12.

19. Hyman's translation, p. 285; Arabic, pp. 281, l. 10–283, l.3.

20. Hyman's translation, pp. 285–86; Arabic, p. 283, ll. 4–8.

21. Hyman's translation, pp. 286–87; Arabic, pp. 285, l.7–p. 286, l. 11.

22. Van de Bergh's translation, op. cit., p. 318; Arabic, op. cit., p. 519, ll. 12–15.

23. Van den Bergh's translation, pp. 319–20; Arabic, p. 522, l. 15–p. 524, l.1.

24. Van den Bergh's translation, pp. 321–23; Arabic, p. 526, l.3–p. 528, l. 5.

25. See, op. cit., p. 73.

26. Van den Bergh's translation with a modification, p. 323; Arabic, p. 529, ll. 1–4.

27. *Decisive Treatise*, Hourani's translation, p. 70 and Hourani's edition, p. 39.

25

"The Future Life" and Averroës's *Long Commentary on the De Anima of Aristotle*

Richard C. Taylor
Professor of Philosophy,
Marquette University (USA)

"**I**n this matter [of a future life] only the negation of existence is unbelief (*kufr*), because it concerns one of the principles of religion and one of those points to which assent is attainable through the three methods common"[1] to all. In this comment found in his *Decisive Treatise* (1179/80 C.E.[2]) Averroës refers to the methods he had previously indicated as appropriate for the people of the rhetorical, dialectical and demonstrative classes.[3] This was the third matter on which al-Ghazali had leveled at the philosophers the charge of unbelief. The others were the philosophers' teachings on the eternity of the world and on God's knowledge of particulars. But only concerning a future life and its existence does Averroës allow that the charge of unbelief is correctly leveled and that the assertion of the existence of the future life can be rightly expected from all persons regardless of their placement in classes as rhetorical, dialectical, or demonstrative people.

Averroës deals with this in a similar way in the *Tahafut al-tahafut*, written at about the same time. In regard to al-Ghazali's accusation that the final resurrection of the body is denied by the philosophers, Averroës holds that the philosophers regard this teaching as important and strongly believe in it because it gives order to human life, makes the attainment of happiness possible, and "is a necessity for the existence of the moral and speculative virtues and of the practical sciences in men."[4] Here Averroës highlights the value of religious guidelines for human beings across cultures and commonly for all religions. Religion is essential to politics and it is by way of the political arts that humanity as a whole can be aided in achieving fulfillment and excellence in accord with the natural dispositions of each individual. In this context he asserts that

> it must be admitted that the soul is immortal, as is proved by rational and
> religious proofs, and it must be assumed that what arises from the dead
> is a simulacra of these earthly bodies, not these bodies themselves, for
> that which has perished does not return individually.[5]

In each of these works explicitly Averroës holds for the existence of the future life. But also evident in each of these works is Averroës's well-known doctrine on the three classifications of people mentioned earlier. For he asserts that there are those persuaded by rhetorical argument, those swayed by the dialectical, and those convinced by the demonstrative. This last group consists of the philosophers, the only people who can comprehend truth most perfectly.[6] But what group is Averroës addressing in these works? In each it is the people only capable of the dialectical grasp of truth. The *Decisive Treatise* is a monograph on religious law and as such presupposes the truth of certain starting points of discussion and argument on the basis of revelation, tradition, and faith. Although it is a commentary and partial response,[7] it seems best to characterize the *Tahafut al-tahafut* as dialectical as well. This is clear when Averroës explicitly points to the way of understanding for the people of demonstration and philosophical proof. In the context of a discussion of the divine attributes, he writes:

> All this is the theory of the philosophers on this problem and in the way
> we have stated it here with its proofs, it is a persuasive not a demonstra-
> tive statement. It is for you to inquire about these questions in the places
> where they are treated in the books of demonstration, if you are one of
> the people of perfect eudaemonia, and if you are one of those who learn
> the arts the function of which is proof. . . . The kinds of statements . . . are
> many, some demonstrative, others not, and since non-demonstrative state-
> ments can be adduced without knowledge of the art, it was thought that
> this is the case with demonstrative statements; but this is a great

error. And therefore in the spheres of the demonstrative arts, no other statement is possible but a technical statement which only the student of this art can bring, just as is the case with the art of geometry. Nothing therefore of what we have said in this book is a technical demonstrative proof; they are all non-technical statements, some of them having greater persuasion than others, and it is in this spirit that what we have written here must be understood.[8]

What we need to seek out, then, are Averroës's demonstrative philosophical statements on the existence of the future life. And evidently a likely candidate for containing these is one or more of his philosophical commentaries. Let us give careful consideration to his discussion in his *Long Commentary on the De Anima of Aristotle* where the nature of the soul is directly discussed in philosophical terms. This work is most suitable because it contains his most complete psychological account of human beings and because it is one of his most mature works.[9] Moreover, the need for thoughtful consideration of this work seems all the more important in light of conflicting interpretations of Averroës's thought and recent efforts to portray his purportedly philosophical arguments about the nature of the soul as being founded on principles taken from the Qur'an. For it has recently been contended that his *Long Commentary on the De Anima of Aristotle* contains doctrines reconciling the Qur'anic conception of death and the Aristotelian conception of soul on the matter of the future life.

Ovey Mohammed asserted in a 1993 article in *International Philosophical Quarterly* that Averroës's view is that eternal life comes about for people when their earthly bodies are replaced by other bodies at resurrection.[10] He sets forth the interpretation that there can be a reconciliation of teachings and an understanding of Averroës's notion of a future existence of human beings from study of the *Long Commentary on the De Anima of Aristotle* if scholars will only bring the correct viewpoint to consideration of the texts of Averroës, namely that there is a single understanding of human beings and their afterlife common to the Qur'an and the *Long Commentary on the De Anima of Aristotle*.[11] Modern researchers, in spite of profound efforts made in work toward the grasp of his philosophy and theology, have struggled without success in dealing with his admissions of personal immortality. What has escaped them is the religious character of Averroës's *Long Commentary on the De Anima*, for "their unfamiliarity with Qur'anic anthropology has left them unable to reconcile this finding with Averroës's theory of the intellect as found in the Long Commentary on the *De Anima*."[12] He further writes that Averroës clarifies his understanding of soul and intellect thanks to revelation[13] even to the extent that "One may say that it is Averroës's concern with the Qur'anic conception of human beings and their relationship with God that furnishes in part the reason why the intellect is conjoined or united (*copulatur*) to us. Moreover, as we shall see, this theory of conjunction is of great importance in understanding how human beatitude in this life is related to a system of reward and punishment in the next."[14] And on the topic of body and soul, "In fact, it is because of this Qur'anic teaching [on body and soul] that Averroës can state categorically that the use of a corporeal instrument is the decisive factor in determining whether a particular power should be called "soul" or not."[15] This entire approach, he contends, is confirmed by a careful reading of the *Long Commentary on the De Anima*, for "When Averroës shows emotion in defending his interpretation of the soul against Alexander, this surely indicates that it is because he has certain knowledge of it from a source other than philosophy, that is, from revelation."[16]

Obviously, we need to consider these statements in conjunction with direct examination of the texts of *Long Commentary on the De Anima of Aristotle*. This will be best accomplished if we first spell out in some detail Averroës's understanding of the nature of intellect and of the particular human being, for key to the entire discussion is the grasp of the nature of rationality and intellect as these are used of each. That accomplished, we will study the unique text of the *Long Commentary on the De Anima of Aristotle* in which religion and human immortality are explicitly discussed in order better to determine the role of religion in his philosophical account. We will then conclude with a brief but pointed and critical examination of just three of the several claims of Ovey Mohammed.

Aristotle's metaphysical approach to epistemology openly takes it for granted that the soul is able to know universals,[17] that is, to know things by means of their forms following sensation.[18] In connection with this Averroës follows Greek and Islamic Peripatetic tradition in arguing for the need of a separate intellect for there to be knowing on the part of individual human beings. In this philosophical context there must be an Agent Intellect—separate in being from the individual—bringing intelligibles which exist in the sensible world as potentially intelligible for human beings to the state of being actual intelligibles. This was described by Aristotle as acting in a fashion analogous to the way he understood light, to act in his natural philosophy. Light is understood to be a cause of sight by actualizing the medium of intervening air in such a way as to make what was transparent in potency transparent in actuality, thereby allowing the colors and sensible objects to be actually sensible to and sensed by the receptive sensory power.[19] Similarly, the Agent Intellect is a cause of actuality which enables the potential intelligibles to become actual intelligibles and actually to be understood intellectually by the knower.

Intelligibles as universals cannot be received by means of a material power which is individual since this would render them particular in the recipient and destroy their natures as universals. For Averroës, the intelligibles are received into an immaterial but receptive nature, an intellect, which preserves their natures as intelligibles in actuality.[20] In conjunction with this, it was evident to Averroës that an intelligible universal could be received only into one intellect, for its reception into a plurality of different intellects having receptive potency would yield a plurality of intelligibles, not a single universal. But for there to be the universal knowledge of essences assumed in the Peripatetic tradition, it must be the case that there is only one essence or universal of each kind of thing. If this actual intelligible were received into different intellects, the purported intelligible in those individual intellects would in fact be a particular intelligible noted in a particular intellect. This would then require that there be another intelligible over and above these particulars by reference to which the intelligibles in the particular intellects are said to be the same. But, of course, this version of the Aristotelian "Third Man" argument would have to continue to infinity unless a final intellect in which existed the unique intelligible universal were finally reached. In this way, it is evident that for Averroës, in accordance with his understanding of the demands of the Peripatetic tradition of epistemological realism, the universal as actual intelligible or intelligible in act had to be received into an immaterial intellectual power that is intellectually receptive, that is, in an intellect the nature of which is a distinctively intellectual potency for intelligibles.[21] The receptive intellect, that is, the Material Intellect which plays a role in the psychology of Averroës radically different from what is found in Ancient and Medieval thinkers prior to him, proceeds from a state of potency for receiving intelligibles to a state of possessing these intelligibles in act due to the Agent Intellect's activity upon the potential intelligibles found in the imagination following upon sense perception. It is this activity which causes those intelligibles to come to be actual intelligibles in the Material Intellect.

By sense perception of physical objects and their material intelligibles, the individual rational animal generates images in the imaginative power of the soul. A twofold role is then played by the soul's imaginative power in reference to potential intelligibles and in reference to actual intelligibles. The images—potential intelligibles which have been "spiritualized," that is, made less particular insofar as they have been taken away from the physical particulars in which they primarily exist as forms and intentions of things[22]—are then presented to the separate intellects. The Agent intellect actualizes them as intelligibles by its "light" and these intelligibles are received as actual intelligibles into the directed or determinate potentiality for intelligibles, the Material Intellect. Human beings provide the images and thereby play a positive and active role in this actualization of which they too are recipients in virtue of their connection with the Material Intellect, in which knowledge in the fullest sense comes to be. After this a human being can call upon knowledge using images in studying new particulars of the world and in understanding and classifying them.

The Aristotelian doctrine of intellect was born of the simple view that human beings actually do come to be knowing after not knowing in a way which allows for a grasp of intelligibles. This is a way different from that of sense perception in which particulars are grasped. Consequently, in light of the reality of human knowing the doctrine of separate Agent Intellect and separate Material Intellect in the thought of Averroës explains the way in which knowledge comes to be and how this way is congruous with the metaphysical and epistemological teaching as a coherent philosophy. The intelligibles *qua* actual intelligibles can only be received into something immaterial so as to forestall their particularization. In the particular human being what is received is an image.

Termed speculative intellect and speculative intelligibles by Averroës, the actual intelligibles come to exist in the separate Material Intellect and have an eternal nature as a consequence of the nature of that into which they are received. But in the individual human passive and passible intellect, which is the imaginative power in human beings, [23] they have the nature of generable and corruptible things. Seemingly functioning as signs, these images or speculative intelligibles in particular individuals are not the eternal speculative intelligibles in the separate Material Intellect. Those eternal speculative intelligibles in act could not exist in a human being's particular intellectual power. What, then, is this power in the individual human being by which she thinks or understands as commonly meant by the use of those terms? This is the cogitative power, one of the internal senses, which employs images in its activity.[24] The internal sense powers are four: the common sense, the imaginative power, the cogitative power, and the power of memory. Averroës is explicit in his view that the cogitative power is a corporeal power, in Book III, Comment to Text 6 of his *Long Commentary on the De Anima*: "The cogitative power...is of the genus of powers existing in the body."[25] And while he clearly rejects Avicenna's understanding of the internal senses, in this Comment it is clear for Averroës that the cogitative power functions much as it does in Avicenna, namely as a discriminating power actively composing images from sense prior to the grasp of intelligibles and actively utilizing intelligibles received from the intellect in its formation of propositions of science, morality and the like, in a rational person.[26] It is the human imaginative faculty which is characterized as rational or intellectual. The cogitative power, then, is in a sense intellect. In his Comment on Text 5 of Book III of the *Long Commentary on the De Anima*, Averroës remarks that intellect is properly "that part by which we draw distinctions and cogitate,"[27] even though the Greeks sometimes would use the term intellect in a general sense whereby it denoted the imaginative power. For Averroës intellect is that by which these activities take place; what uses intellect in the formation of propositions, distinctions, cogitations is the particular human being. In the Comment to Book III Text 6 Averroës says:

> Although, therefore, a human being properly has a cogitative power, nevertheless this does not make it that this power is rational and discerning, for it discerns universal intentions, not individual ones. . . . If, therefore, the distinguishing rational power were a power in a body, it would happen that it would be one of those four powers, and so it would have a bodily organ. Or it would be an individual distinguishing power different from those four. But it was already explained there that this is impossible. And because Galen thought that this cogitative power is rational and material, it made him err in regard to this with respect to the place of the consequent. For because the rational power belongs to human beings and the cogitative belongs to them, it was thought on account of the conversion of the universal affirmative that the cogitative power is the rational power.[28]

Galen's mistake was one of the second figure of the syllogism in the affirmative, for this does not give rise to a necessary conclusion. Only equivocally can a human being be or have the "distinguishing rational power," for this resides primarily and properly in the separate intellects upon which human beings must draw when they carry out their cogitative activity commonly called thinking or understanding. Consequently, when Aristotle speaks of the passible intellect Averroës explains that this intellect in particular human beings is "the forms of imagination insofar as the cogitative power proper to human beings acts upon those forms."[29] Imagination, cogitation, and memory exist in human beings and have as their function the presentation of the form of an imagined thing in the absence of sense. In the representation of a particular thing to the individual human being when the thing is absent from sense, these function in a cooperative way.

Averroës's understanding of the activity of cogitation is clearly presented when a text of Aristotle prompts him to provide an explanation. At Text 33 of Book III Averroës reads Aristotle as saying, "*For one cogitates, as it were, and sees a thing in the ways of the imagination, and cogitation of it in reference to future things is according to things present.*"[30] (431b7-8) In his Comment Averroës states clearly his understanding of cogitation:

> The meaning of cogitation is nothing but that the cogitative power presents a thing absent from sense as it if were a sensed thing. For this reason things able to be grasped by human beings are divided into these two, namely into the comprehensible which has as its principle sensation and the comprehensible which has as its principle cogitation. We already said that the cogitative power is neither the material intellect nor the intellect which is in act,[31] but it is a particular material power. This is evident from the things said in *Sense and sensibilia*. It is necessary to know this, since the custom is to attribute the cogitative power to the intellect. It should not be the case that someone says that the cogitative power composes singular intelligibles. It was already explained that the material intellect composed them. For cogitation is only for distinguishing individual instances among those intelligibles and to present them in act as if they were existent in sensation. For this reason when they are present in sensation, then cogitation will diminish and the activity of intellect in regard to them will remain. From this it is explained that the activity of intellect is different from the activity of the cogitative power, which Aristotle called the passible intellect, which he said is generable and corruptible. This is evident concerning this [power], since it has a determinate organ, namely the middle chamber of the brain. A human being is not generable and corruptible except in virtue of this power and without this power and the imaginative power {477} the material intellect thinks nothing. For this

reason, as Aristotle says, we do not remember after death, not because the intellect is generable and corruptible, as one can believe.[32]

Our use and exercise of this faculty is directly relevant to our ability to initiate activity on the part of the Agent in order for us to come to have knowledge.[33] Will and voluntary action on the part of the individual has as its source this cogitative power. This is further emphasized by Averroës in another Comment on a Text of Aristotle in which cogitation is discussed. Averroës reads that *"The cogitative power ... is in rational [animals] alone. To choose to do this or that belongs to cogitative activity."* in Book III Text 57 (*De Anima* 434a6-8) The Greek *hê bouleutikê* , the power of willing or wishing, here is found rendered as *virtus cogitativa* and *de actione cogitativa*. Hence we find Averroës commenting as follows:

> Imagination exists in other animals, while cogitation exists in rational animals. For choosing to do this imagined thing and not another is of the activity of cogitation, not of the activity of imagination. For what judges that this imagined thing is more pleasant than another ought to be of necessity the same power which reckons imaginations in which it judges what is more pleasurable. .... [I]t is necessary that one power reckon those imaginations until it grasps from them what is more pleasant, as one thing reckons unequal numbers until it grasps which is the greater. Likewise, cogitation reckons imaginations and compares them until it is able to be affected by the imagination of some one of these. This is the reason why a rational animal has opinion, for opinion is a response which arises from cogitation. .... [A]side from the rational animal, none has cogitation because none has reason. The motion of animals is due to pleasure and it is simple motion, not complex [motion]. This is because it does not have the cogitative power together with appetite in such a way that these two powers command one another to the extent that the animal is moved sometimes on account of will as [is the case] in regard to the rational animal.[34]

Choice and will as well as knowledge are available to the individual human being thanks to the cogitative power which is itself responsible for the choices for Averroës. Averroës rejects Avicenna's estimative power in animals and his conception of the per se immortality of the rational soul is by no means accepted by Averroës in his mature work. For Averroës the self responsible for intellectual and moral development of the whole per-

son, including the physical body, is to be located in the cogitative power
found in the brain. The human self or soul is concerned with particulars
when it acts rightly or when it errs, so what else would one expect? In the
Aristotelian context, intellect most properly concerns universals and does
not err with regard to them.[35] Averroës's understanding is all the more cred-
ible since Aristotle himself does speak of this human power as being *nous*
or "mind" even though the power of *boulesis* or "will" is bodily.[36] Averroës
rightly states that in Greek intellect is sometimes used to denote imagination or a power of imagination such as cogitation.[37]

With this understanding of Averroës's human psychology in the *Long
Commentary on the De Anima,* how could he be viewed as espousing any
sort of human immortality? Averroës, in fact, holds for human immortality, something quite clearly evident in his treatment of the question of the
necessity that knowledge always be in actuality. He asserts that the metaphysics of the Agent and Material Intellects requires that there always be
thinking human beings, that is, people exercising their imaginative and
cogitative powers, in the world so that philosophy is always being carried
on. In this way the speculative intellect is always in actuality even if the individuals are themselves generable and corruptible.[38] Commenting on Aristotle's notion of the passive intellect, Averroës explains that the notion "that
the soul, that is, the speculative intellect [in the individual human being],
is immortal" is one which arose from considerations which are not necessary.[39] Averroës remarks then that Plato's account "that the universals are
neither generable nor corruptible and that they exist outside the mind"
was in a way true and in a way false. Aristotle refuted the notion that universals are outside mind in his *Metaphysics*. Still, it is true that they are neither generable nor corruptible. Now "it is impossible for probable things
to be completely false. The Ancients recounted this and all the religious
laws alike reflect it."[40] The same applies in the case of the soul and probable propositions about it: "probable propositions . . . attribute to the soul
both kinds of being, mortal and nonmortal." And the understanding of the
soul as mortal and corruptible Averroës here asserts as the true part in these
probable propositions.[41] Religion's probable propositions on the immortality of the human soul are not completely false, for there is a sense in
which propositions asserting the immortality of the soul are true. But they
are not true in the way they are asserted by religion, namely as true of particular human beings. Rather, they are true in that the speculative intellect
through which all human beings are rational and intellectual is eternally ac-

tive and by this particular rational humans are in a sense eternal as members of an eternal species.

In light of this account of the thought of Averroës in the *Long Commentary on the De Anima* let us consider now the statements of Ovey Mohammed on the value of this work for giving proof of the religious character of the thought of Averroës on the nature of the soul. Consider just three assertions from his article.

First, we saw the assertion that "One may say that it is Averroës's concern with the Qur'anic conception of human beings and their relationship with God that furnishes in part the reason why the intellect is conjoined or united (*copulatur*) to us." The argument for this assertion is simple: The Qur'an is concerned with human beings and their relationship with the transcendent. Averroës's doctrine on the intellect is concerned with human beings and the transcendent. Therefore, Averroës's doctrine is founded on Qur'anic concerns. Yet, the assertion that both Averroës and the Qur'an are concerned with the same matters yields no necessary connection between the philosophical thought of Averroës on this issue and what is found in the Qur'an. In regard to this assertion that it is the Qur'anic conception of human beings and God that furnishes part of the reason for Averroës's concern over the matter of conjunction with the separate intellects, there is no evidence in the *Long Commentary in the De Anima* for this view. Rather, the arguments of the Commentary are philosophical through and through.

What sort of fallacy is involved here? This is just the sort of fallacy of which Averroës makes special note several times in his *Long Commentary on the De Anima*. It is one of the syllogisms in the Second Figure with two affirmative premises. This is a version of False Cause or *post hoc ergo propter hoc*. Once he notes Aristotle's use of this to undermine the view of those who assert that the imagination must be the intellect since each is sometimes true and sometimes false.[42] Another time he notes that some have held that, since fire causes change and the principle of growth and nutrition causes change, then the principle of growth and nutrition must be fire.[43] It is ironic that just this sort of difficulty afflicts the arguments of Ovey Mohammed

Secondly, he stated that "In fact, it is because of this Qur'anic teaching [on body and soul] that Averroës can state categorically that the use of a corporeal instrument is the decisive factor in determining whether a particular power should be called 'soul' or not."[44] But to note that Averroës puts forth this general understanding of the soul and that this general understanding of the soul can be found in the Qur'an hardly allows one to conclude that the Qur'an must be the source for Averroës on this. This is the same difficulty of the syllogism in the Second Figure with two affirmative premises. There is no necessity in this argument. In fact, it is clear that Averroës's conception of the soul comes directly out of the Aristotelian tradition's reflections on the definition of soul in *De Anima* II 1 where soul is described as a first actuality of a natural organic body.[45]

Finally, "When Averroës shows emotion in defending his interpretation of the soul against Alexander, this surely indicates that it is because he has certain knowledge of it from a source other than philosophy, that is, from revelation."[46] The premises (a) that strong emotion is indicative of certain knowledge and (b) that revelation is a source of certain knowledge, are taken to yield the conclusion (c) that the source or grounds for Averroës's strong emotion is revelation. Yet again we find here a syllogism in the Second Figure with two affirmative premises. In this instance as in the case of the doctrine cited in the previous paragraph, Averroës's expression of his philosophical understanding is consequent upon argument of a *philosophical* sort and thoughtful reflection on the *philosophical* tradition. His words are most likely an expression of his own frustration over the many years he spent pondering the issue of the intellect.

Critique of the logic of this recent attempt to understand Averroës's philosophical thought as religiously founded is an important reminder for us of the necessity for careful argumentation regarding the teachings found in Averroës's philosophical works on the topic of the future life. While it can be concluded that there is no room explicitly made for personal immortality or a personal future life in the philosophical teachings found in the *Long Commentary in the De Anima*, there remains the logical and psychological possibility for him to have held the particular soul to be personally immortal. His teachings in the *Long Commentary* might be read as supportive of such a view if it were possible to argue that he asserted the existence of the future life on philosophical grounds with clarity and resolve. But such is not the case. If it were, one would have to argue that he holds for personal immortality on the basis of persuasive rhetorical or dialectical arguments, not demonstrative arguments. But the assertion of immortality in the *Tahafut al-tahafut* and the strict statement of the religious necessity of affirming the future life in the *Decisive Treatise*, are not the consequences of demonstrative arguments and so only have the necessity appropriate to rhetorical or, at best, dialectical arguments. Yet such "necessity" is in fact no logically compelling necessity at all. On the basis of his discussions in the *Long Commentary in the De Anima* there is no reason to believe that Averroës held for a personal immortality on philosophical grounds. In this work there is strong deductive reasoning for the necessity of human immortality with argument founded on the basis of his understanding of intellect and its nature, that is, for the eternal sequential existence of perishable human souls which by their imaginative powers provide images for the eternal intellects. A philosophical doctrine of personal immortality is not found in the *Long Commentary in the De Anima* nor is it asserted there on religious grounds.

Notes

1. Ibn Rushd (Averroës), *Kitab fasl al-maqal with its appendix (Damima) and an extract from Kitab al-kashf fi al-manahij al-adilla*, Arabic text, ed. by George F. Hourani (Leiden: Brill, 1959), hereafter *Fasl*, p.17; *Averroës. On the Harmony of Religion and Philosophy: A translation, with introduction and notes, of Ibn Rushd's Kitab Fasl al-Maqal with its appendix (Damima) and an extract from Kitab al-kashf fi al-manahij al-adilla*, by George F. Hourani (London: Luzac & Co., 1967), hereafter Hourani, p.61.

2. In dating the works discussed here I follow Miguel Cruz Hernandez, *Abû-l-Walid ibn Rušd (Averroës) : vida, obra, pensamiento, influencia* (Cordoba, 1986), pp. 56-57.

3. *Fasl*, pp.6-7; Hourani, p.49.

4. *Tahafut al-tahafut* (TT) 581; Van Den Bergh, trans., *Averroës' Tahafut Al-Tahafut: The Incoherence of the Incoherence* (London: Aris and Phillips, 1978), p.359.

5. TT 586; Van Den Bergh, p.362.

6. *Fasl*, p. 2; Hourani, p.45.

7. Averroës critiques the arguments of al-Ghazali but does not hesitate to side with him against the excesses of philosophers of the Islamic tradition, Avicenna in particular, who have strayed from soundness of Peripatetic philosophical argumentation.

8. TT 427–28; Van Den Bergh pp. 257–58.

9. In his edition of the Arabic *Middle Commentary on Aristotle's de Anima* (Cairo 1994), Alfred Ivry holds that "In general...the *Long Commentary* represents Averroës's most thorough and definitive treatment of Aristotle's text" (p.10) but still believes that the *Middle Commentary* is posterior to the *Long Commentary* (pp. 10-11). In the matter of the dating of these works he is in disagreement with the generally accepted chronology (see the work cited in note 2 above) and with Herbert Davidson. See the latter's *Alfarabi, Avicenna, and Averroës on Intellect* (New York and Oxford 1992), pp. 276–81, 296–97. Both agree, however, that the

Long Commentary on the De Anima contains Averroës's mature positions on the issues at stake.

10. "Human beings will enter eternal life when the resurrection body takes the place of our earthly body at the new creation." Ovey N. Mohammed, S.J., "Averroës, Aristotle, and the Qur'an on Immortality," *International Philosophical Quarterly* (IPQ) 33 (1993): 37–55, see p.54. This statement repeats what was written in *Averroës's Doctrine of Immortality: A Matter of Controversy* (Ottawa, 1984), p. 113. There it is also stated that "Averroës' exposition of the soul is an explanation of the future life guaranteed by the Qur'an in Aristotelian terms. It is a defence of the monistic conception of man found in Aristotle and the Qur'an."

11. "Averroës' doctrine of the future life can be reconstructed from his Long Commentary on the *De Anima* alone if we accept a monistic conception of human beings and the future life as dependent on God." IPQ 1993, p. 54.

12. IPQ 1993, p. 41.

13. ". . . Averroës has already clarified the ambiguity between soul and intellect with the help of revelation . . ." IPQ 1993, p. 50

14. IPQ 1993, p.50.

15. IPQ 1993, p.50.

16. IPQ 1993, p.51.

17. *Posterior Analytics* II 19, 100a13–14

18. *De Anima* III 8, 432a3–7.

19. *De Anima* III 5, 430a14–17; II 7, 418b3ff.

20. Averrois Cordubensis Commentarium Magnum in *Aristotelis De Anima Libros,* ed. F. Stuart Crawford (Cambridge, 1953), hereafter Crawford, pp.387.23–388.56. Also see pp. 416; 491. Cf. pp. 384–85. All translations of Averroës's *Long Commentary on the De Anima of Aristotle* found in this article are mine from this edition.

21. Crawford, p. 388.45–56.

22. Crawford, p. 388.37–49. Also see pp. 416; 491. Cf. pp. 384–85.

23. Crawford, p. 409.640–41.

24. See H. A. Wolfson, "The Internal Senses in Latin, Arabic and Hebrew Philosophic Texts," *Harvard Theological Review* 28 (1935): 69–133.

25. Crawford, p. 415.67–68.

26. See Wolfson 1935 for a general account of the historical development of teachings on the internal senses. Re. Avicenna, see Davidson 1992, pp. 95–102.

27. Crawford, p. 387.3–4.

28. Crawford, p. 416.75–89.

29. Crawford p. 449.173–75.

30. Note that the Greek *logizetai kai bouleuetai* which is rendered by Smith and Barnes (*The Complete Works of Aristotle: The revised Oxford Translation,* ed. J. Barnes, Princeton, 1984, vol. I.) as "it calculates and deliberates" is conveyed in Averroës's text of Aristotle by a verb and a noun indicating the activity of cogitation: *Cogitat enim quasi videret rem per modos imaginationis, et cogitatio eius in rebus futuris est secundum presentes. Cogitare, cogitativus* and *cogitatio* usually render forms of the Arabic root *f-k-r.*

31. That is, it is neither the Material Intellect nor the Agent Intellect.

32. Crawford, p. 476.57–477.85.

33. Crawford, pp. 453.301–454.320.

34. Crawford. pp. 529.16–530.39.

35. *De Anima* III 6. Cf. Crawford p. 464.17–22.

36. *De Anima* III 10, 433a14.

37. Crawford, p. 387.17–22.

38. Crawford, pp. 407.597–409.643; 469.25–27.

39. Crawford, p. 409.640–644. On the meaning of *a remotis* here see Crawford, p.16.53–55.

40. Crawford, p. 409.652–53.

41. At Crawford, p. 408.610–29, he remarks: "For, since it is the case that wisdom exists in some way proper to human beings, just as it is the case that [various] kinds of arts exist in ways proper to human beings, it is thought that it is impossible that the whole habitable world shun philosophy, just as one should hold the opinion that it is impossible for [the whole habitable world] to shun the natural arts. For if some part of [the habitable world], for example, the northern quarter of the earth, is devoid of them, namely the arts, the other quarters will not be devoid of them, because it was explained that habitation is possible in the southern as in the northern quarters. Perhaps, then, philosophy is found in the greater part of the subject in every era, as a human being is found [to come about] from a human being and a horse from a horse. The speculative intellect, therefore, is neither generable nor corruptible in this way. And generally it is for the agent intellect creating the intelligibles just as [it is] for the distinguishing recipient intellect. For, insofar as the agent intellect never ceases generating and creating absolutely speaking, even if some subject is removed from this, namely [from] generation, so it is concerning the distinguishing intellect."

42. Crawford, p. 368.19–23.

43. Crawford, p. 193.13–19.

44. IPQ 1993, p. 50.

45. *De Anima* II 1, 412b4–8.

46. IPQ 1993, p.5 1.

26

Some Remarks on Averroës's Statements on the Soul

M. E. Marmura
Professor of Philosophy,
University of Toronto (Canada)

I

In the Introduction of his English translation of Averroës's *Fasl al-Maqal* (The Decisive Treatise)[1] and in an article entitled, "The Early Growth of the Secular Sciences in Andalusia,"[2] the late George Hourani sums up for us the religious and cultural situation in Islamic Spain leading to the period in which Averroës (Ibn Rushd) (d. 1198) lived and wrote. True enough, the al-Muwahhid ruler, Abu Ya'qub Yusuf (d. 1184), a man of learning with a genuine love of philosophy, took Averroës under his wing. But, as Professor Hourani remarked, both he and Averroës had to be circumspect. We also know that in 1194, the son and successor of this ruler, al-Mansur, probably under pressure from the religiously conservative, banished Averroës, to restore him shortly thereafter.

The realm of the al-Muwahhids was religiously conservative. In Spain the dominant Islamic scholars followed the traditional Malikite school of Islamic law. And although these scholars were hardly in favor of Islamic speculative theology, *kalam*, the opposition of this discipline to philosophy, forcefully expressed in the Ash'arite works of Ghazali (al-Ghazali) (d.

1111), notably his *Tahafut al-falasifa* (*The Incoherence of the Philosophers*
), was becoming known in the Islamic West. And Averroës himself tells us
that most Muslims have come to regard the adherents of the Ash'arite
school of theology as *ahl al-sunna*, the people who follow the customary
practice of the prophet, that is, as "orthodox."³

This is not to say that the tension between Islamic speculative theology
and philosophy did not exist before Ghazali. There is a suggestion that the
earliest of the Islamic philosophers, Kindi (al-Kindi) (d. ca. 860), was targeting Mu'tazilite theologians in one of his critical remarks.⁴ Much later, the
Mu'tazilite theologian 'Abd al-Jabbar (d. 1025) had some adverse criticism
of Kindi.⁵ Alfarabi (Al-Farabi) (d. 950) criticized *kalam*;⁶ and the writings
of Avicenna (Ibn Sina) (d. 1037) abound with criticisms, often unobtrusive,
of this discipline. Professor Hourani quotes the statement of the Isma'ili theologian, Nasir-e Khosraw (d.1067) about the tension between these two dis-
ciplines.⁷ And Ghazali's teacher, the prominent Ash'arite theologian and
Shaif'i lawyer, al-Juwayni (d. 1085), had criticized philosophy.⁸ But it was
Ghazali who brought things to a head. To begin with, he devoted an entire
work, *The Incoherence of the Philosophers*, to a closely argued logical critique of twenty theses of the Islamic philosophers Alfarabi and, particularly,
Avicenna. Moreover, he denounced seventeen of these theses as constitut-
ing heretical innovations, and singled out three as being totally opposed to
religious principles, charging those who upheld them as unbelievers, pun-
ishable by death. This charge, which he repeated again in later writings, was
not a rhetorical utterance, but a legal pronouncement. Philosophy was put
on the defensive as it had never been before. Both Ghazali's logical criticisms and his legal charge called for an answer.

Averroës offered the fullest answer. He offered it in three complementary treatises, forming in effect a trilogy,⁹ and a much larger work. The
trilogy consists of a short epistle on divine knowledge, followed respectively by *Fasl al-maqal* (*The Decisive Treatise*), that addresses itself to the
legal charge raised by Ghazali, and *Kitab al-kashf 'an manahij al-adilla fa
'aqa'id al-milla* (*The Book of the Exposition of the Methods of Proofs Regarding the Beliefs of the [Islamic] Religion*).¹⁰ The latter offers an alternative theology to that of such Ash'arite thinkers as al-Juwayni and Ghazali. It is very much a critique of Ash'arism. The large work is his famed
Tahafut al-tahafut, (*The Incoherence of the Incoherence*). Most of it is
written in the form of a long commentary: it quotes the bulk of Ghazali's
Tahafut, paragraph by paragraph, commenting critically on each. The crit-

icisms are directed for the most part at Ghazali. But Averroës's book also includes criticisms of Avicenna. As we shall see, sometimes Averroës sides with Ghazali against Avicenna.

Now, the first of the theses which Ghazali denounced as irreligious is the Aristotelian doctrine of a pre-eternal world, espoused by both Alfarabi and Avicenna. The two other theses, the doctrine that God knows particulars "in a universal way," and the doctrine that upholds the individual immortality of human souls, but denies bodily resurrection, are distinctively Avicennan. This latter doctrine maintains that all human souls are immortal. This is where it differs from Alfarabi's theory that confines individual immortality to certain groups. The philosophical systems of both these philosophers, however, cannot accommodate a doctrine of bodily resurrection. And this is the issue that concerns Ghazali.

With this as reminder, we will now turn to Averroës's discussion of the question of the hereafter, first in *Fasl* and *Kashf*, and then in his *Tahafut*.

II

In *Fasl*, Averroës elaborates a theory of scriptural interpretation that forms an integral part of his response to Ghazali. The background of this theory is to be found in the political philosophy of Alfarabi. According to Alfarabi, religion, which includes the prescriptions of the law, necessary for governing the virtuous state, "is the imitation of philosophy." It gives the same truth as philosophy but in a language which the nonphilosopher majority of mankind can understand. This is the language of the concrete instance, of the image and symbol, rather than the abstract idea. It is largely the language of metaphor which can only be understood philosophically by the philosopher. The nonphilosopher must not be exposed to its philosophical interpretation.

Averroës brings to this theory something distinctively Islamic. He sets the problem at issue in Islamic legal terms and informs his discussion with arguments that constantly refer us back to the Qur'an which he frequently quotes. Underlying this—and this is made quite explicit in the *Kashf*—is a philosophy of language. We must begin, Averroës argues, by understanding Qur'anic language in the most natural and ordinary way. He argues, in effect, that the Qur'an tells us that nature is endowed by God with causal powers that lead us to Him as the cause of all causes. The Ash'arite denial of causal efficacy in created things, assigning all causal action directly to divine power, is artificial and a distortion of the Qur'anic cosmic view.

A philosophical interpretation of this language must be confined to the few, those "well grounded in knowledge," *al-rasikhun fi al-'ilm*, those who belong to the demonstrative class. There are two other classes of believers, the dialectical and the rhetorical, the latter forming the majority. These two classes must interpret scriptural language on the dialectical and rhetorical levels, respectively. Related to this is Averroës's classification of scriptural language:

Scriptural texts, he argues in *Fasl*, fall into three classes. In the first class the meaning must be understood in the same way by the rhetorical, dialectical and demonstrative classes. These texts must hence be accepted literally by all. The second class of texts are ambiguous and should be understood by the demonstrative method. But they should be so interpreted only by the philosopher. The unqualified scholar, the nonphilosopher, must not be permitted to access them. Then there is a third class of text whose classification, in terms of the other two, is not certain. This class is interpreted by some allegorically, by others literally. It is, however, the qualified scholars, the philosophers, who should decide whether or not to take them allegorically. Now, should such scholars err in deeming such texts open to allegorical interpretation and should they also err in the interpretation they offer, in either case the error is permissible and those who commit it ought not to be condemned as infidels.

This brings us to the question of those scriptural texts that speak of the hereafter. All three classes of men should accept literally the statement that there is a hereafter. But whether one should accept literally the descriptions of this hereafter or not is another matter. If the scholar errs in maintaining that such descriptions are allegorical and should be interpreted philosophically by the philosopher, his error is permissible. Again, if the philosopher errs in his interpretation, this also is permissible. In either case, the philosopher must be absolved from the charge of unbelief. As long as one accepts the fact of a hereafter, Ghazali's charge that a rejection of bodily resurrection constitutes Islamic unbelief is baseless.

This point is repeated and elaborated in the *Kashf*. Averroës devotes the fifth and final chapter of this treatise to the question of the hereafter. His position in the *Kashf* is summed up in an opening statement:

> The resurrection is one of the things concerning whose existence [all] religions agree and for which there has been demonstrative proof among scholars. Religions have only differed on the nature of its existence,

though, in reality they do not differ [so much] regarding the nature of its existence, [as they do] regarding the observable things [they have used] to symbolize this unseen state.[11]

Averroës then argues for the belief in the hereafter on both philosophical and scriptural grounds. This belief is an obligation on all Muslims. But it is the duty of the believer to interpret scriptural texts pertaining to the resurrection according to where his own reflection leads him. This reflection should be commensurate with his individual intellectual capacity. Indeed, Averroës points out, Muslims have interpreted the resurrection in three different ways. Some have held it to be corporeal, life in the hereafter being identical in kind with the mundane, differing only in permanence. Others have maintained that the afterlife is corporeal but different from the mundane both in kind and in permanence. A third group have denied bodily resurrection, affirming survival only for individual souls.

Taken at its face value, the *Kashf* seems to be affirming a doctrine of individual immortality in the hereafter, whether this involves bodily resurrection or only the survival of immaterial souls. At one point, he seems to be reiterating Avicenna's doctrine of reward and punishment of the immaterial souls in the hereafter. There is ambiguity in Averroës's statements, which we also encounter in his *Tahafut*, to which we will now turn

III

Ghazali devotes the last three discussions of his *Incoherence*, that is, the eighteenth, nineteenth, and twentieth, to the question of the hereafter. The eighteenth includes a critique of ten Avicennan proofs for the immateriality of the soul. None of these, Ghazali endeavors to show, demonstrate such an immateriality. Averroës reproduces Ghazali's discussion, commenting on it section by section, pointing out ambiguities and giving sober assessments of the arguments pro and con. The Avicennan proofs strive to show the immateriality of the human soul considered in its earthly existence. This is a necessary condition for his argument that the individual soul is immortal, which Ghazali criticizes in the nineteenth discussion.

Now, as we shall shortly see, the question of the individual immortality of the immaterial soul, discussed in the nineteenth discussion and, by implication, in the twentieth, is raised much earlier in the *Tahafut*. One must note at this stage, however, that in both the nineteenth and twentieth dis-

cussions, Averroës departs from the pattern he had been following throughout the *Tahafut* of quoting Ghazali's work section by section and commenting on it. In the nineteenth discussion he simply gives a summary of
what he conceives to be the main argument, answers it, and then raises the
question of the individual immorality of souls. In the twentieth discussion
Averroës does not really summarize or discuss Ghazali's arguments. He simply takes up Ghazali's charge that the philosophers deny bodily resurrection
and, in a somewhat rhetorical essay, tries to show in effect that the philosophers hold that it is necessary that the masses should believe this doctrine.

As already indicated, the question of the soul's individual immortality
appears much earlier in the *Tahafut*. It appears in the first discussion where
Ghazali is engaged in refuting the doctrine of a pre-eternal world. He argues that, given the Aristotelian view that the world is pre-eternal and that
humans have always existed, and given the Avicennan doctrine that the individual human soul is immaterial and immortal, this leads necessarily to
the conclusion that at any point in time there would have to be an infinity
of coexisting souls. But, Ghazali points out, all agree that such an infinity
is impossible. Avicenna, who was well aware of this difficulty, had argued
that since these souls are immaterial and have no position in space and
since they are not related to each other in the way the coexisting essential
causes and effects are related, the infinity they form, though coexisting, has
no order. As such, the infinity of these souls, is possible.[12] Ghazali dis-
agrees. In the fourth discussion where he tries to show that the philosophers
have failed to prove God's existence, he points out that their proof is based
on the impossibility of an infinity of coexisting essential causes. But how
can they maintain that this is impossible when they allow an infinite number of *coexisting* souls? Avicenna's argument *that these souls have no
order is unacceptable. For, Ghazali argues, if we suppose the birth of one
individual a day, there would be a chronological order of Avicennan created souls, those that have left their bodies, and those still existing with the
body. And this order renders the infinity of such souls impossible.*

In his comments, Averroës begins by taking Ghazali to task for the dialectical way in which he introduces his initial objection.[13] But when it
comes to the substance of Ghazali's criticism, Averroës agrees with Ghazali and raises his own objection to Avicenna's theory. He, first of all, injects
into the discussion the Aristotelian dictum that matter is the individuating
principle. If these souls that survive the death of the body are immaterial,
how can they be individual? He writes:

As for positing numerically many souls without matter, [this is some-thing] unknown in the doctrine of "the people," *al-qawm*. For, according to them, the cause of the numerically many is matter. The cause of agree-ment in numerical multiplicity is form. But for things to exist as many in number, one in form, without matter is impossible.[14]

We notice that in his answer Averroës refers us to the doctrine of "the people," presumably, the philosophers. But which philosophers? Here he seems to be speaking of the true followers of Aristotle. These, then, would not include Avicenna, unless the latter is propounding a doctrine of the im-mortal individual immaterial soul only "for public consumption." Averroës himself suggests that this is what Avicenna may well be doing. For on the question of whether or not the supposition of these individual immortal souls would lead to upholding an impossible conclusion, a coexisting or-dered infinite, he sides with Ghazali. He rejects Avicenna's argument that since such souls have no position in space, their infinite coexistence is pos-sible. "We know no one," he writes, "who has differentiated between what has position and what does not in this connection except Avicenna. . . . For the people (*al-qawm*) deny the existence of the actual infinite regardless of whether this constitutes a body or not a body because from this it nec-essarily follows that [one] infinite is more numerous (*akthar*) than [an-other] infinite." He then adds: "Perhaps Avicenna only intended by it to convince the masses concerning what they are accustomed to hear regard-ing the soul."[15]

Going back to the argument that matter is the principle of individuation, Averroës in the *Tahafut* clearly maintains that if there is to be individual im-mortality, this would require bodies. He suggests, however, that these need not be earthly bodies, as we shall shortly see when we turn to the nineteenth dis-cussion. But to continue with the first discussion, in response to one of Ghaz-ali's arguments,[16] Averroës makes the following key statement:

The soul of Zayd and 'Amr is one in form. Numerical multiplicity, I mean, division, only attaches to the one in form with respect to matter.[17] If the soul, then, does not perish when the body perishes, or has in it something of this [imperishable] quality,[18] then it becomes necessary that when it separates from bodies it should be numerically one. But there is no way for divulging this knowledge in this place (*wa hadha al-'ilm la sabiila ila ifsha'hi*[19]*fi hadha al-mawdi'*."[20]

Although he says it almost in passing, unobtrusively, Averroës in this passage affirms, in effect, a unitary doctrine of the immaterial soul, stating at the same time that such knowledge ought not to be divuldged "in this place."[21] With this in mind, we will now turn to his discussion of the souls' individuation in the nineteenth discussion.[22]

IV

In his own *Tahafut*, Ghazali had argued that the Islamic philosophers have not demonstrated that the immaterial soul must continue to exist after separation from the body. According to one of his arguments, as restated by Averroës, if the soul was individuated by the body in this life, it is connected with it. As such, it cannot continue to exist after the body's corruption. Averroës remarks that this need not be the case. It does not always follow that when one of two related things, for example, lover and beloved, magnet and iron, ceases to exist, the other must cease to exist.[23] The real point the disputant should raise, Averroës maintains, is to ask how such souls can retain their individuality in the absence of the principle of individuation, matter. He then writes:

> But it is for those who claim the immortality of the soul and its numerical multiplicity to say that it is in a subtle matter, namely the animate soul that emanates from the celestial bodies. This is the heat which is neither fire nor includes the principle of fire. But within it lies the souls that bring about the bodies that are here and the souls that come to inhere in these bodies.[24]

Averroës elaborates this theory, drawing on Neoplatonic and Stoic ideas, stating that none of the philosophers deny that the elements also possess creative souls that give birth to each of the existing species. These souls are viewed as either something that is intermediary between the souls of the celestial bodies and human souls, or else as entities that connect with the human souls they create so that when the bodies are corrupted these souls return to their spiritual matter and their imperceptible subtle bodies. All the ancient philosophers, he then adds, have acknowledged the existence of such souls, but differed as to whether they are identical with those in human bodies or constitute another genus.[25]

Then in what seems to be a shift from the question of individuation, he states that the Islamic philosophers who uphold the doctrine of "the giver of forms" have made these powers (*al-quwa*) a separate intellect. He criticizes this doctrine of "the giver of forms."[26] He then states that this is one of the most difficult of problems. It is not clear, however, which problem he is referring to: Is it the problem of individuation, of the existence of celestial, nonmaterial souls, or the problem of immortality in general? He then declares that "one of the strongest [things] to which one can appeal as evidence (*wa aqwa ma yustashhadu bihi*)" with respect to this topic is that the material intellect apprehends "infinite things in the one intelligible and judges them universally," adding that that "whose substance is such a substance is basically nonmaterial and for this reason Aristotle praises Anaxogoras in making the first mover an intellect, that is, a form free from matter."[27] The interposition of this statement is puzzling. Its intention is not entirely clear. Does it relate at all to the doctrine of the subtle material celestial entities that serve as a principle of individuation for the departed human souls? Alternatively, is Averroës in introducing it hinting at something else—a theory of an eternal active and passive intellect that cannot accommodate individual immortality?

To return to the theory of individual immortality that he introduced, is Averroës subscribing to it? It is virtually certain that he is not. There is, to begin with the statement we quoted from the first discussion where he defends a unitary doctrine of the soul. Then there is the manner in which he introduces the theory: "But it is for those who claim the immortality of the soul and its numerical multiplicity to say (*Lakin liman yadda'i baqa' al-nafs was ta'addudiha an yaqul*)." In other words, those who claim that the souls are individually immortal could argue that they are individuated by the subtle celestial matter. This wording says nothing about Averroës himself being one of these claimants. Finally, there is a philosophical reason for doubting that he upholds such a theory. This theory was introduced to resolve the problem of the individuation of the human souls after they leave their earthly existence. It does not, however, resolve the problem of their infinite number. For, if we follow Averroës's arguments in the *Tahafut*, he subscribes to the doctrine of an eternal world and does not deny the Aristotelian view that humans have always existed in the eternal past.[28]

V

The twentieth discussion[29] on bodily resurrection is rhetorical and polemical. It gives eloquent expression to Averroës's political philosophy as it reiterates many an idea encountered in *Fasl* and *Kashf*.

Averroës begins by challenging Ghazali's charge that the philosophers deny bodily resurrection. None of the ancient philosophers had had anything to say about the matter, even though the doctrine of bodily resurrection had been proclaimed in the various religions long before philosophy. The philosophers, of all people, Averroës states, have shown the greatest reverence for it "and belief in it." (The "it," *laha*, is in the feminine and refers to religion, not to the doctrine of bodily resurrection.) For religion "moves towards (*tanh, nahwa*) the governance of people (*tadbir al-nas*) through which the existence of the human as a human comes about and which brings about the happiness proper to the human."[30] For religion is necessary for the existence of "moral virtues, theoretical virtues and practical arts,"[31] without which people can have no life in this world and hence no resurrected life beyond. The moral virtues are thus attainable through "knowledge of God and [through] magnifying Him in the acts of worship prescribed for them in each religion, such as offerings, prayers, supplications and the like."[32] The laws, the philosophers hold, "are necessary civic arts whose principles are taken from [both] reason and scriptures,"[33] especially those principles that are common to all religions.

All religions, he continues, agree that there is a hereafter but differ in describing it.[34] Moreover, all religions have "alerted" (*nabbahat*) people to the belief that is peculiar to the philosophers, but have stressed the belief held in common by the philosophers and the masses.[35] It is not clear at this point in the exposition whether Averroës intends by this common belief, belief in bodily resurrection, or simply a general belief in the hereafter. As he continues, however, he seems to be intending by it the belief in bodily resurrection. He argues, in effect, that this common belief is the basis of the law and order, necessary for the survival and well-being of everyone, including the philosophers. Philosophers must not disparage this common belief, a belief on which they were nurtured, before becoming philosophers capable of its philosophical interpretation. Descriptions of the hereafter in the *Qur'an*, as compared with its description in other religions, give mankind in general a greater incentive to act virtuously. This is because the *Qur'an* represents the hereafter in physical terms,[36] in the language that the commonality understands.[37]

Averroës ends the twentieth discussion[38] by actually commending Ghazali for his opposition to those who reject an afterlife.[39] Such opposition must posit that the soul is immortal and that at the resurrection it will join, not the original body, but a replica thereof, as Ghazali has shown.[40] Averroës, then uses the argument that the resurrected bodies would have to be replicas of the original bodies to criticize the Ash'arite doctrine that the soul is an accident. Averroës leaves it unclear whether he is endorsing the resurrection theory he attributes to Ghazali, or whether he is simply commending Ghazali for scoring a point against those who deny the afterlife. His vagueness seems quite intentional.

As with the nineteenth discussion, the twentieth is not free from the ambiguous and the evasive. This is not unexpected considering the cultural and religious circumstances of the times, so succinctly outlined by Professor Hourani. But ambiguity and evasion are also used by Averroës as a means for adhering to that basic Farabian principle of his political philosophy, namely that demonstrative knowledge must not be divulged to the public. His *Tahafut* was written for philosophers and nonphilosophers alike. It was written in response to Ghazali who, from Averroës's point of view, had "let the cat out of the bag," so to speak, by going public on matters that should be confined to the qualified few. This, for Averroës, was Ghazali's cardinal sin.

Notes

1. *Averroës on the Harmony of Religion and Philosophy* (London; Luzac and Co., for E.J. W. Gibb Memorial Series and UNESCO, 196l).
2. *Studia Islamica* 32 (1970): 143–56
3. Ibn Rushd, *Kitab al-kashf 'an manahij al-adilla fi 'aqa"id al-milla*, Arabic text in M. J. Müller's edition in *Philosophie und Theologie von Averroës* (Munich, 1859), p. 118. References to this work will be abbreviated, *Kashf. Kashf,* in effect, forms the third and longest part of a trilogy that begins with a short work, *The Epistle on Divine* Knowledge followed by *Fasl.* See M. S.Mahdi, "Averroës on Divine Law and Human Wisdom," in J. Cropsey, ed., *Ancient and Modern Essays on the Tradition of Political Philosophy in Honor of Leo Strauss* (New York, 1964), pp. 114-31; and "Remarks on Averroës's Decisive Treatise," in M.E. Marmura, ed., *Islamic Theology and Philosophy: Studies in Honor of George F. Hourani* (Albany, N.Y., 1984), pp. 189-202; C. S. Butterworth, "The Source that Nourishes, Averroës's Decisive Determination," *Arabic Science and Philosophy,* vol. 5 (1995), pp. 93-ll9.
4. Al-Kindi, *Fi al-falsafa al-ula* in *Rasail al-Kindi al-falsaiyya,* ed. M. Abu Rida (Cairo, 1955), pp. 103–104.

5. 'Abd al-Jabbar, *Tathbit dala'il al-nubuwwa*, ed. M. A. K. 'Uthman (2 vols.: Beirut, 1966), vol. 2, pp. 274, 508, 629–30.

6. Al-Farabi, *Ihsa' al-'ulum,* ed. O. Amin (Cairo, 1949), p. 108 ff.

7. G. F. Hourani, *Averroës on the Harmony of Religion and Philosophy,* pp. 4-5.

8. Al-Juwayni, *al-Irshad,* ed. M.Y. Musa and A.A. Abd al-Hamiid (Cairo, 1950), pp. 234–37.

9. See above note 3.

10. See above, note 3.

11. *Kashf,* p. 118.

12. Avicenna, *al-Najat* (Cairo, 1938), pp.117, 124.

13. Ghazali had argued that the philosophers cannot claim that his theory that an eternal will relates to creation in time is known to be false by "the necessity of thought," that is, to be self-evidently false, when their theory of a pre-eternal world leads to consequences that are known to be false by "the necessity of thought." Averroës is critical of this methodological approach. For a closely related discussion, see my article, "Le Modèle demonstratif: étude sure une bréve critique par Averroës d'une question Ghazalienne," in M.A. Sinaceur, ed., *Penser Avec Aristotle* (Ouvrage publié avec UNESCO, Toulouse, 1991), pp. 678–86.

14. Ibn Rushd, *Tahafut al-Tahafut*, ed. M. Bouyges (Beirut, 1930), pp. 26–27. References to this work will be abbreviated TT in the notes.

15. Ibid., p. 27

16. After objecting with his argument that the doctrine of a pre-eternal world must have as its contradictory consequence the existence of an infinity of souls, Ghazali puts in the mouth of the philosophers an affirmation of an alternative theory, he attributes to Plato, namely that the soul in all of us is one and hence that the question of the number of souls after separation from the body does not arise. Ghazali responds that since the individual Zayd experiences himself as distinct from 'Amr, their souls cannot be one and the same. Averroës maintains that Ghazali has not realized that the souls of Zayd and 'Amr are distinct accidentally, but are essentially one in form. The above quote is a follow-up on this.

17. More literally, "from the direction of materials."

18. Cf. Aristotle's *De Anima* I, 4, 408b 24–29; III, 5 430a20–25.

19. Averroës's use of the term *ifsha'*, that normally signifies the disclosing of a secret, is very significant.

20. TT, p. 29

21. The reference here is not merely the context of the above argument, but to the *Tahafut* as a whole—this when considering the ambiguities of his statements on the hereafter in both the nineteenth and twentieth discussions.

22. Ibid., p.29

23. Ibid.,p. 577

24. Ibid.

25. Ibid., pp. 577–79.

26. Ibid., p. 579. The ancient philosophers would not accept this theory,

Averroës states, because it is one of their principles that the separate celestial principles by their essences do not change terrestrial matters by way of transformation and primarily. For that which transforms is the opposite of what is transformed. In other words, if the celestial principles "by their essence" cause transformations in the terrestrial world, then the principles would themselves be undergoing transformations, which cannot be the case.

27. Ibid. Averroës does not make a direct reference either to Aristotle's *Metaphysics* or his *De Anima*. See, however, *Metaphysics*, I, 3, 984b13; also *De Anima*, III, 4, 429a

28. *Physics*, ii, 1, 193b 8; 2, 194b 13.

29. TT, pp. 580–86

30. TT, p. 581

31. Ibid. For the use of such expressions, see Alfarabi, T*he Attainment of Happiness,* translated with Introduction and Notes by Muhsin Mahdi (New York, 1962), p.13.

32. TT, p. 581. See Avicenna, *Al-shifa' (Healing); Al-Ilahiyyat (Metaphysics)*, ed. G.C. Anawati, S. Dunya, M. Y. Musa, and S. Zayid (2 vols.: Cairo, 1960), Madkour, Bk. X, ch. 2, p. 442; ch. 3, pp. 444–45.

33. TT, p. 581.

34. TT, p. 582.

35. Ibid.

36. Ibid., p. 585.

37. This is implied in Averroës's statement. He does not state it explicitly.

38. Ibid., p. 586.

39. Ghazali's criticisms, however, were directed against Avicenna who believed in individual immortality, but an indidvidual immortality confined to immaterial souls.

40. Ghazali had only "shown" this in the sense that he had explained Avicenna's argument against bodily resurrection. Averroës gives a mistaken impression that Ghazali is expressing his own view. For Ghazali's position, see the author's, "Al-Ghazali on Bodily Resurrection and Causality in the Tahafut and the Iqtisad," *Aligarh Journal of Islamic Thought* 2 (1989): 46–75; 58–59.

MOURAD WAHBA is professor emeritus of philosophy at the University of Ain Shams in Cairo, Egypt, and the founder and honorary president of the Afro-Asian Philosophy Association.

MONA ABOUSENNA is professor of English at the University of Ain Shams in Cairo, Egypt.